OWARD THE GEOPOLITICAL NOVEL

Literature Now

Literature Now

Matthew Hart, David James, and Rebecca L. Walkowitz, Series Editors

Literature Now offers a distinct vision of late-twentieth- and early-twenty-first-century literary culture. Addressing contemporary literature and the ways we understand its meaning, the series includes books that are comparative and transnational in scope as well as those that focus on national and regional literary cultures.

TOWARD THE

GEOPOLITICAL NOVEL

U. S. Fiction in the Twenty-First Century

CAREN IRR

COLUMBIA UNIVERSITY PRESS   *New York*

COLUMBIA UNIVERSITY PRESS
Publishers Since 1893
NEW YORK   CHICHESTER, WEST SUSSEX
cup.columbia.edu

Library of Congress Cataloging-in-Publication Data
Irr, Caren.
  Toward the geopolitical novel : U.S. fiction in the twenty-first century / Caren Irr.
    pages cm. — (Literature Now)
  Includes bibliographical references and index.
  ISBN 978-0-231-16440-5 (cloth : acid-free paper)
  ISBN 978-0-231-16441-2 (pbk. : acid-free paper)
  ISBN 978-0-231-53631-8 (e-book)
  1. Political fiction, American—History and criticism.   2. American fiction—21st century—
History and criticism.   3. Politics and literature—United States.   4. Globalization in
literature.   I. Title.
  PS374.P6177 2013
  813.099'358—dc23

                                                                        2013027558

Columbia University Press books are printed on permanent and durable acid-free paper.
This book is printed on paper with recycled content.

Printed in the United States of America

c 10 9 8 7 6 5 4 3 2 1
p 10 9 8 7 6 5 4 3 2 1

COVER IMAGE: © Noel McLaughlin / Gallery Stock
COVER DESIGN: Chang Jae Lee

CONTENTS

ACKNOWLEDGMENTS

THIS BOOK AROSE from conversations that took place during my year at Masaryk University in the Czech Republic. For that invaluable opportunity, I have the generosity of the Fulbright Commission as well as my affable hosts in the Department of English and American Studies to thank. Students in several contemporary literature courses at Brandeis gamely continued the conversation—especially those in my fall 2011 seminar on the literature of revolution. Laura Hill's research eased early stages of my writing process.

For their rigorous reading of the bulk of the manuscript, I am very grateful to Aliyyah Abdur-Rahman, Ulka Anjaria, Dave Sherman, Faith Smith, and Lisa Swanstrom. Michael T. Gilmore and Paul Morrison also provided pep talks at just the right moments. The scrupulous commentary offered by the anonymous readers for Columbia University Press was invaluable during revision, and special gratitude goes to Philip Leventhal and the editors of the Literature Now series for giving this book such a good home. Irene Pavitt's copyediting was also amazingly thorough and helpful.

An early version of chapter 1 was published as "Media and Migration: Danticat, Díaz, Eugenides, and Scibona," in *Wretched Refuge: Immigrants and Itinerants in the Postmodern* (Newcastle upon Tyne: Cambridge Scholars Press, 2010), a collection of essays thoughtfully edited by Jessica Datema and Diane Krumrey. A small portion of chapter 4 appeared as "Postmodernism in Reverse: American National Allegories and the 21st Century Political Novel," in "Postmodernism, Then," ed. Daniel Worden and Jason Gladstone, special issue, *Twentieth Century Literature* 57, nos. 3–4 (2011): 516–546. Gordon Hutner kindly published an earlier version of chapter 6 as "Toward the World Novel: Genre Shifts in 21st-Century Expatriate Fiction," *American Literary History* 23, no. 3 (2011): 660–679. Finally, I dedicate this book to my daughter Lonso, whose irrepressible joy and energy brighten every day.

TOWARD THE GEOPOLITICAL NOVEL

INTRODUCTION

The Resurgence of the Political Novel

ON THE AUSPICIOUS date of January 1, 1984, in the *New York Times Book Review*, Mary McCarthy described the effect that the first volume of John Dos Passos's *U.S.A.* trilogy (1930–1936) had on her more than fifty years earlier: "I fell madly in love with that book. . . . I responded. . . . I went to the library and looked up every line that Dos Passos had published that was in the card catalogue. I read them all."[1] Immersing herself in the causes, people, and publications mentioned in Dos Passos's writing launched McCarthy's own remarkable literary career. "Like a Japanese paper flower dropped into a glass of water," she recalls, "it all unfolded, magically, from Dos Passos."

These recollections open McCarthy' case in defense of the political novel. Far from "our home product [being] primarily domestic, unconcerned with public affairs," she argues, American fiction has had a long, healthy tradition of engaging with issues of the day. McCarthy testifies to the effects of this writing before presenting her own common-sense definition of the genre. Making persuasive arguments, describing political figures, and exploring problems are the three tasks of the political novel, McCarthy asserts. Their frequent adoption ensures that "the political novel in this country is certainly no fringe phenomenon." Almost any novel about anti-Semitism, race, or women counts as political for McCarthy, as do pacifist-leaning books on war and veterans. She points to tendentious novels by John Steinbeck, Richard Wright, and Robert Penn Warren as well as more recent offerings by Norman Mailer, Kurt Vonnegut, and Joseph Heller to support her thesis. These powerful, even life-changing works ground her conclusion that the political novel was alive and well in 1984.

McCarthy's confidence about the vitality of the political novel remains entirely justified in the early twenty-first century. Since 2000, the political novel has experienced a marked resurgence in U.S. fiction. Its major themes, figures, and narratives have been reinvigorated in hundreds of works that address the interconnected global environment of the new millennium. The more than 125 novels examined in this book participate, in one manner or another, in a concerted movement toward a new literary form: the geopolitical novel.

Observers across the literary field have already noticed signs of the return of the political novel. In *Reality Hunger*, creative writing professor David Shields argues that contemporary fiction is greatly enlivened by intentional efforts to make "other people interested, empathetic, questioning, or even antipathetic to what they're seeing."[2] Bill Marx endorses the same tendency from a more explicitly global perspective; his polemical essay in *Ploughshares*, published in 2000, urges readers to reshape their "expectations of what a novel is supposed to be" by exploring the social questions at the heart of international fiction.[3] Finally, in his remarks on submissions for *Granta*'s "Best of Young American Novelists 2" issue, published in 2007, Edmund White gave this phenomenon a name. White, rather archly, summed up the international and idealistic preoccupations of young authors by designating them "Peace Corps" writers.[4]

The whiff of distaste expressed by White and some others for the new fiction relates to their sense of how far (or not) it has moved from its origins in the nationally grounded political novel. White suggests that much of the new fiction reproduces 1960s-era political clichés and adopts a naïve relationship to neocolonial American foreign policy. Bruce Robbins agrees, chastising contemporary novelists for the brevity of their forays into the international scene and their reduction of non-American history to a litany of atrocities.[5] From a different angle, Tim Parks in the *New York Review of Books* also stresses the "dullness" of the "new global novel."[6] Parks's main concern is the limited linguistic creativity manageable in writing that is intended to be translated and accessible to an international audience (think Stieg Larsson), but these formal objections imply a political critique as well. To the extent that the twenty-first-century geopolitical novel aspires to success in a ready-made international market dominated by publishing conglomerates that are oriented toward readers in the United States, it may fail to innovate sufficiently, he suggests. These skeptical observers find would-be global fiction too uncritically American. They worry that the new fiction reflects, rather than reverses, the preoccupations of a conservative national culture—especially the "Edenic myth" of American innocence in a dangerous world.[7]

A broad survey of contemporary fiction reveals, however, that these fears are largely unfounded. Reading widely and synthetically demonstrates that the new geopolitical fiction resists reproducing the least appealing features of American fiction of recent decades. Instead, the twenty-first-century political novel actively reorganizes existing literary forms. More than a hundred writers have twisted and stretched conventional versions of the political novel, testing its durability as they encourage new mutations. These energetic efforts to create new genres are the sign of a culture in contest. After all, neither American culture nor the literary genres that codify cultural trends is static. To the contrary: fiction of the past decade actively seeks creative ways to move beyond existing national forms, and does so because it participates in an active social process in which new political positions and attitudes are emerging.

Although it may be premature to describe the positions expressed in twenty-first-century fiction as full-blown ideologies, the consistent matrix of possibilities evident in this writing does suggest a worldview or a proto-political orientation. Less often than in McCarthy's day is recent work by astute internationally minded authors concerned primarily with political ideas or persuasion; that version of the genre tends to rely on a high level of extra-literary political organization—such as party platforms and journals of opinion. In recent decades, literary authors have ceded much of this terrain to political professionals. McCarthy's second variety of political novel—the literary vision of a public figure—is somewhat more common. But most often, the twenty-first-century geopolitical novel presents detailed descriptions of ordinary, dedicated people wrestling with the problems of the new millennium. In these problem novels, common tropes repeatedly appear, and interpreting these scenes, figures, and conflicts reveals some key features of contemporary political experience.

Although any literary work may be said to be political at an unconscious level, contemporary problem novels are explicitly political in their subject matter. Politically charged characters, settings, conflicts, and styles of narration comprise the foreground of the narrative as well as the background of the geopolitical novel. This fiction directly addresses questions of collective identity and power, appropriate means of collective action, and the struggle to articulate ideals and goals that orient action. It makes a political problem fundamental to the story. Whether authors of the geopolitical novel ask, for example, how assimilation comes about in a media-saturated environment, how American idealists can effectively respond to crises in the developing world, what safe spaces the nation provides in the context of neoliberalism, when and how revolutions happen, or how we might recognize the hero of globalization, they tackle core questions of the new century. They rarely provide dogmatically clear solutions to their problems—preferring the exploration of narrative dilemmas to the making of propagandistic speeches. Nonetheless, the twenty-first-century geopolitical novel edifies contemporary readers in several senses. It shatters isolationist myths, updates national narratives, provides points of access for global identifications, and, perhaps most important, allows reflection on the emerging subjects of consensus (for better or worse) in the United States.

THE FALL AND RISE OF THE POLITICAL NOVEL

The resurgence of the political novel in the twenty-first century is partially atavistic, reviving antecedents that had almost disappeared from view. In the last decades of the twentieth century, many political narratives (from Soviet Communism to ethnocentric nationalism) were discarded or discredited. By 2000, their literary expression had become a historical curiosity rather than an urgent issue, and consequently those who identified the political novel solely with radical leftist propaganda or conversion fiction[8] regarded the form as obsolete. In its place, many sought new political narratives that would express the situation created by the collapse of the Soviet bloc, the initiation of a potentially endless war on terror, and the global enforcement of neoliberal ideologies. Far from eliminating the political novel, however, this shift in the geopolitical terrain renewed a thirst for social fiction. To meet this need and craft their own fresh responses to the global scene, twenty-first-century authors have returned to received genres and begun to overhaul them. In so doing, they have paid special attention to those elements of the political novel that were grounded in the increasingly dated ideal of the territorially defined sovereign nation.

The version of the political novel that fell into such disrepute and is now being revived in a more international manner is that defined by Irving Howe in *Politics and the Novel* (1957). In a wide-ranging series of essays, Howe asserts that the central concern of the genre is an individual's psychologically rich struggle to articulate political ideas adequate to meet the social concerns of his or her day. Far from expressing a rigid scheme for interpreting the world (a common complaint directed toward socially conscious fiction during the 1950s), the political novel as Howe understands it places the psychic, intellectual, and pragmatic complexity of formulating responsible political ideas at the center of the form. In his essay on Conrad, for instance, Howe explains the author's stoicism and embrace of a typically English brand of conservatism in terms of both Conrad's membership in a class that was falling from power and his reaction to his Polish father's revolutionary zeal. The antipathy to anarchist activism so readily on display in several of Conrad's short novels is thus read as a symptom; the deep content of this (and many other novels with explicitly political content) Howe directly attributes to specific national conditions. In Conrad's case, the latent content of the Polish independence movement determined his later apparently English attitudes. The terrifying abyss of revolutionary upheaval that opened during Conrad's youth shaped the distinctive worldview expressed in his mature fiction.

Howe's definition of the political novel as the result of a struggle to craft a psychologically satisfying response to national conditions was especially well suited to the existentially tinged protest fiction of the mid-twentieth century. He championed authors such as Richard Wright and Harvey Swados who wrote passionately and philosophically on behalf of populations excluded from the national public sphere. This concept of the political novel came under attack later in the century. In a review of the reissue of *Politics and the Novel* in 1992, William Sharpe, for one, expresses disappointment in Howe's lack of attention to "the politics of everyday life" and the intermeshing of "public issues and private lives."[9] For Sharpe and others influenced by certain versions of feminist theory,[10] Howe's concern with public expression had become antithetical and antipolitical. For Howe's critics, the only viable political fiction is that which explores the character of a subnational (usually explicitly private) sphere. Pervasive estrangement became, for some, the only viable political attitude for literature to express.[11]

The shift away from the novel of ideology was accelerated by a preoccupation in the late twentieth century with the politics of literary form. Since the 1960s, complex postmodern styles have been at the center of debates over the political implications, if any, of formal experimentation.[12] In these discussions, those who associated politics with private life often advocated psychological realism, while pro-postmodernists considered the most challenging experimental works to be the most political. Despite their disagreements, though, both of these late-twentieth-century positions disparaged the nationally oriented novel of political and ideological expression as defined by Howe.

By the end of the century, his version of the political novel had shrunk down to topical Washington exposés, such as the anonymously authored Clinton-era exposé *Primary Colors: A Novel of Politics* (1996) or the Obama-era *O: A Presidential Novel* (2011).[13] For many readers, writers, and critics, it seemed as though politics as a manifest content of U.S. fiction could be addressed only through ironies of form (as in Robert Coover's Nixon satire *The Public Burning* [1977] or Joan Didion's rewriting of Henry Adams's *Democracy* [1984]) or privately (as in Toni Morrison's novels of traumatic re-memory, such as *Beloved* [1987]). According to the orthodoxy of the era, both the persuasive and the problem novel versions of the genre risked an "authoritarian" overkill if the protagonist developed an ideological attitude endorsed by the narrator.[14] In short, the political novel as understood by Howe did not simply fade from favor; it was actively repudiated by those who found its basic premises dangerous and obsolete.

Since the heyday of the rejection of the political novel, a number of critics have recovered an essentially liberal sensibility in domestic fiction in particular.[15] Without the political novel proper as an antagonist, this form no longer seems subversively nonpolitical so much as centrist. At the same time, calls for an oppositional political fiction more compatible with Howe's vision of the conversion novel have begun to reemerge in the twenty-first century. Since the late 1980s, Fredric Jameson has sought a political aesthetic of the multinational system—a project he calls "cognitive mapping"—while more recently, Walter Benn Michaels has urged a return to the kind of critical and cultural discourse that allows for genuine disagreement, rather than an ever-proliferating expression of inarguable cultural differences.[16] Together, these influential positions prompt inquiry into confrontational and socially engaged writing that is attentive to the environment of the present. In the past decade, much writing of this variety has engaged the global, rather than the domestic, scene. Directly addressing public political questions—such as the utility of foreign aid, the prospects of revolutionary movements, and the effects of neoliberal economic policy—dozens of twenty-first-century authors have published new narratives of political life. Their stories revisit Howe's focus on the drama of political engagement, even as they expand their range beyond local or national questions.

In particular, authors of twenty-first-century geopolitical fiction tinker with the conventions of the so-called program era. As described and defended by Mark McGurl, the fiction produced by professors and students in the more than three hundred MFA programs in the United States is characterized by "high cultural pluralism and technomodernism."[17] That is, this fiction reflects a preoccupation with writing as a craft. Regarding culture as a system and an industry, authors of program fiction experiment in an essentially technological manner. They downplay the flamboyance of the heroic author in favor of a more anonymous professionalism that reflexively supports the institutional context for their writing. McGurl also stresses cultural pluralism and the role of ethnic or racial spokespeople, arguing that identity becomes a form of expertise: "[W]hat Roth knows about Jewishness, and Morrison knows about blackness, writers like Powers, DeLillo, and Pynchon know about the second law of thermodynamics, cybernetic causality, communications and media theory, and the like."[18] These parallel forms of expertise are cultivated in institutions of higher education, and the fiction they generate should be valued by proponents of the university, McGurl concludes.

This account of program fiction suggests that the politics of program-sponsored suburban realism can be affiliated with mid-century efforts to diversify the American middle class through education.[19] Pluralistic and technical models of authorship may be understood as displacing forms of creativity premised on the decoding of tacit class-based norms. Observers of middle-brow culture similarly stress the therapeutic self-reflection allowed by domestic realism, suggesting that it has an ameliorative politics.[20] Nonetheless, the same works also contain some asocial or antisocial elements.[21] Program fiction's interest in technical competence can endorse neoliberal market logic just as easily as liberal pluralism. As the so-called crisis of the humanities has revealed,[22] American universities consistently align middle-class professionalism with capitalist market pragmatism. However idealistic the vision of single works of program fiction might be, program writing in general can also participate in the reduction of education to a narrowly immediate concept of economic self-interest. Precisely because this writing so often repackages its endorsement of dominant values as technical expertise, it can reinforce a status quo interpretation of the self and home, even while claiming to have moved beyond the critical consciousness of the political novel.

Perhaps for this reason, explicit efforts to resuscitate the political novel often turn to alternative literary traditions. One major competitor to the program model is described in Chad Harbach's lively survey of the contemporary literary landscape, "MFA vs. NYC." Harbach sketches a celebrity-oriented, New York model of writing, characterized by "long books . . . [that] address large-scale societal change and engage in sharp but affable satire of same."[23] These works are often titled "with [a] sweeping, often faintly nationalist simplicity" that is at odds with the more ironic and imagistic preferences of program writers. In works by Jonathan Franzen, Gary Shteyngart, and Nicole Krauss, among others, Horbach finds evidence of a less institutionally minded, more embattled, and somewhat riskier literary practice. He stresses the openness to political expression in contemporary social fiction.

Harbach's New York strain of writing reminds us that literary norms other than those of the program model can still be influential, even if a particular writer works or studies at a university. This is particularly true of writers born, raised, and educated abroad but currently teaching part- or full time at American universities. Authors such as Helon Habila, Amitav Ghosh, Junot Díaz, Daniel Alarcón, and Daniyal Mueenuddin may have spent time in MFA programs in the U.S. and their work may signal "high cultural pluralism" to some readers. Nonetheless, their writing also engages with other traditions—such as Nigerian popular fiction, the Indian nationalist novel, and Latin American neorealism. It does not do justice to their varied and inventive work to frame it solely in relation to the American university. This is especially true with authors such as Ghosh who enjoy a broad readership outside the United States and practice a self-conscious version of literary cosmopolitanism.

Even writers who are not migrants themselves often have institutional affiliations beyond the MFA program. Many international novels have been penned by returned Peace Corps volunteers and aid workers or by journalists-turned-novelists such as Ian Buruma, Ken Kalfus, and James Meek—not to mention career diplomats such as Mark Jacobs and Shirley Hazzard. The work of these authors provides ample evidence of the influence of ideals, worldviews, and writing practices associated with institutions other than the university. Although these institutions produce fewer fiction writers than do MFA programs, they have distinct voices and concerns worthy of critical attention.

A fourth non-MFA strain of writing is also sporadically important for the authors of geopolitical fiction. Alongside New Yorkers, migrants, and affiliates of international institutions are self-consciously "indie" authors associated with small publishers such as McSweeney's, Graywolf Press, and Coffee House Press. Frequently exhibiting an experimentalism more eccentric and personal than the technomodernism of program writers, indie authors tend to shatter the syntax of academically sanctioned genres fairly aggressively while frequently embracing a necessarily collective language of generational antagonism.[24] Their work thus aligns with the project of the geopolitical novel, to the extent that authors such as David Wong Louie, Maile Chapman, Salvatore Scibona, William T. Vollmann, Vendela Vida, and Dave Eggers are interested in testing the assumptions of the nationally grounded writing in which they were schooled. Indie writers may be less explicitly committed to reviving the political novel as a genre than are authors strongly influenced by postcolonial literature; their work shows less evidence of conflict with institutional values than does that of career diplomats who moonlight as novelists; and their writing often tests aesthetic extremes more fully than does that of the socially minded New York authors. However, some indie authors still join these contemporaries in exploring the space available for a newly public, engaged form of writing.

Thanks to the labors of urban, migrant, extra-university, and indie authors, then, in the past decade or so, a new type of U.S. fiction has emerged. This writing engages actively with international literary scenes and traditions and revises the political novel in particular as a form, testing its capacity to express vital conflicts in the present. This emerging genre—which we can call the geopolitical novel—presents an important, invigorating challenge to the market dominance of suburban realism and program fiction. No matter how innovative or moving the explorations of white middle-class angst may prove to be in the work of Rick Moody, Carole Maso, and Ben Marcus, say, a programmatic emphasis on craft and the personal experiences of those with enough social capital to attend graduate programs in writing has, for some experienced readers, also contributed to the formation of a "lackluster," "mediocre," and "uninspiring" body of work.[25] Disrupting those patterns to various degrees, authors of the international novel have begun to formulate political narratives appropriate to the twenty-first century. Recognizing that "it's damn hard to figure out who's [or what's] an American," the new geopolitical fiction does not look inward to confirm fidelity to received national ideologies.[26] Instead, it tests the viability and boundaries of domestic literary conventions. The geopolitical novel draws on several alternative strains of writing in order to revive the problem of representing the world in a new, lively form.

THE SCOPE OF THIS BOOK

To define and explain the concerted movement toward the geopolitical novel, it was necessary to examine many works. When assembling the list of more than 125 novels that serve as the primary texts for this book, I began with winners of literary prizes, such as the National Book Award, the Pulitzer Prize, the National Book Critics Circle Award, and the Lannan Literary Awards.

From the twenty-first-century finalists and winners of each award, I culled those works with explicitly international subjects. I then supplemented that list with fiction that had received positive reviews in the *New York Times Book Review*, the *Washington Post*, the *Los Angeles Times*, the *New Yorker*, and *Publishers Weekly*. I also consulted the review sections of such influential digital sources as *Bookslut*, *Slate*, and *Salon* as well as recommendations made by independent booksellers with strong literary reputations. My goal was to identify a broad sample of international novels addressed to an American audience.

From this long list, I organized clusters sorted by genre. Only genres with at least ten examples were included. For this reason, interesting new forms, such as the nanny novel and the backpacker novel, that have as yet inspired only a few works with international content did not become the subject of whole chapters. Once a viable genre cluster emerged, some novels that contributed less directly to the category could be included—such as works that mix several genres; are directed toward an English, a Canadian, or an Australian audience; or were published during the last years of the 1990s. The five genres of the international novel that ultimately became central to this study are the migrant novel, the Peace Corps thriller, the national allegory, the revolutionary novel, and the expatriate satire.

For each of these genre clusters, I then identified a genre-defining predecessor. The significance of Ernest Hemingway is inescapable for the expatriate novel, for example, just as Graham Greene casts a long shadow over the thriller and Chinua Achebe continues to influence the national allegory. These forerunners established precedents that twenty-first-century authors test. For each genre, I provide a schema explaining the perceived limitations of older models as well as the new motifs, characterizations, conflicts, and modes of resolution. Each chapter of this book begins with a taxonomy of the most common developments in each genre of twenty-first-century writing. An effort has certainly been made to recognize individual works that move beyond these emerging norms as well as their twentieth-century predecessors. However, my interest lies in the norms as well as the exceptions. Both are crucial to my effort to infer emerging ideologies.

Beyond the five genres selected for extended discussion, a few others did suggest themselves as promising candidates. Contemporary developments in travel literature, spiritual-quest narratives, exploration novels, and prose documentaries all seemed viable subjects. However, they were ultimately excluded, mainly because they muddy the discussion of literary form by mixing conventions of fiction and nonfiction. Similarly, genres with a very well-established tradition independent of "literary" fiction—such as science fiction and the detective novel—are mentioned only in passing, as the audience questions they generate differ markedly from those raised by mainstream realism. Finally, a few subgenres were omitted simply because too few examples could be located. William T. Vollmann's globe-trotting narratives concerned with prostitution and the very poor, for example, are enormously compelling but ultimately too unique to sit comfortably in a genre.

Another important question has already been alluded to: How should "American" be defined? My thesis about the rise of the geopolitical novel does not encompass all contemporary English-language writing but is limited to what I call "U.S. fiction." For my purposes, a work counts as part of "U.S. fiction" not on the basis of the author's birthplace, citizenship, current residence, or workplace. Any one of these biographical factors may be pertinent to any individual author's narrative, but no single data point (or combination) defines Americanness. My category of "U.S. fiction" includes works by authors such as Samrat Upadhyay who were born and educated abroad but now teach writing in the United States as well as fiction by Mohsin Hamid, who was born in Pakistan, educated in the United States, and now lives in Great Britain and holds a British passport. More important than biographical markers for my purposes is an explicit effort to address a North American audience. The inclusion of major or minor American characters who are in some way educated by the international scene but are otherwise incidental to the story is one major indication that an author is addressing an American audience. Other signals of this concern include the preoccupation with correcting stereotypical American ideas about a particular region or the (often inverted or displaced) use of a common American narrative, such as the upwardly mobile immigrant story. In general, I view internal evidence such as voice, style, and narrative frame as more reliable indicators of a particular work's having an American reference point than authorial biography.

Inclusion in "U.S. fiction" is a matter of genre. It is the use and revision of historically American narratives for making sense of the rest of the world that marks individual works as examples of "U.S. fiction." These genre commitments easily coexist with participation in other national or regional traditions as well. Like bumper stickers that read "God bless the rest of the world, too," "U.S. fiction" in a geopolitical mood refers to and revises explicitly national assumptions, such as the ever-present desire (or is it a demand?) that "God bless America." The new geopolitical fiction revises and ironizes the national tradition by recasting it in a more international context.

In the same spirit, I chose the purely calendrical marker of 2000 as the starting point for my project, rather than the domestically significant date of September 11, 2001. The attacks on the World Trade Center and the Pentagon were obviously significant events that triggered a blitz of media attention to the relationship between the United States and the rest of the world; these events also inspired some new variations on the city novel almost immediately (as in the growing genre of September 11 fiction, which includes Ken Kalfus's *Disorder Peculiar to the Country* [2006], Don DeLillo's *Falling Man: A Novel* [2007], and Claire Messud's *Emperor's Children* [2007]). The attacks of September 11 have also arguably contributed to a modest internationalization of Americans' reading habits—with somewhat more lip service being paid in the United States to literature by and about Muslims around the world. Nonetheless, I concur with Phillip Wegner, who argues that September 11 closed the short period of American history launched by the collapse of the Soviet Union.[27] Like Wegner, I regard September 11 more as the end of the twentieth century than the beginning of the twenty-first. I do not consider novels about September 11 to be a new species of political fiction but a subset of the national trauma writing discussed in chapter 2. For this reason, the somewhat more arbitrary but also more "global" (though obviously still Christian) date of 2000 serves as the starting point for this study of contemporary literature.

To sum up, then, this book examines five thriving genres of contemporary fiction that revive and revise twentieth-century literary conventions associated with the political novel. It understands national literature as an ideological and institutional effect of genres, rather than as a feature of authorial identity. It explores only genres that have accumulated numerous respected examples in the twenty-first century. Collectively, the more than 125 works of fiction it examines suggest the emergence of a set of new motifs, figures, and attitudes definitive of the geopolitical novel.

A Few Words on Critical Methods

The methods of analysis used in this study are not limited to close reading. While recognizing the value of close reading for certain kinds of interpretive questions and occasionally indulging in its pleasures, I do not believe that it is the only tool useful to the literary and cultural critic. My working assumption is that making a responsible argument about a large-scale change in literary culture, such as the rise or fall of a genre, requires some resistance to the hagiographic tendencies of close reading. Detailed explication of exceptional masterworks rarely provides illuminating accounts of the underlying genre norms. For my purposes, tracking the repeated appearance of typical figures, conflicts, and attitudes has been more productive, even if it risks overgeneralization. In places, attention to unoccupied positions in a matrix of possible approaches to a genre has also proved useful; close reading is obviously not possible in such a case, since no texts are available to interpret. Because my aim is to establish the axioms of genres as well as to recognize the singular genre bender, I have had to do more than study the inner workings of individual texts.

For these tasks, I have found a version of "distant reading" helpful. I do not endorse the wholesale detachment from primary texts that Franco Moretti describes, nor does this study duplicate Moretti's experiments with empiricism.[28] I do, however, make regular use of other scholars' critical statements and surveys to map the literary landscape. I also aim in reading any individual novel to elucidate the features that it shares with other works, rather than prizing only those that distinguish it. For this project, it has been necessary to patiently accumulate multiple instances that point toward patterns more clearly observed, as it were, from afar.

My understanding of genre derives from the work of Tzvetan Todorov, Mikhail Bakhtin, György Lukács, and Fredric Jameson, all of whom attend to the historically mutable character of literary form. Structuralist accounts such as Todorov's (or, rather differently, Northrop Frye's) suggest helpful ways to define the signature tensions of any particular genre at the moment of its emergence.[29] Bakhtin and Lukács add to this descriptive vocabulary a range of useful tools for relating the waxing and waning fortunes of particular genres to their historical circumstances.[30] Jameson pulls these insights together with a classic formulation, describing literary genre as the imaginary resolution to certain concrete social issues of a particular moment, a resolution that can be sustained past the moment of its origin and updated to meet new needs.[31] At certain moments, however, as genre theorists in film studies have also reminded us, the old resolutions must strain too hard to incorporate new conditions or to crossbreed with alternative literary traditions.[32] In these instances, the imaginary solution that successfully responded to earlier conditions begins to break down, and a new genre—one that imagines a new ideological framework for social concerns—begins to emerge. These exciting moments at the crossroads of literary and social history reveal the specific work that genre performs as an institutional and social mediation.

By understanding genre as a historically mutable negotiation between social needs and literary history, I hope to move past classic poststructuralist critiques of the category, such as those offered by Maurice Blanchot. Like Jacques Derrida in "The Law of Genre,"[33] Blanchot was concerned in his theoretical and literary writing with the danger of genre rules that function as limits and/or prescriptions; regarding genre as inherently repressive and authoritarian, he favored a radical singularity of expression.[34] My own view draws more from film theory, a field in which genre is often understood as a malleable starting point and as an expression of institutional creativity.[35] For many film theorists, auteurist individualism and uniqueness of style are important to recognize but insufficient for a full account of particular works. Genre, understood as an effect of criticism as an institution as well as studio and post-studio production, has in film theory a lively status—one from which scholars making a turn toward the analysis of literary institutions might usefully learn. My aim is to draw selectively from the accounts of genre developed in film theory in order to advance a literary critical appreciation for collective forms of creativity. Literary analysis informed by close reading often excels at particularizing and individualizing; I understand genre analysis as the logical complement to that activity.

The second major method employed in this study is ideology critique. Well established in the mid-twentieth century, ideological criticism—or political analysis more generally—has, for some readers, recently acquired a very bad name, as it is often hastily subsumed under the category of politically correct moralism.[36] In that sort of reading, a litmus test is applied (or so critics hostile to political interpretation imagine), and individual works are supposedly valued or repudiated to the degree that their own assumptions match those of the critic. Others believe ideology critique to consist of sweeping attacks on static political enemies, attacks pursued in ignorance of the historical factors influencing discussion of particular issues as well as the literary and cultural aspects of political expression.[37] This is not what I mean by ideology critique.

Instead, my approach builds on the insights of Jameson when he asserts that "ideology-critique begins at home, with the so-called self and its baggage and furnishings, and can only thereafter be trained with some accuracy and precision on the outside world and its doings."[38] That is, beginning with internal, often psychological and/or characterological categories of single works or genres, my readings move out to establish the unique features of ideological positions that are beginning to cohere in the present. I am not particularly concerned with the validity of these positions or their internal coherence; instead, it is the way in which literature serves as an "antenna" (to use Ezra Pound's image) for a range of opinions, attitudes, and intuitions that have not yet fully congealed in public discourse that I want to track.[39] Ideology critique in this version pulls into the open air the as yet hidden range of reactions to contemporary problems that are shared by many thoughtful observers, presenting their etiology and logic as clearly as possible. It is not concerned with evaluation so much as formation; its founding assumption is the mutability and openness of seeming historical inevitabilities. In this spirit, this book stresses the novel literary effects accompanying the return of the political problem as a subject for contemporary fiction. The resurgence of the political novel is, in my view, such a widespread phenomenon that we cannot generalize responsibly about contemporary fiction without attending to it; nor do I believe that a narrowly formalist account can properly explain the distinctive genre mutations that political subjects have triggered in fiction of the past decade. Despite passing disagreements on local points, this project shares with those of Mark McGurl, Sean McCann, Suzanne Keen, David Cowart, Gordon Hutner, James Annesley, and Walter Benn Michaels the assumption that a synthetic, historical, and institutional approach to contemporary fiction reveals important insights. My understanding of ideology critique (derived mainly from Jameson and Adorno) is premised on attention to the formation of ideologies in the present rather than their imagined effects in the future.

After all, "stupidity," as Max Horkheimer and Theodor Adorno wrote in the moving final paragraph of *The Dialectic of Enlightenment*, "is a scar" that "marks a spot where the awakening play of muscles has been inhibited instead of fostered."[40] These inhibitions can trigger repetitions, redirections, or deformations that harden into character types, personal blind spots, or intellectual positions. In this account of scarring, Horkheimer and Adorno mainly have in mind the perverse fanaticism of the fascist self that Adorno elsewhere describes as the authoritarian personality.[41] However, their account may be usefully extended to many different ideologies, each of which involves—if it is not too crude to put it this way—a characteristic type of stupidity. The critic's task when facing a stupid scar, especially a scar that is still in the process of forming, is not to berate the bearer of the scar (still less the scar itself!) but to examine the inhibitions that led to its formation as well as the generic repetitions that make that scar a permanent feature of the social self. This, at least, has been my effort—to read the repeated tics and habits of various genres as stages in an ongoing process of ideological interaction in which all subjects are to some degree mangled. We are all rendered generically repetitive and stupid, it seems to me, by our participation in a global system premised on enormous economic inequality, widespread social fragmentation, and the narrow concept of self allowed by consumerism. It is my hope that creating a taxonomy of these contemporary scars will make them more legible as symptoms of a social disease.

The Ideological Matrix of Twenty-First-Century Geopolitical Fiction

An ideology critique examines ideologies in formation, but defining the concept of ideology is notoriously difficult.[42] Some scholars follow Theodor Adorno in placing the positions that interest them along a spectrum that moves from left to right or from less to more authoritarian, for example.[43] Others use a two-axis scheme like that of the World Values Survey. This ambitious. ongoing project plots the world's nations on a grid that arrays individual versus collective values on one axis and adherence to versus deviation from "traditional" authority on the other.[44] While both schemes have their merits, a growing number of political scientists have begun to argue that focusing exclusively on domestic social questions obscures some of the most pressing contemporary global issues. Citing the need to recognize attitudes toward ecological challenges and the demise of Third Worldist politics in favor of new globalisms, they have called for new tools to describe and assess emerging political viewpoints.[45] So far, no single simple visualization of these positions has been widely adopted, although verbal descriptions have appeared.[46] A memorable arrangement of emergent, residual, and dominant attitudes toward the global system would be very useful.

What follows are the results of one attempt to code the much smaller subset of attitudes expressed by authors of geopolitical fiction. As Richard Ohmann has argued, literary intellectuals often hold a narrower range of positions than the populace as a whole, even though this group has significant internal disagreements. Certain norms are embedded in the profession and institutions of authorship.[47] To portray the consistent array of geopolitical attitudes shared by contemporary authors, I have borrowed a working definition of "ideology" from the editors of a special issue of *New Political Science*.[48]

Using their definition, I assigned each work a score on three fundamental questions:

1. What kind of world do we inhabit now?
2. What does an ideal world look like?
3. How should we move from the actual to the ideal?

Each question had one of four answers, ranging from entirely local to entirely global for the first two and from entirely individual to entirely collective forms of action for the last. The results of this coding appear in tables 1 and 2. (For the sake of brevity, the results are designated by the author's surname, although the coding relied on textual evidence rather than authorial statements.)

When first examining table 1, many immediately notice the empty and/or under-populated boxes. Those in the far-right column represent the small number of authors who understand the world they inhabit as already fully global and integrated. Similarly, very few take extreme localism as an ideal. No authors discussed in this study see the world as both actually and ideally fully global or actually and ideally fully local. Also, none want to move from an overlapping network of cultures to local isolation. These are positions that theorists of ideology refer to as "decontested"; that is, they are inarguable and nonnegotiable foundations that shore up other more conventional positions.[49] In the future, these relatively eccentric positions could be sites of literary exploration, but to date those options have not been taken by the geopolitical novel.

A second observation: the diagonal connecting the upper-left corner of the table to the lower-right corner is the emptiest; these boxes represent the alignment of the actual and the ideal world. Few authors regard the actual and the ideal as being in harmony. The opposite diagonal (lower left to upper right) is more heavily populated; these authors identify a major gap between the actual and the ideal world. Most of them seek greater degrees of global interconnection. The readily apparent difference between these two diagonals, then, is one way of visualizing the ubiquity of explicitly political narratives in contemporary fiction. If happy acceptance of the status quo were the norm and politically charged fiction were obsolete, this pattern would be reversed. That said, the fullest boxes are those representing authors who take only one greater degree of globalization as their ideal. This pattern suggests that most authors of the geopolitical novel understand the present as a moderate crisis, not a severe catastrophe.

TABLE 1 Actual and Ideal Worlds in Contemporary Fiction

IDEAL WORLD	ACTUAL WORLD			
	LOCAL INCLUDES WHOLE WORLD (STRONG LOCALISTS)	WORLD AS PATCHWORK OF NATIONS (MODERATE LOCALISTS)	WORLD AS OVERLAPPING NATIONS AND CULTURES (MODERATE GLOBALISTS)	ONE INTEGRATED WORLD (STRONG GLOBALISTS)
LOCAL INCLUDES WHOLE WORLD (STRONG LOCALISTS)		Berberian, Brommell, Mda, Rachman, Russo, Sofer, Vida		Atwood
WORLD AS PATCHWORK OF NATIONS (MODERATE LOCALISTS)	Adichie, Anam, Cameron, Firouz, Gunesekera, McCarthy, Pasulka, Theroux, Tuck, Upadhyay, Wicomb	Franzen, Toutonghis	Choi, Galchen, Hamid, Iweala, Kunzru, Lee, McCann, Vollmann	Mountford
WORLD AS OVERLAPPING NATIONS AND CULTURES (MODERATE GLOBALISTS)	Abani, Chabon, Grushin, Haslett, Jen, Khadivi, Mantel, Meek, Meyer, Patchett, Shand, Yamashita	Alvarez, Banks, De Robertis, Doerr, D. Eggers, P. Eggers, Farah, Foer, Freudenberger, García, Habila, Hobbet, Jacobs, Jin, Kalfus, Kunzru, Kushner, Menéndez, Mengiste, Nwaubani, Raban, Rosenberg, Simpson, Syjuco, Verghese, Wayne	Davis, Ghosh, Hagedorn, Powers	Allison, Hazzard

ONE INTEGRATED WORLD (STRONG GLOBALISTS)	Bell, Chikwava, Isegawa, Messud, Min, Ochsner, Philips, Rush, Stefaniak, Wray	Caputo, Coleman, Dooling, D'Souza, Matar, Meidav, Mishra, Wiley	Alarcón, Aridjis, Berlinski, Brockmeier, Buruma, Carey, Chandra, Cole, Dasgupta, Díaz, Eugenides, Hemon, Mengestu, Mueenuddin, O'Neill, Shteyngart, Suri

Table 2 presents the preferred political methods imagined in contemporary geopolitical fiction in relation to the ideal world. It allows us to see whether there is a correlation between authors' ideals and preferred political methods.

Like table 1, table 2 demonstrates that certain combinations are very common. Many authors view the world as a patchwork of nations at present while idealizing an overlapping flow of cultures; the passage from this moderately local to a moderately globalized condition is most commonly thought to occur when small groups of individuals cluster together or combine into larger units having no predetermined motive. This cluster of positions I call contemporary *mainstream liberalism*, at least as expressed by writers of U.S. fiction. Well-known authors writing from this viewpoint include Dave Eggers, Christina García, Ha Jin, Ken Kalfus, Hari Kunzru, Rachel Kushner, Ana Menéndez, Jonathan Raban, Mona Simpson, and Abraham Verghese. Even though their views on other matters might diverge considerably, in the very simple schema proposed here, these authors share a major and central position.

Despite the preponderance of authors who express mainstream liberal attitudes, other important clusters also appear. Among those who take an overlapping international condition (or moderate globalism) as their ideal, many describe individualist and symbolic forms of action as being most effective. Authors in this group include Chris Abani, Michael Chabon, Olga Grushin, Adam Haslett, Gish Jen, Laleh Khadivi, Hilary Mantel, James Meek, and

TABLE 2 Ideal Worlds and Political Methods

IDEAL WORLD	PLAN OF ACTION			
	SOLELY INDIVIDUAL (AESTHETIC)	INDIVIDUAL ADDITIVE (LIBERAL REFORMERS)	ANTAGONISM BETWEEN IDENTITY BLOCS (COLLECTIVSTS)	ONE WORLD HOLISM (UNIVERSALISTS)
LOCAL INCLUDES WHOLE WORLD (STRONG LOCALISTS)	Berberian, Sofer, Vida	Atwood, Brommell, Deb, Rachman, Russo	Mda	
WORLD AS PATCHWORK OF NATIONS (MODERATE LOCALISTS)	Hamid, Marcom, Vollmann *Radical aesthetes*	Cameron, Choi, Firouz, Franzen, Galchen, Gunesekera, Iweala, Lee, McCann, McCarthy, Pasulka, Theroux, Toutonghi *Mainstream liberals*	Adichie, Anam, Mountford, Prose, Tuck, Upadhyay, Wicomb	
WORLD AS OVERLAPPING NATIONS AND CULTURES (MODERATE GLOBALISTS)	Abani, Alvarez, Chabon, Davis, Freudenberger, Grushin, Hagedorn, Haslett, Jacobs, Jen, Khadivi, Mantel, Meek, Shand, Syjuco	Alison, Doerr, D. Eggers, García, Hazzard, Hobbet, Jin, Kalfus, Krauss, Kunzru, Kushner, Menéndez, Mengiste, Nwaubani, Oyeyemi, Raban, Rosenberg, Shacochis, Simpson, Thomas, Vapnyar, Verghese	Banks, De Robertis, P. Eggers, Farah, Ghosh, Habila, Meyer, Patchett, Wayne, Yamashita	Foer, Powers

ONE INTEGRATED WORLD (STRONG GLOBALISTS)			
Aridjis, Chikwava, Cole, Dasgupta, Eugenides, Messud, Philips	Berlinski, Buruma, Carey, Chandra, Díaz, D'Souza, Hemon, Matar, Meidav, Mengestu, Min, Mishra, Ochsner, O'Neill, Shteyngart, Stefaniak, Wiley, Wray	Alarcón, Bell, Caputo, Isegawa, Rush	Brockmeier, Coleman, Dooling, Muenuddin, Suri
		Collectivist globalists	
Moderate aesthetes			Hard-core globalists
	Liberal globalists		

Rosa Shand. This subset demonstrates that liberals are not necessarily unified in their understanding of political action, even if they share similar ideals. We might call this group the *moderate aesthetes*, since they tend to avoid explicit descriptions of political processes, placing faith instead in aesthetic mechanisms for moving from local to more interconnected global scenes.

A third significant cluster in table 2 is composed of those who aspire to a more unified one-world ideal by individualist means. It includes authors such as Mischa Berlinski, Ian Buruma, Peter Carey, Vikram Chandra, Junot Díaz, Aleksandar Hemon, Dinaw Mengestu, Joseph O'Neill, and Gary Shteyngart. Critics have often celebrated the apparently edgier point of view expressed by these authors, and the writings of these *liberal globalists* usually feel significantly different from those of mainstream liberals, even though the two groups share many fundamental assumptions. One of the goals of this book is to show how these authors' serious assaults on genre conventions serve their more temperate political purposes.

Finally, the fourth major cluster is made up of those who favor collective action as a means to create a more integrated world. This group of authors includes Russell Banks, Madison Smartt Bell, Philip Caputo, Carolina De Robertis, Paul Eggers, Nuruddin Farah, Helon Habila, Moses Isegawa, Philipp Meyer, Norman Rush, Teddy Wayne, and Karen Tei Yamashita. Most of these authors explicitly depict some form of left-wing politics in their writing. This *collectivist globalism* does not differ enormously from liberal globalism in substance, but it demonstrates far less stylistic consistency. The continuing presence of a diverse group of leftist outliers is a recurring theme in the chapters that follow, too, as we ask whether fidelity to emerging norms constrains political expression.

On the whole, then, authors of geopolitical fiction tend to support pro-global ideals in combination with liberal individualism or moderate collectivism in political action. They diverge considerably in their depictions of the present, however, and liberal individualists in particular imagine a very wide range of ideal worlds. They are not necessarily committed to a universalizing globalism, any more than collectivists are necessarily committed to localism (as they may have been during the heyday of Third Worldist delinking). These tables also suggest that very few radical aesthetes write geopolitical fiction; that is, few imagine a global holism resulting from isolated aesthetic rebellion. However, this is not an entirely uninhabited position. *Radical aesthetes* and *hardcore globalists* are actually about evenly matched in terms of number. Finally, if one were to color-code these tables in order to isolate authors by genre, very little significant clustering would appear. All of the emerging genres of geopolitical fiction have an ideological range; none is formulaically attached to a single position, even though each has certain important recurring features and decontested blank spaces, as subsequent chapters will demonstrate.

The most important point, however, to take away from these tables is that the twenty-first-century geopolitical novel consistently differentiates between actual and ideal worlds. In recent writing, the novel remains a form that expresses a social critique and envisions mechanisms for change. The novel persists in being, in other words, importantly political in ambition across a matrix of positions. The visions offered in the geopolitical novel may not be routinely attached to a particular political party or program or repeated in the slogans of street protests, but they are patterned and principled. The geopolitical novel works with the building blocks of twenty-first-century ideologies. In this resurging genre, collectivist ideologies appear alongside liberal individualist and aestheticist positions because the novel continues to make room for vigorous, continued debate. The ideological struggles expressed in the geopolitical novel exceed the constraints installed by the publishing industry, the ingrained prejudices of readers, and the influences of recent landmark events. Geopolitical fiction creates a vivid world waiting to be mapped and explored. This is a world in formation, open to the future, and ready for the reader's full engagement. Culture as an active, ongoing process rather than a museum of rarified objects is under way in the twenty-first-century geopolitical novel.

1 FROM ROUTES TO ROUTERS

The Digital Migrant Novel

Who more sci fi than us?
Junot Díaz, *The Brief Wondrous Life of Oscar Wao*

DURING THE 1980s and 1990s, narratives about immigration to the United States were frequently routed through trauma. Figuring immigration as the agonizing loss of a home culture, Maxine Hong Kingston, Julia Alvarez, and Jhumpa Lahiri, among others, developed a lexicon of wounds and scars. In widely read works such as *The Woman Warrior* (1975), *How the García Girls Lost Their Accent* (1991), and *The Interpreter of Maladies* (1999), the protagonists waver between a painful past and social exclusion in the American present. The migrant subject remains unincorporated and alien, and mourners, ghosts, and zombies proliferate. The migration narrative of the 1980s substitutes personal traumas for politics.

This version of the migration novel aims to recover culturally repressed or disavowed memories. Revisiting the traumas of migration is imagined as healing for the authorial subject and instructive for the nation. An "emancipatory politics of memory," Ali Behdad argues, "works through past traumas and injustices by way of adjudicating or 'properly' forgetting them."[1] For Behdad, that process concludes when healthy forgetfulness replaces the perpetual melancholic reopening of the traumatic wounds of migration. After the migrant's story is therapeutically recalled, it can drift into a more authentic amnesia. Proponents of trauma theory consider this process emancipatory because it focuses on private and autobiographical experiences of loss while refusing the social concerns of previous generations of dissidents and exiles.[2] The trauma theory of immigration sets Kingston's ghosts in the place of Anzia Yezierska's struggling garment workers in *Bread Givers* (1925), Abraham Cahan's enterprising businessmen in *The Rise of David Levinsky* (1917), and even Mario Puzo's capitalist gangsters in *The Godfather* (1969).[3]

These early-twentieth-century stories often stressed the discontinuity between pre- and post-migration scenes; they also tended to represent American culture as homogeneously white.[4] As summarized in the table, the traumatic migration novel attaches these inherited spatial and cultural figures to the memory-infused temporality of the genealogical narratives that flourished during the mid-twentieth century. Borrowing the tropes of fractured memory from the fictional neo-slave narratives such as Toni Morrison's *Beloved* (1987), Charles Johnson's *Middle Passage* (1990), and Octavia Butler's *Kindred* (1979), they turn their attention to the persistence of pre-migration culture and use trauma as a figure for temporal confusion and geographical distance.[5] In James Clifford's often-cited phrase, they combine "roots" and "routes."[6] Always en route, never finally arriving, the traumatized migrant maintains an insecure relationship to both sending and receiving cultures—an instability commonly figured through psychological doubles, mental and physical disorders, vulnerability to manipulation, homesickness, nostalgia, and unresolved family conflicts.[7] These figures ensure that "it is not private life that is subject to and interpreted in light of social and political events, but rather the other way around."[8] Trauma creates an inward-looking ethnic enclave largely defined by its hostile relation to an American environment organized around a binary system of race that disturbs the migrant's self-identity without replacing it.

The 1980s-era traumatic migration novel renounces the qualified optimism of earlier versions of the genre while retaining their national frame. Like the heroes of assimilation and roots narratives, traumatized migrants undergo an identity crisis triggered by passage over the border and incomplete assimilation into a racially marked national culture. Although rarely transcending the patriarchal ethnic enclave or successfully entering the capitalist marketplace as do the heroes of earlier generations, they continue the romantic approach to the self in crisis. Traumatized migrants also celebrate personal experience and free speech while traveling a landscape in which nations and cultures are closed, congruent spaces. The trauma of migration rests, after all, on the assumption that the home territory is inaccessible. Time may have become an echo chamber of private memories for the immigrant, but space does not yet share that feature.

The generic status of the traumatic migration narrative has attracted a good deal of critical attention—much of which points out political and aes-

The Traumatic Versus the Digital Migration Novel

	TRAUMATIC MIGRATION	DIGITAL MIGRATION
TIME	Memory and the past dominate the present	Accelerated, multidirectional, new eternity
SPACE	Bounded nations, place makes culture, displacement is limbo	Layered, phantasmagoric, discontinuous
SOCIETY	Inward-looking enclave, United States = racial binary	Dispersed families, ruptured enclaves, multiple racial divisions, resistance to conviviality, institutional focus
PLOT	Recovery, self-discovery	Code-switching, navigation, defining a public
HERO	Weak, disorganized, scarred, orphaned	Disembedded, in flight, publicly engaged
NARRATOR	Empathetic therapist, extends personal narrative	Archivist, router, multiple literacies
OBJECTS	Cultural fetish, memento	Recently obsolete technologies
TONE	Melancholic, mournful	Satiric, comic

thetic limits to this genre. In his comprehensive study of the cinema of exile, for instance, Hamid Naficy dissects the claustrophobic nationalist nostalgia that pervades immigrant and diasporic filmmaking.[9] Similarly, Pheng Cheah, Aihwa Ong, Timothy Brennan, Amitava Kumar, and Rosemary George have urged a reconsideration of the political visions advanced by celebrated authors of migration narratives, stressing the need to temper the self-representations of elites with narratives that consider the mass of less prosperous migrants.[10] In a related critique, David Morley argues that taking migration as the prototypical contemporary experience distorts the understanding of non-migrants in receiving cultures, making an effective analysis of First World xenophobia that much more difficult.[11] More broadly, Paul Gilroy refuses the "unhappy, archaic domain . . . populated by the timeless iconic ciphers of postcolonial melancholia," urging a turn toward the condition he calls "conviviality": "the processes of cohabitation and interaction that have made multiculture an ordinary feature of social life" in Britain and elsewhere.[12] For Gilroy and like-minded critics, the traumatized narrative of immigration is not only recognizable but also exhausted. Perpetually reconstituting the private world of the migrant's trauma, they argue, reproduces elite nationalism and precludes a more contestatory and pragmatic focus on interethnic coexistence in the present. The content, form, and tone of traumatic migration narratives require, on this account, some serious rethinking.

Although the trauma subgenre has not disappeared, a significant number of contemporary novelists have begun to move beyond it. Novels by Edwidge Danticat, Junot Díaz, Jeffrey Eugenides, Salvatore Scibona, Aleksandar Hemon, Francine Prose, Michael Chabon, Dinaw Mengestu, Teju Cole, Chris Abani, Hari Kunzru, and Mohsin Hamid, for example, replace the romance of migrant psychology with a focus on the media. More specifically, these twenty-first-century migration novels consistently take media systems as figures for transnational cultural exchanges. They occupy a spectrum of positions—ranging from those still wrestling with the trauma narrative to those rejecting it more fully—but all tackle media-related topics. This preoccupation with the digital-media economy in particular suggests that a genre shift is under way. The twenty-first-century migration novel is moving from the discrete geography of nations to the overlapping and virtual spaces of communication technologies.

Of course, media systems also appear in earlier immigration novels. Early-twentieth-century assimilation narratives often invoke broadcast media as figures of homogeneity, holism, and deracination that are at odds with the immigrant's cultural specificity and long historical traditions. Henry Roth's *Call It Sleep* (1934), for example, begins with the arrival on Ellis Island of immigrants whose clothes, food, and postures distinguish them from the mass of native-born, turn-of-the-century New Yorkers; only a life-threatening experience of near electrocution converts David Schearl into a modern American. Roth's semiconscious hero receives a wild array of fragmented sensory impressions, and he is remade into a triumphant modern hero when he attunes himself to their incessant call. For Roth, Yezierska, Cahan, Pietro di Donato, Sui sin Far (Edith Maude Eaton), and a host of other authors who published their works before 1945, media systems rewire the migrant; indeed, they arguably represent the Americanization process as a whole.[13] Media—understood as a cluster of semiotic systems ranging from radio, newspapers, movies, and popular literature to fashion and food—repeatedly serve in prewar migration literature as the sign of assimilation into a nationally delimited modernity.

Mass media is still used to figure American homogeneity in twenty-first-century migration fiction. Building on a tradition of media skepticism that stretches from Ralph Ellison's *Invisible Man* (1952) to Don DeLillo's *White Noise* (1985), Thomas Pynchon's *Vineland* (1990), and David Foster Wallace's *Infinite Jest* (1996), recent works such as David Wong Louie's *Barbarians Are Coming* (2000) invoke television as a reservoir of images for supposedly American norms and the deforming self-parodies involved in media representations of ethnicity.[14] Similarly, Susan Sontag's *In America* (2000) presents American culture through the eyes of a Polish actress appalled at the uniformly low standards of the maudlin melodramas that she encounters after immigrating to California. Often this figure has political connotations. Khaled Hosseini's best seller *The Kite Runner* (2003), for instance, uses popular song and film quite conventionally to represent a sphere of liberal toleration at odds with the Taliban's perverse prohibitions, while recent works by Díaz, Danticat, and Mengestu associate broadcast media with dictators. Reflecting a digital sensibility, these twenty-first-century authors look back at centralized media systems from vaudeville, radio, and the popular press to television and use these forms as figures for political as well as cultural dogmatism. They invoke early-twentieth-century depictions of mass media as a tool of assimilation but often stretch that analogy to its metaphysical extremes.

Another media motif common in earlier versions of the migration novel is an independent, community voice that coexists with and sometimes repudiates mass media. In reference to cinema, Naficy calls these practices interstitial, collective, and artisanal.[15] In American literature, a comparable practice involves presses that target specific populations and/or languages—such as the bilingual Arte Público and the Before Columbus Foundation at the University of California, Berkeley. Aiming for differentiation rather than assimilation, these "narrowcasting" projects use media practices for community empowerment, and they are actively involved in the publication of the roots-oriented immigrant writing that began to proliferate in the late 1970s.

Contemporary migration writing, however, scrutinizes the empowerment approach to ethnic media as often as it endorses it. In the new fiction, a pattern of immigrants exploiting newer immigrants undercuts the intra-ethnic solidarity necessary for artisanal media. Concerns about clichés and tokenism also challenge community media's enclave sensibility. Rather than retreating from the homogeneity of the dominant media, twenty-first-century authors reframe "mainstream" media as an ethnically specific practice: Michael Chabon converts superheroes into golems, Hari Kunzru analogizes the computer virus and Bollywood cinema, while Junot Díaz insists that science fiction is inherently Antillean (and vice versa). These authors replace alternative media production with an oppositional reading of media history. In this respect, whether or not it directly figures digital media, the new migration novel relies on the premise of a dispersed, peer-to-peer media system, rather than broadcasting or narrowcasting logics.

For the authors of early-twenty-first-century migration fiction, in other words, "roots" become "routes," and then "routes" become "routers." This writing is well acquainted with multimedia networks organized around nodes that allow multidirectional transmissions of coded signals. Establishing patterns of overlapping links, frequency, and "stickiness" is as important in these works as announcing a unified theme. The digital-media system, as I understand it, enfolds broadcasting and narrowcasting within a network of telecommunications, reducing even further any absolute distinctions among technologies, as all become interconnected components of a mobile system.[16] In this apparatus, the router is vital because it can send and receive packages of data simultaneously to and from multiple devices using different protocols. Whether in home-office personal computers or building-size megacomputers, routers serve as translation machines that encode, decode, and recode. Networks do not function without these points of contact, and the firewalls installed on routers protect the network itself from the data overloads that can occur when router capacities are exceeded. Routers connect, translate, and filter; routers—or, in Manuel Castells's word, "switchers"—are the "the privileged instruments of power."[17] In all these senses, the new migration fiction positions the narrator as a router, filtering and processing an overwhelming multisensory global system. The narrator as router is distributed across the system rather than looking inward or backward in the romantic sense. Whether or not they directly take digital media as a topic, the new works borrow the organizational logic of digital-media systems and, in so doing, reformulate the basic premises of migration fiction.

The narrator as router is embedded in a distinctive social logic. The digital system provides an enormous archive of the recent past alongside a much thinner array of copyright-protected materials from the preceding two generations. This pattern arguably reinforces an accelerated sense of temporality, as well as a geography organized by compression, rapidity, urban density, and radical inequalities of access.[18] Digital temporality and spatiality extend the organization of historical time and territorial space while introducing such new components as the experiences of disembedded placelessness that geographer Aharon Kellerman has called "phantasmagoric."[19] Some observers consider wired youth to be a new social and political subject of liberation (while others feel that new forms of social fragmentation and radical solipsism are the primary effects of digital media).[20] Similarly dualistic evaluations of new forms of text, literacy, and attention also arise in assessments of the digital environment.[21] Regardless of whether we like it or not, though, in this phantasmagoric, socially disorganized textual space, the strong omniscient narrator tends to dissolve into the archivist, bookmarker, detective, traveler, or surfer—that is, the router. The digital system not only enfolds pre-digital forms of communication (epistolary, telegraphic, telephonic, televisual, and so on) but also requires stories to navigate among these nodes by means of code switching, translation, and a continual re-routing of vital processes. Thus a significant number of migration narratives produced in the first decade of the twenty-first century reduce their investment in the motif of trauma, turning instead to an exploration of a digital-media space.

Borrowing some pieces from narratives of traumatic migration, the digital migrant novel wrenches them into a new shape. Generational differences, for instance, are often marked by styles of media engagement, as well as by the geographic dispersal and degrees of linguistic assimilation used in earlier writing. The new migrant heroes are less often psychologically wounded recipients of demoralizing messages and more often mobile subjects who receive and interpret cultural codes while actively transmitting and translating their own information. Often reaching a crisis point in a public space (such as a church, prison, palace, street, monument, festival, or café), the navigational plots of these works frequently turn on the characters' discovery of maps of transnational arenas rather than the revelation of secrets so crucial to romantic fictions of self-discovery. Also, the tone of this writing downplays traumatic melancholy, striking a sharper, satiric note. These novels shift away from the personal universe of trauma and toward a public and political effort to think life stories that exceed those provided by the sending or receiving nations. Digital migrant fiction, in short, moves toward the geopolitical novel.

Many variations arise in the new migration novels, some of which can be traced to the regionally specific literary precedents with which authors struggle. Migration from the Caribbean and the Mediterranean regions, central Europe, sub-Saharan Africa, and South Asia has not only occurred at different historical moments but also triggered different narrative dilemmas. Consequently, writers concerned with these regions have taken diverse approaches to the common problem of reshaping the U.S. immigration narrative for the digital environment. Nonetheless, when read together, these works also reveal a kind of transnational conviviality that is only partially evident in individual texts.

The Divided Island: Edwidge Danticat, Junot Díaz, and Caribbean Migration

To illustrate the range of the new migrant narrative, one could do worse than to turn to two writers and friends born on the island of Hispaniola: Edwidge Danticat and Junot Díaz. While Haitian American Danticat's writing makes much freer use of the motifs of trauma to narrate immigrant lives, her lyric prose in *The Dew Breaker* (2004) also subtly tests those conventions. It shares more than one might initially imagine with the much more ecstatic turn away from trauma in Díaz's debut novel, *The Brief Wondrous Life of Oscar Wao* (2007). This Pulitzer Prize winner makes free use of "narratives of the impossible: sci fi, horror, fantasy."[22] Díaz's long and multidimensional detour through genre fiction leads the way toward the new migration novel. His writing rebounds from the stalemates of immigrant trauma tales by expanding their geographic and generic vision simultaneously.

Despite their considerable stylistic differences, Díaz and Danticat share a concern with Caribbean versions of revolutionary nationalism. In the post-colonial Caribbean, nationalism has been crucial for writers interested in articulating a New World sensibility distinct from the culture of the former colonists, the neocolonial presence of the United States, and any techno-global forms of historical amnesia.[23] Literary nationalisms in the Caribbean are also quite diverse. Those deriving from Aimé Césaire's Négritude often displace the heart of the nation to the African diaspora, while indigenists ground their efforts in the particular forms of racial and cultural *mestizaje* that have arisen in the Caribbean.[24] Many indigenist works were written by men living in exile, and they tend toward a paradoxically romantic nostalgia for a Caribbean nation understood as incomplete or even imaginary. The contradictions inherent in this exilic nationalism have been addressed in recent writings by Caribbean women—many of whom are economic migrants, rather than political exiles.[25]

Deepening this gender critique, in *House/Garden/Nation*, Ileana Rodríguez distinguishes revolutionary Caribbean nationalism from bourgeois approaches to the nation and elite cosmopolitanism.[26] She argues that contemporary men's and women's fictions of dispossession and migration expose the idealist underpinnings of the revolutionary tradition, and she prefers these projects to the amnesia that results from a purely American approach to the migrant's story. The engagement of contemporary Caribbean writers with a nest of issues centered on the home, private space, and experience, Rodríguez argues, should be understood as a politically charged moment in an ongoing discussion of the nation as home, rather than as a retreat from public life.

This approach illuminates Danticat's *Dew Breaker*, a novel that directly addresses "the most celebrated literary work of Haitian indigenism": Jacques Roumain's *Gouverneurs de la rosée* (*Masters of the Dew*, 1944).[27] The exile Roumain was a romantic nationalist who considered the landed peasant to be the ideal citizen, and Danticat updates and complicates his vision. Instead of a dewy pastoral retreat, her fiction makes a twenty-first-century layered, urban, and transnational space the migrant's home. She replaces a utopian drive for mastery with a politically skeptical and mediated sensibility.

Danticat's revision of a specifically Haitian version of the national novel coexists, however, with her investment in the American Anglophone context that has granted her a "stepmother" tongue.[28] Much of her earlier work addresses this context in the language of trauma. *Krik, Krak!* (1996) is a story cycle informed by a receding oral culture; *Breath, Eyes, Memory* (1998) considers sexual anxieties linked to the Haitian practice of "testing" a girl's hymen; *The Farming of Bones* (1999) describes genocidal massacres at the Haitian–Dominican border; and *Brother, I'm Dying* (2008) recalls the life of a beloved uncle who died in detention facilities run by the Immigration and Nationalization Service. Critics often read these works as affirming an ethnically bound female solidarity.[29] Some even feel that Dandicat's work rejects the tropes of transnational migration and hybridity altogether.[30] However, while therapeutic figures do recur in her prose, even influencing the treatment of landscape in *The Dew Breaker*, roots and racination are not her only themes. As Valerie Kaussen has argued, Danticat playfully experiments with indigenism in a media-savvy manner.[31] Her version of the Haitian countryside as well as the metropolitan United States is saturated with urban graffiti, prison tattoos, telephone calls, answering machines, community radio, and newspaper reports. Authentic, indigenous, and matrilineal orality are carefully filtered through the communication technologies of the modern state in Danticat's most recent writing. This is especially true in *The Dew Breaker*, a story cycle that explores the titular father's compromised legacy, not the mother's. Detailing media systems that circulate traumatic histories, Danticat complements the individualist preoccupation with memory with the public concerns of the twenty-first-century migration novel.

The significance of the media in *The Dew Breaker* is accentuated by Danticat's lyric minimalism. In prose characterized by brevity of statement, carefully selected detail, thematic and rhythmic use of silence, and symbolic internal monologues, the few passages in which dense descriptions of physical objects occurs attract particular notice. For example, in a crucial passage, the protagonist's family attends a Christmas Eve Mass at a Haitian American church in Brooklyn. There they imagine that they recognize Emmanuel Constant, the organizer of death squads in the 1990s.[32] This passage introduces a sort of historical data (number of victims, names of political organizations, proper names of the enemy) that is unusual in Danticat's spare and symbolic prose, and it presents a microcosm of the primal scene of the volume (the daughter's new view of her father). It also uses a recognizably "postmodern" layering of mediated images. The characters do not simply point and see. Anne, the mother and focalizer of this passage, has only a "limited view of the man's profile" (78). She does not experience the instantaneous flood of memory and sensation that Danticat has elsewhere identified as an effect of trauma.[33] Instead, Anne compares her view to "the picture a community group had printed on the WANTED FOR CRIMES AGAINST THE HAITIAN PEOPLE flyers, which had been stapled to lampposts all along Nostrand Avenue a month before" (78). The flyer as an informal medium of communication authorizes this moment of recognition (later revealed as a misrecognition). It also keeps in circulation the knowledge of Constant's crimes as they are reported "through Haitian newspapers, Creole radio and cable access programs" (79). The flyer signals the migrant community's networked sensibility, and it is itself repeatedly rewritten. A "fragmented collage with as many additions as erasures," the flyer acquires "demonic-looking horns" that later fade, much as its inflammatory writing "started disappearing so that the word rape became ape and the 5 vanished from 5,000, leaving a trio of zeros as the number of Constant's casualties" (79). In this unusually detailed description of the ephemeral flyer, Danticat documents the faulty circuits of transmission that undergird memories of trauma as well as purportedly cathartic moments of recognition. Zeros and faded demons are the unreliable substance of public memory, according to this story—which is ironically titled "The Book of Miracles." Firmly stapled to a lamppost on Nostrand Avenue in the Bedford-Stuyvesant neighborhood of Brooklyn, the flyer also insists on the tangibly American location of the mediated migrant's experiences and memory.

Media-inspired misrecognition also organizes *The Dew Breaker*'s framing narratives and provides the volume's thematic core. In the opening story, "The Book of the Dead," the author figure (a sculptor named Ka) discovers that she has misrecognized her own father, taking him for a victim of the *tonton macoutes* (death squads) rather than a member. This discovery is presented through a sequence of inverted media motifs during a journey to deliver a statue of the father to a Haitian American celebrity. The father dumps the statue in a body of water and disappears from their hotel, only to be tracked down by the police. While searching for her father, Ka recalls his repeated readings of "The Negative Confession" from *The Book of the Dead*, an ancient Egyptian funerary text. "I should have removed the negatives" from the passage's litany of nonviolence and renunciation of culpability, she concludes (23). Rather than moving with the breaks in the grain of the wood in which she has too easily found an analogy for her father's scarred back, Ka, as well as her actress-patron, begin the more counter-intuitive practice of reading and listening against the grain of repeated stories. This media skepticism is necessary because, in *The Dew Breaker*, repetition is strongly associated with dictatorial communication, as well as with deceptive silence. Crucial scenes recall an insulting ritual in which food was distributed to the poorest citizens (winners in the "poverty Olympics") as well as the "daylong speeches [that] were continually rebroadcast on the radio each year" (171, 150). Besieged by that one-way communication, Ka and other receptive narrators in *The Dew Breaker* learn to reroute mediated signs.

Some of this peer-to-peer communication occurs by telephone. On discovering her father's past, Ka calls her mother in Brooklyn. "Manman, how do you love him?" she asks (24). Rather than an explanation of her mother's (or father's) life in Haiti, this question triggers a reflection on the parents' complicity with each other—the way they "echo each other, in their speech, their actions, even in their businesses . . . they were a society of two, sharing a series of private codes and associations, a past that even if [she]'d been born in the country of their birth [she] still wouldn't have known" (25). Excluded from this dyad and unable to access the secret of her own origins, the daughter Ka is overcome by the sensation "that something else besides [her] brain and muscles is moving [her] fingers," and she hangs up the telephone (25). Once the broadcast system is disrupted, in other words, a channel is opened for possession by Vodun Loa, or spirits. In the grip of Loa, Ka begins to interpret family "codes and associations" to which her access had been limited. The encounter results in a new multidirectional Haitian American media.

This new media practice aligns Ka with the second-generation journalist who interviews one of her father's torture victims; Aline "had never imagined that people like [her interviewee] existed, men and women whose tremendous agonies filled every blank space in their lives," and she discovers that "maybe there were hundreds, even thousands, of people like this, men and women chasing fragments of themselves long lost to others" and that "maybe [she] herself was one of them" (137–138). However, Aline's reconstruction of the fractured story of her traumatized interviewee is not the story of *The Dew Breaker*.

Not the innocent daughter but the patricidal ex-con, Claude, serves as Danticat's emblem of a new mediated migrant sensibility. Claude appears in "Night Talkers," a tale in which one of several torture victims travels to the mountaintop village of his youth. "Too young, it seemed, to have been expatriated twice, from both his native country and his adopted land" (100) and covered in heavily tattooed skin reminiscent of the graffiti-scarred flyer, Claude is learning to speak Creole as well as English and, more crucially, learning to understand himself. "It's like a puzzle, a weird-ass kind of puzzle, man," he explains. "I'm the puzzle and these people are putting me back together, telling me things about myself and my family that I never knew or gave a fuck about" (102). His interlocutor concludes that "Claude was even luckier than he realized, for he was able to speak his nightmares to himself as well as to others" (120). Unlike village matriarchs who murmur in their sleep, the notably masculine, multiply migratory, and heavily encoded Claude can speak distinctly "in the nighttime as well as in the hours past dawn" (120). This utopian figure suggests the possibility of a successful, hybridized communication system and style emerging from the experience of migration. He is neither an assimilated entrant into the hegemonic American system, like Ka and Aline, nor an unsullied representative of a pure Haitian oral culture. His speech, as well as his skin and history, are pieces of a "weird-ass puzzle" that is not yet solved. He is memorable and visible—unlike the tortured prisoner who (according to radio reports that close the volume) set himself on fire at dawn, "leaving behind no corpse to bury, no trace of himself at all" (242). Through this emphasis on a new interlingual, multimedia communication, then, Danticat effectively shifts her focus in *The Dew Breaker* from the traumatic memories of individual victims of torture to the public and political questions surrounding media systems that report (or fail to do so) on the existence of torture.

Díaz begins where Danticat concludes, making a version of her Claude the tragic-comic title character of *The Brief Wondrous Life of Oscar Wao*. A science fiction–obsessed, overweight "ghetto nerd" whose story bridges Santo Domingo and suburban New Jersey, Oscar vividly exemplifies some of the most characteristic tendencies of the twenty-first-century mediated migration narrative. His story sketches the political history of the Dominican Republic and investigates the responsibilities of writers in a geopolitically charged situation. As the novel proceeds, its narration becomes increasingly elaborate, until finally the politics of contemporary media systems supplant any nostalgic or affirmative approach to the past. Genre fiction, comic books, role-playing games, and science fiction films vividly convey the absurdity of the geopolitical present for Díaz's contemporary migrant.

In *Oscar Wao*, as to a lesser extent in *The Dew Breaker*, the excess of mass media displaces the authority of indigenous folklore. Rather than disturbing a banal calendrical realism with the spookier temporality and causality of myth (as in magical realism), Díaz repeatedly mixes an array of postmodern media images and supposedly premodern figures, refusing the differentiations required for magical effects. At the sentence level as well as in his claiming of the territory previously claimed by Mario Vargas Llosa's *Feast of the Goat* (2000) (a gruesome depiction of the assassination of Rafael Trujillo), Díaz revises some of the most influential conventions for representing Hispanophone Latin America in general and the Dominican Republic in particular.

After all, although depicting the wounds inflicted on the Dominican Republic by Trujillo's regime, *Oscar Wao* is not a dictator novel. In fact, it is profoundly skeptical of any opposition between writers and dictators. As the title indicates, Díaz is at least as interested in addressing an American literary tradition as he is in wrestling with indigenist magical realism. Borrowing syntax as well plot devices from Hemingway's widely read story "The Short Happy Life of Francis Macomber" (1936), Díaz tackles a prototypically American narrative that celebrates the revelatory powers of travel. Hemingway's narrator is an expatriate hunter in Tanzania who denounces the romantic clichés of safari films while allowing that they may have granted the doomed title character a twinge of masculine self-mastery in the moment immediately preceding his death. Similarly, Díaz's hip-hop-loving, Web-surfing narrator, Yunior, finally reconciles himself to the less than macho Oscar and his nerdy media habits. Like Hemingway's hunter, Díaz's narrator becomes importantly complicit in the story he conveys—a simultaneously American and Dominican narrative of displacement.

Díaz's interest in crafting a new hybrid and mass-mediated language for migration is evident from the first clauses of the novel: "They say it came first from Africa, carried in the screams of the enslaved; that it was the death bane of the Tainos, uttered just as one world perished and another began; that it was a demon drawn into Creation through the nightmare door that was cracked open in the Antilles. *Fukú americanus*, or more colloquially, *fukú*—generally a curse or a doom of some kind; specifically the Curse and the Doom of the New World" (1). Creative and colloquial, Díaz's narration rapidly transitions from Africa to the Antilles and from historical horrors to mock-scientific classification and everyday slang. These registers fuse together to forge the capitalized, patterned logic of myth, but that seemingly folkloristic ritual for closing "the nightmare door" quickly mutates into a comic book fantasy of death banes and demons—a fantasy refined in the Tolkien reference to "the Curse and the Doom."

As this paragraph and novel unfold, these hyperbolic passages become less frequent, but we still return occasionally to the voice of popular rumor, with which the novel begins ("They say"). What "they say" in *Oscar Wao*, however, is always a mixture of folk mythology and mass-produced elements. Oscar's grandmother La Inca, for instance, imagines the United States through the conventions of both film noir and the catechism as "nothing more and nothing less than a *país* overrun by gangsters, *putas*, and no-accounts. Its cities swarmed with machines and industry, as thick with *sinvergüencería* as Santo Domingo was with heat" (158). Although facing north rather than south, her multilingual and multigenre speech is no less complex than Yunior's narration.

Yunior is, after all, the Watcher, who, like the DC Comics alien, cannot (yet occasionally does) venture beyond the "Source Wall" separating him from the humanoids he observes. As the Watcher, he also notes the appearance of "a creature that would have been an amiable mongoose if not for its golden lion eyes and the absolute black of its pelt" (149). Seemingly a totemic protector straight out of Afro-centric folklore, this recurring figure of the black mongoose also sings popular songs in an unplaceable accent, "maybe Venezuelan, maybe Colombian"—especially the well-known lyric "sueño, sueño, sueño, como tú te llamas. . . . Yo me llamo sueño de la madrugada" (150). This creature with the "chabine eyes," indicating its mixed-race roots,[34] is characterized in the narrator's footnote as "one of the great unstable particles of the Universe and also one of its greatest travelers" (151n.18). Like the *fukú*, its passage from Africa to the Caribbean goes by way of India and possibly has extraterrestrial aspects as well. The ultimate migrant as well as a salvational force on a par with La Inca's miraculous prayers, then, the mongoose installs media consciousness at the origins of folkloristic myth (and vice versa).

This hybridized folk–media sensibility defines the first-person plural of "we postmodern plátanos" (144). "Who more sci-fi than us?" Yunior memorably, though rhetorically, asks (21). Oscar's privilege in this scenario lies in his writerly capacity for appreciating the wild extremes and beauty of the Dominican

Republic. He perceives the economic needs of Dominicans while fulfilling his own erotic longings on a return journey. But from the point of view of Yunior's narration, the real wonder is Oscar's transition from the shamed social outcast to the type of the ideal writer. Intensely creative, he pours out pages of narrative during his island sojourn and, in essence, writes his magical *chabine*, his mongoose-like and salvational "golden mulata," into existence (279). Yunior as narrator reemphasizes this pairing of nerd and folk culture in one of many meta-fictional reflections. "I know I've thrown a lot of fantasy and sci-fi in the mix," he asserts, "but this is supposed to be a *true* account of the Brief Wondrous Life of Oscar Wao. Can't we believe that [Oscar's erotic object] Ybón can exist and that a brother like Oscar might be due a little luck after twenty-three years" (285). The truth of the narrative, as well as whatever possibilities for fulfillment it presents, appear in this title passage by means of the fantasy and science fiction elements, not in spite of them. Unlike Oscar's culturally and historically produced bad luck, these popular media genres introduce into the narrative some open doors and necessary magic. True in their effects as well as fantastic in their content, these observations on genre fiction tie questions of media systems inextricably to the political themes of the novel.

After all, it is not only Oscar's prolific, although unpublished, writing that features in the novel. Díaz also repeatedly illustrates the writing process of states. Contesting Salman Rushdie's assumption that writers and dictators are inherently opposed, Yunior suggests the possibility of their alignment in an early footnote explaining the novel's efforts at polyvocality. As monovocal texts, the writings of dictators contain many censored, silent moments that Díaz exposes, expands, and explores, reading them as instances of repressed mediation. Most notably, the Dominican Republic's former dictator Trujillo not only is presented in *Oscar Wao* as wrongly and unfairly adopting popular representations (such as the Vodun Loa Baron Samedi) for his own purposes, making them speak his language of terror, but also is concerned with editing from a distance—controlling the circulation of scholarly dissertations by assassinating their authors and, Yunior speculates, arresting the patriarch of Oscar's family (the bookish Abelard) because of "a book about the Dark Powers of the President, a book in which Abelard argued that the tales the common people told about the president—that he was supernatural, that he was not human—may in some ways [have] been *true*" (245). Complicating any easy story of erotic drives governing history, Yunior/Díaz finds writing fundamental to political power. Writing reveals the truth contained in the supernatural tales of the "common people," and that is why dictators aim to control it, we are told. The dictatorial state acts not in opposition to any and all writers but, in particular, against those writers who stand in solidarity with the population, a solidarity manifested in a politicized approach to popular tales. The state is an editor and a censor whose perfect book is the blank that appears repeatedly in dreams and visions in several passages in the last third of the novel. Substituting for Abelard's explanatory *grimoire*, the blank book correlates with the horrifying "man with no face" that both Oscar and his mother confront immediately after their experiences of torture. These terrifying dream images represent the anti-writing performed by the dictatorial state. A monovocal text is the dictator's blank text, according to Yunior.

In opposition to dictatorial singularity and blankness, Díaz positions not the unfiltered excesses of either supernatural folk tales or genre fiction. It is instead in popular media archived, researched, retooled, and recombined by a "literary" writer that we find the most utopian moments of the novel. As the Hemingwayesque title reminds us, the narrative is built around the irony of a potentially insincere narrator reflecting on the death of a naïve hero. Yunior, after all, is not only the classic Dominican playboy, Oscar's roommate, and Oscar's sister's one-time boyfriend but also, we learn toward the close of the novel, a struggling creative writer who teaches composition at Middlesex Community College, and he serves as an archivist of sorts for Oscar's many unpublished volumes, a researcher who posts to Dominican-themed Listserves, and the bearer of Oscar's dream. Yunior literally dreams Oscar's dreams for him after his death; Yunior is haunted by the blank book, the man with no face, and his own unspoken words of love: "——— ——— ———" (327). As a middle-class, literate, domesticated married migrant, Yunior takes up Abelard's mantle, producing his own postmodern *grimoire*, a form in which both excesses and blanks appear on the page before the reader.

Yunior's emergence, in short, as the exemplary migrant—akin to Danticat's repatriated Claude—depends on neither full assimilation into the capitalist culture industries of the United States nor enthusiastic embrace of an authentic sending culture. Instead, Díaz's mediated migrant is multivocal, having disruptive, difficult relations with dictatorial writing in the context of an economically stratified consumerist society. He recalls the truths told by popular narrative (recast as science fiction) and the repressive, terrorizing hand of the censor. This media-savvy narrator allows Díaz to highlight, first, his shift from the psychologizing language of trauma and, second, his turn toward a strongly politicized and anti-statist approach to writing. By no means do all of

Díaz's companions in the project of retooling the migration novel share these arguably anarchist concerns; a range of responses to the dominant trauma narrative appears in twenty-first-century fiction. Nonetheless, Díaz's emphasis on the political benefits of overcoming individual psychological wounding grounds many works in the emerging genre of the digital migrant novel.

MEDITERRANEAN MIGRANTS: JEFFREY EUGENIDES AND SALVATORE SCIBONA

Fiction that describes the voyages of migrants from the Mediterranean also wrestles with its political and literary predecessors, searching for those subjects occluded by narratives popular in the United States. Italian American authors, in particular, confront a distinctive cultural nationalism organized around Catholicism, family identity, and failed imperial ambition. This powerful in-group narrative is both caricatured and reinforced by pop-culture representations of Italian Americans as patriarchal Mafiosi.[35] In the 1980s, this tradition had settled so solidly in place that a counter-narrative could appear—including some revisionist fiction exploring maternal and grand-maternal relationships, for example (such as Tina De Rosa's *Paper Fish* [1980] and Helen Barolini's *Umbertina* [1979]).

This self-referential and critical sense of ethnicity is less evident in narratives describing migration from Greece. According to Ioanna Laliotou, mid-twentieth-century Greek immigrant autobiographies and Greek-language publications in the United States tended to remain focused on the homeland; they described community rituals and the motives for migration rather than a new hybridized ethnic identity.[36] But, more recently, a more pronounced, self-conscious struggle with media images (from Elia Kazan's immigration epic *America, America* [1963] to the more sentimental and suburban pastoral narratives of *Zorba the Greek* [1964] and *My Big Fat Greek Wedding* [2002]) has emerged. Several of the popular comic essays by David Sedaris—for instance, *Naked* (1997) and When *You Are Engulfed in Flames* (2008)—play on ethnic stereotypes, undercutting clichéd portraits of a warmly supportive Mediterranean family life by portraying Greeks as serial litterers, for example, or homophobic followers of Orthodox Christian dogma. In writing like Sedaris's, normative versions of an ethnicity forged by the trauma of migration begin to cede to a more cosmopolitan sensibility skeptical of in-group identity. Although this new cosmopolitanism may not always culminate in the kind of pan-Mediterranean sensibility suggested by Fernand Braudel,[37] it does suggest that a degree of media critique informs some recent Mediterranean migration narratives. Often using family-saga frameworks that establish some distance between the trauma of migration and the present, twenty-first-century Mediterranean migration narratives locate themselves in a potentially post-ethnic media landscape.

This pattern certainly organizes Jeffrey Eugenides's *Middlesex* (2002). The novel parodies the assimilationist ideals of the melting pot in a sequence that pairs a performance of Israel Zangwill's famous play *The Melting Pot* (1908) with intrusive Fordist scrutiny of the immigrant's home life. But its main concern is the emptiness of ethnicity as a genetic category.[38] *Middlesex* takes as its hero a single mutated gene expressed as hermaphroditic genitalia, tracing the fortunes of this pair of chromosomes as it moves from a mountain village in Asia Minor to early-twentieth-century Detroit, New York, and San Francisco before moving finally into expatriation in a contemporary-sounding Berlin. Although enabled by the inbred isolation of the village and the immigrant enclave, as well as the social upheaval and possibility for self-invention allowed by the burning of Smyrna, the mutation itself is presented as having no particular culture. Only the accidental illogic of Greek folk practices and the specific contingencies of an American hospital birth, allow the narrator, Cal/Calliope, to be miscategorized as a girl, albeit a hairy and flat-chested one; a specifically American and 1970s practice of gender-assignment surgery figures in the novel as coercive misrecognition as well. Cal escapes from family and doctor alike to forge a new identity on the road and ultimately in exile. Both ethnic tradition and the supposedly cultureless institutions of the United States are dangerously restrictive in *Middlesex*. As the title indicates, the positive term in Eugenides's new migration novel is the excluded middle between male and female, Greek and American, and—more contentiously— black and white.

The latter theme emerges when the protagonist's family establishes a home base in Detroit in the Greek-only Zebra Lounge, a space that is figuratively black and white. This segregated establishment soon mutates into a thriving Greek restaurant with black employees and, finally, into a lucrative, deracinated hot-dog chain. Similarly, recognizing the absurdity of the ethnic conflict motivating the novel's primal scene (the burning of Smyrna) becomes a condition of Americanization. Far from being the inevitable and timeless antagonists described by older members of the community in the novel, Greeks and Turks become in the United States nearly indistinguishable. They intermarry and, in one of the great comic sequences of this sprawling novel, their supposed status as intermediaries in a white–black racial binary is planted at the heart of Eugenides's depiction of the Black Muslim movement. Cal's grandmother Desdemona not only overcomes stifling Depression-era racial prejudices by taking a job in a black neighborhood but also discovers that Wallace Fard, the mysterious leader of the Nation of Islam before Elijah Muhammed, apparently shared her ethnic, racial, and geographic origins.[39] The revelations of *Middlesex*, in short, derive from access to continuities that lie deeper than perceived ideology or national culture, including the nationally specific American views of race and gender.

These continuities emerge through media systems. The most utopian and affirmative moments of Eugenides's novel invoke a developing system of mass media that anticipates the cosmopolitan sensibility of the expatriate narrator and his new beloved, an Asian American artist and photographer. Mass media, especially popular music, permeate and unify the world of Eugenides's novel in a way that nation and/or culture (understood as ethnically demarcated tradition) never do. At the outset, Desdemona woos her brother by recreating pages from an underwear catalog, just as Lefty seeks escape from his provisionally thwarted desires in the Greek version of urban blues known as *rembetika*. In the next generation, Cal's father keeps the genetic mutation in circulation by seducing his cousin with medleys played on the jazz clarinet. Even Cal/Calliope's erotic life is filtered through the media—from the prepschool vampire film that frames her first fumbling heterosexual encounter to the much more vivid stage performances that bring the female Obscure Object of Desire (an obvious homage to the film of the same title directed by Luis Buñuel) into view. Even after Calliope hits the road as Cal, she resurfaces, literally, in the context of a Tom Waits–inspired carnival. In short, you know not only who you are but also who you want in this novel because of the media.

Perhaps the most memorable moment, however, of media permeation and reorientation of culture and identity in *Middlesex* is not erotic but political. While Desdemona tends the silkworms in the temple, she hears Fard's speeches filtering up through the floorboards. Every day at one o'clock, the grate began to rumble: "PERHAPS YOU RECALL, IN OUR LAST LECTURE, HOW I TOLD YOU ABOUT THE DEPORTATION OF THE MOON? . . . SIXTY TRILLION YEARS AGO A GOD-SCIENTIST DRILLED A HOLE THROUGH THE EARTH, FILLED IT WITH DYNAMITE AND BLEW THE EARTH IN TWO. THE SMALLER OF THESE PIECES BECAME THE MOON. DO YOU RECALL THAT?" (153).

In addition to emphasizing in its content the creative power of fantasies of origins, Fard's rhetorically excessive reported speech provides a crucial image of the situation of interethnic entanglement that makes his separatist vision possible. Once we understand them as the work of the Mediterranean Jimmy Zizmo, these politically charged Afro-futurist meditations double as racial/ethnic performances premised on the migrant's mobility, and like the heroic funk sensibility that inspires a young Cal during the race riots of the 1960s, Fard's speeches anticipate *Oscar Wao*'s even deeper investment in the same science-fictional status of the migrant. Together with Eugenides's repeated descriptions of the clitoris/penis as a budding crocus and the narrative emphasis on flight, this ecstatic passage reinforces the novel's commitment to the emergence of new, mobile, and voluntary stories, rather than a coercive, collective fidelity to a traumatic past. *Middlesex* finds wild new media narratives exhilarating even if they are also sometimes monstrous and disturbing.

A similarly ambivalent relation to ethnic tradition appears in Salvatore Scibona's impressive debut novel, the National Book Award nominee *The End* (2008). Set in the fictional Elephant Park section of Cleveland, Ohio, between 1905 and 1953, *The End* takes as its subject the interlocking lives and desires of a group of immigrants from Sicily and southern Italy. The novel is organized around events that transpire during the Feast of the Assumption. All six primary characters undergo private transformations and changes in their relationships during the festival, and social bonds animate the novel. Intergroup relations are also changing; a ripple of rumor passes through the procession, and the faithful react to the presence of African Americans in the crowd and ultimately in the neighborhood. In short, *The End* employs Faulknerian and Woolfian devices to build up a textured account of community life in an early-twentieth-century immigrant enclave.[40] The novel's depiction of this community is, however, not remotely nostalgic.

The repetitious daily life of Rocco the baker, the hero of the opening section, for example, is clearly oppressive and torturous. Rocco's fidelity to the wife and three sons who have abandoned him—in short, his devotion to a family ideal—troubles him enormously. Although Scibona honors the baker's labors with gorgeous descriptive detail, his real heroism emerges in the moments of sublime anxiety experienced during an eastward journey to reclaim his wife. In a subtle and characteristically twenty-first-century reformulation of tropes of the migration novel, Scibona places Rocco at Niagara Falls, jangling his car keys, tempted to leave the United States, "an act that represented, yes, the terminus of the path along which Providence had been leading him. He had entered the United States one morning forty years before and had yet to leave. The pattern of these last two days, the instruction he was receiving, was to take the long view, and longer. The next step, yes, was to get out of the country altogether and turn around and see it for what it was" (53).

It is not the baker's initial departure from Italy that matters here, dramatic and complete as it is repeatedly understood to be, but the way in which the migrant himself might reverse his course and "take the long view" of his own history. *The End* suggests that this retrospective vision will ultimately be eschatological. In this scene, as in the novel as a whole (which returns to the vertiginous, suicidal temptations of bridges near its close), the emphasis shifts outward from individual consciousness to the "instruction" received from Providence. Travel and mobility are translated into a distinctly Catholic universalism.

This philosophically complex element of Scibona's novel arises most directly in the passages describing the education of Ciccio, a teenager conceived during the rape of an Italian immigrant woman by a WASPy Kentuckian. As a figure for assimilation, Ciccio is clearly ambiguous. As in *Middlesex*, reproduction and heritage are vexed figures inside the ethnic enclave and at its borders. Ciccio remains largely unaware of the manner of his own conception, focusing instead on learning for the future. Through his education, Ciccio simultaneously abandons his immediate circumstances for the international world of the Jesuits and reaffirms the fundamental premises of the Italian community through his exploration of faith. His position as an intellectual version of Rocco, hovering on the border, excited by uncertainty, is underscored in a scene in which his tutor Father Manfred gives him an oral examination. Taking Aristotle's definition of motion as its subject, the exam follows a typically Jesuit path that Scibona has already sketched—attempting to deflect the desirous teenage boy into a Thomist resolution of Greek and Pauline learning by inviting his opposition to the largely mechanical Aristotelian universe. "All of this fills you with a terrific sense of misgiving, but you don't know about what you have this misgiving. Tell me what you feel at the edge of your brain," the priest demands (221). Rather than closing with a confession that might stabilize the boy's wobbly mental geography, the passage swerves away from the Jesuit script when Ciccio chooses feeling over faith. This deviation anticipates his own final flight by train away from Elephant Park on the day of the feast. Ciccio's flight duplicates the movements of his mother from Italy to the United States and later across the United States by train, and in so doing also suggests that her migration was a stage in a continuing multigenerational journey. Ciccio's flight also makes him a hinge figure, joining the intellectual and theological universe of medieval Catholicism to contemporary geopolitical visions of the interlinked globe. He perceives "at the edge of [his] brain" the "bogusness" of the priest's solution, but that revelation also occurs in part because of the priest's attention to him. As in the passage with Rocco at Niagara Falls, in this crisis passage, Scibona reconstructs a moment of discovery of the larger world, crafting it out of the sensibilities of a migrant enclave about to be abandoned.

That this depiction of the discovery of a post-national and potentially post-ethnic world occurs in a pedagogical scene should not mislead us into conflating Scibona's novel with the assimilation-by-literacy narrative so ably sketched by Thomas Ferraro, among others.[41] Scibona's Ciccio does not represent the upward mobility of a newly literate and multilingual victor over the parochial authority of the enclave, nor does he stand in for the integration of the dominant culture's business ethic with local values—the two major narrative options that Ferraro examines. Instead, his is a lateral flight outward, and his hyper-literacy derives from his participation in the migrant community. He flees, in a sense, from his position as a studious reader of the classic works of the Western canon, moving out into the creative and strange terrain of a largely unknown popular culture. In *The End*, after all, opera is what the local abortionist buys access to with the proceeds of her business, and a fixation on the archive of the past is one of the primary attributes of the disturbing consciousness of the rapist, a character who obsessively collects letters from Civil War soldiers. Against these preoccupations with tradition, Scibona sets a world of genre fiction and popular literacy—the novels of Zane Grey, the daily crossword, and the local newspaper. These components of an emerging multinational media system appear at the periphery of Scibona's novel, but they are important enough to color the book's last images. In Ciccio's final reflections before disembarking in Chicago, memories of a dying priest mingle with a sensual experience of language and a move into the present. Ciccio ponders the "two long os, two short as" of Oklahoma, the doubled-up, excessive sign of the "home country, to which he belonged regardless of his desire to belong to it" (279). He longs for someone to talk to until his inner monologue finds an external correlative: "There was a used-car lot flying past him with a hundred plastic yellow pennants flapping, and the prices were painted on the windshields of the cars" (280). This oddly hopeful sequence strongly suggests that Ciccio's desire for an interlocutor will be fulfilled in the unglamorous, second-hand, and commercial world outside the ethnic enclave. As an authorial figure, Ciccio bridges the eschatology of the dying priest and the potentially post-ethnic world of twenty-first-century mobility.

Stories of Slavic Central Europe: Aleksandar Hemon, Francine Prose, and Michael Chabon

A somewhat stronger attachment to regional predecessors characterizes recent migration fiction that treats the passage from Slavic central Europe to the United States. Like Mediterranean migration narratives, these stories are often historiographic—reviewing narratives of early and mid-century migration from the region with a critical eye. However, they more frequently retain elements of the 1980s-era trauma narrative than do Mediterranean tales, and they evaluate a post-ethnic media culture more ambivalently. In many novels, the historical experiences of the Holocaust and the collapse of Soviet Communism continue to be framed by aspects of trauma writing.[42] At the same time, the warm rewards of an in-group solidarity founded on a shared relation to traumatic wounding are sometimes linked to the dangers of vigorous nationalism. Doubts about the coherence of ethnic identity shadow several twenty-first-century central European migration narratives, even those scarred by trauma, because in the post-Yugoslav era, cultural nationalism is the scandalous crisis as often as it is a solution.

Antipathy to nationalism and capitalist mass media alike is a common theme in much of the Slavic-language experimental literature that is circulating in the United States in the early twenty-first century. The recent translation into English of work by authors from the former Yugoslavia, in particular (for example, Slavenka Drakulić, Danilo Kis, Miljenko Jergović, Josip Novakovich, Dubravka Ugrešić, Vedrana Rudan, and Ludmila Ulitskaya), has made an important strain of artful irony available as an alternative to trauma narratives. Especially in combination with Vladimir Nabokov's influential example, these authors establish a distinctly Slavic-language literary means for revising American narratives about the traumatic losses exacted by migration or, in an earlier version, by political dissidence.[43]

Aleksandar Hemon (whose writing one critic has described as "a tributary to a powerful tradition of experimental prose initiated by Danilo Kis")[44] shows this line of influence particularly clearly. In *The Lazarus Project* (2008), Hemon presents a double narrative designed to upset any account of traumatic loss. The first strand follows a present-day Bosnian, bedeviled by writer's block and survivor's guilt, who decides to travel with a photographer friend on a return journey to Sarajevo. This out-migration reverses the course of the second narrative strand, set in 1908, which examines the world of a central European Jewish anarchist who is shot by police shortly after his arrival in Chicago.

Both men have lost a world and a set of ideals, and both are seriously under-whelmed by the conditions they encounter on their travels. Brik, the Bosnian, finds himself no more welcome in his home culture than is Lazarus, the 1908 pogrom survivor, and both heroes in different manners finally require a sort of resurrection from the deadly, drifting condition that signals their vulnerability to political violence.

At this thematic level, the powerful gravitational pull of trauma narratives is clearly evident in *The Lazarus Project*; however, the style drifts in another direction. Rather than dwelling on psychological pain, Hemon's writing is suffused with a very contemporary, eyebrow-raising humor even as it repeat-edly probes the bruises left by loss and historical amnesia. When, for example, Lazarus is nearly run down in the street in the first pages of the novel, it is "an enormous automobile, panting like an aroused bull" that threatens him, and he muses that Billy is "a nice name, a name for a fretful, yet happy, dog," while "Pat is weighty, serious like a rusted hammer." The quiet skepti-cism guiding this language learner's verbal fetishism and his bemused view of American convention become inescapably clear when the paragraph con-cludes with a modest moment of irony: "He has never known anybody named Billy or Pat" (6–7). Frequently reversing himself this way, Hemon keeps his narrative in motion, ricocheting between past and present and counter-bal-ancing observation of others with self-scrutiny. The obsessively inward- and backward-looking gaze of the traumatic subject who recovers himself in the present only by finally reconciling with the echoes of the past and account-ing for their consequences is here turned inside out. Hemon's restless ironies make the source of loss difficult to locate because—like Scibona's—his narra-tor resolves conflict by turning outward to the cultural landscape.

Like Ciccio, Hemon's hero pursues his research into Lazarus's origins as deeply as he can, seeking parallels in the horrible events of the siege of Sara-jevo, only to witness the senseless death of his friend—a death that he insists "happen[s] for a reason" (291). He is frustrated, though: there is no seamless fit between deaths in the past and the present; old relatives are not necessarily located; and murderers often have trivial motives. Although operating in a world of existential loneliness, Hemon's narrative refuses the completion ef-fect of trauma narratives—the hasty elision that at one point leads his narrator to misread a tin labeled "sardines" as "sadness" when encountering it in his American kitchen. Finally refusing to fill in all the blanks, resisting the urge to reduce all events to single traumatic causes, releases Hemon's modern-day Lazarus into a weirder limbo world where his own writing can effect change.

A much broader comic treatment of many of the same themes appears in Francine Prose's *My New American Life* (2011), a sharply observed satire of American consumerism narrated by a resilient Albanian nanny named Lula. Like Marina Lewycka's *Short History of Tractors in Ukrainian* (2005) (set in lower-middle-class England), Prose's novel dwells less on memory and nostalgia than on the lighter aspects of former Soviet-bloc citizens accommodating themselves to market logic. Both novels learn more, one might say, from Nabokov's *Pnin* (1955) than from *Speak, Memory* (1951)—dwelling more on frozen food, mini-skirts, and brand names than on folk culture, the lost homeland, and genocide. Despite their differences in tone and focus, however, Prose, Lewycka, and Hemon share a sense that the media provide the landscape for the migrant's entry into a new culture: Hemon's frustrated writing and historical photos are matched by television news in Prose's narrative and a used-car market in Lewycka's. This media surround confuses some migrants in these novels, besieging them with misinformation that is itself misinterpreted, but it also provides common ground and space for exchange, as well as innumerable opportunities for the writer to represent him- or herself as a more fully assimilated participant and achiever in the host society. The immigrant author maintains an important distance from whatever traumas of exclusion and loss the subject of his or her narrative may have endured simply by the fact of publication, and this structural irony is vital to these twenty-first-century tales of migration from Slavic central Europe. By seizing comedic grounds, these authors slowly bury any roots in historical trauma that their narratives might have.

A final twist on the narrative of an immigrant boy's escape from a self-regarding enclave defined by loss, an escape occurring by means of a largely comic commercial popular culture, is memorably presented in Michael Chabon's *Adventures of Kavalier & Clay* (2000). This Pulitzer Prize–winning novel riffs repeatedly on the motif of escape and escapism. The first of its title characters, Josef Kavalier, moves from an interest in Houdini-like escape artistry in Prague to literal escape from the Nazis and a compensatory comic-book battle against fascism in the form of superheroes. Chabon's primary artist hero obsessively depicts the adventures of the costumed Escapist and ultimately decides to embody his hero in order to reconnect with his lost son. Josef's various escapes into and out of characters circulating through the popular media parallel the somewhat different possibilities available to his Americanized cousin Sammy Clay, the closeted gay entrepreneur who escapes first the watchful eye of his mother, then the police who raid the country house where he has his first venture into gay sociability, and ultimately the marriage of convenience to his cousin's object of desire. That is, the novel stitches together two versions of immigrant fiction: the border-crossing flight from traumatic violence and the assimilation/anti-assimilation narrative addressing the migrant family's partial or segmented adherence to purportedly American family norms. The thread that holds these two stories together is the cousins' joint invention, the comic book character The Escapist. Chabon presents this alliance of Old World craft (Josef's draftsmanship) and New World savvy (Sammy's sharp negotiation of the lowbrow-publishing business) as a mock-heroic achievement of upward mobility. The boys literally ascend the Empire State Building as they climb certain social ladders. With this motif, Chabon cheerfully parodies immigrant success stories, drawing attention to their embeddedness in and dependence on mass-media narration. Comic books are the sign of the displaced migrant's vengeance, and they provide the language of the novel's titular adventures as well.

Chabon's adaptation of the tropes of the twentieth-century immigrant novel in light of the post-postmodern media fixation is, however, disrupted by migrant roots in an interesting fashion. Like Díaz's mongoose, Chabon's golem stands in *Kavalier & Clay* at the crossroads between folk/ethnic sensibilities and mass-media narrative; like the mongoose, the golem has obscure origins, fading back into the terrain of myth and religion. While Díaz's figure retains its ambivalence, however, Chabon's golem acquires a more fixed meaning. In the novel, the golem is firmly a part of the traditions of a specific community—the observant Jews of Prague—and its symbolic travels reinforce that association. The golem's coffin allows Josef to escape the Nazis; his identity and survival as an endangered Jew are paired with the golem. Although the golem is subsequently recast as a cultureless superhero and Anglicized as Sammy's beloved, the beefy Tracy Bacon, Chabon always keeps its presumed central European Jewish origins in view—for example, by choosing a name that highlights the not-so-kosher nature of the new incarnation. Even in comic form, the golem remains a reminder of the traumatic central European past. When its dust is finally delivered to Josef's son, it still awaits reanimation through the holy word.

In this respect, then, Chabon's novel shares in the project of extracting a distinctively twenty-first-century migration narrative from its generic predecessors. While definitely centrally concerned with media systems that exceed and overlap national borders (especially the suite of post-vaudeville popular entertainments that includes comics, magic tricks, joke-store gags, and body-building props), *Kavalier & Clay* also underscores its turn away from stories of cultural transition by asserting the identity of mass culture with the diasporic Jews of central Europe. To the extent that Chabon regards superheroes as versions of the golem, then, his novel does not offer either an account of conflicted Jewish assimilation or a story of roots (a postmodern version of which is Jonathan Safran Foer's *Everything Is Illuminated* [2002]) as much as a regrounding of mass culture on the transnational plane of an internationally solvent ethnicity. The Jewish community whose dreams and desires shaped the golem does not disappear, but it is dispersed in Chabon's vision, scattered abroad until it can take some new shape in the future.

Like Eugenides, Scibona, Hemon, and Prose, though, Chabon reflects critically on the conventions of twentieth-century immigrant fiction. All these authors emphasize the increasingly media-saturated texture of immigrant enclaves and underscore a sense of relief associated with escaping that space. In rethinking the conventions of the Europe-to-America immigration novel, then, all of these authors provide figures for an exciting, vigorous, and transnational space of cultural contact and exchange. Although certainly marked by war, poverty, and genocide, that terrain also resembles the map of the Caribbean Basin drawn by Danticat and Díaz in its refusal to allow trauma to be the only story that migrants tell.

New Africas: Dinaw Mengestu, Teju Cole, and Chris Abani

While narratives of migration from southern and eastern Europe tend to revise an existing tradition of immigrant fiction and autobiography, and narratives of migration from the Caribbean tackle a tradition of nationalist writing, twenty-first-century fiction that treats migration from Africa to the United States inhabits a more precarious position. Voluntary migration across the southern Atlantic is a far more recent phenomenon and in many cases is being written into literary history for nearly the first time. Furthermore, for related reasons, most Americans have a far deeper knowledge vacuum concerning African politics, warfare, and social life than they do for Europe,[45] so authors describing the culture shocks experienced by migrants from Africa can rely on fewer landmarks and less shorthand. Neither the motives for migration, the history of earlier waves of migrants, nor a secure—even if grossly clichéd—representation of the successful migrant can be assumed by the author of the African migration novel.

A final challenge faced by these authors relates to the presence of African American writers' visions of Africa. While sympathetic to the politics motivating roots narratives in African American literature, contemporary African-origin authors often react quite skeptically to the visions of Africa this initiative produces. In particular, some of the more romantic ideas of Africa fostered by Afro-centrists during the 1960s and 1970s have become important anti-texts for twenty-first-century authors such as Dinaw Mengestu, Teju Cole, and Chris Abani. They do refer regularly to the "racial wounds" involved in discovering and living with the meaning of blackness in the United States,[46] and for many readers this language immediately recalls Toni Morrison's trauma-inflected narratives of African American life. However, for Mengestu, Cole, and Abani, the more cosmopolitan, exilic, and urban vision of James Baldwin provides the most frequent touchstone.[47] They also supplement even Baldwin's sensibility with additional international referents. V. S. Naipaul, for instance, is crucial for Mengestu, while the Moroccan writer Tahar ben Jalloun plays an important role in Cole's *Open City* (2011) and Latino graffiti artists are vital to Abani's *Virgin of Flames* (2007). As African migration fiction writes itself into being, in short, it turns away from themes of cultural loss and traumatic history. In place of absorption by the historical wound, this fiction elects to map the restless psychology of newly mobile contemporary global subjects.

The Beautiful Things That Heaven Bears (2007), the first novel by Ethiopian immigrant Dinaw Mengestu, illustrates this move toward a post-traumatic narrative of Africans in America most clearly. In the novel's opening pages, a stagnant form of immigrant melancholia predominates; this condition is portrayed and finally cured by means of the shared consumption of community media. Set in the gentrifying Logan Circle neighborhood of Washington, D.C., during the spring of 1997,[48] Mengestu's novel centers on Sepha Stephanos, an immigrant from Ethiopia who inhabits a modest apartment and runs a struggling convenience store in the neighborhood. From a stool planted behind his counter, Sepha observes the comings and goings of his luckless African American neighbors (prostitutes, johns, drunks, and the elderly) as well as the ambitious renovations undertaken by a new crop of white, middle-class property owners. Having long ago relinquished the "hyperinflated optimism" (145) of the new immigrants that he and his African friends once were, at the time of the novel's narrative present, Sepha displays instead the more reserved, resigned attitude of a reader. The novel opens with a scene of reading, a habit indulged in during a routine visit from Sepha's friends Kenneth and Joseph, both of whom have also been transformed by the immigration process: "Kenneth became Ken the Kenyan and Joseph, Joe from the Congo" (1). The well-balanced triangular friendship these men share is anchored by a game in which one provides a name or date and the others identify the relevant African coup. Annotating the map of Africa pinned behind the store's counter, Sepha, Kenneth, and Joseph symbolically revisit the occasions of loss and upheaval that sent each into migration. The terrible, exhausted expertise that this routine creates underscores the theme of melancholic repetition, which permeates many other aspects of the novel as well.[49] Scarred by past injuries—in Sepha's case, the murder of his father—these immigrants have a profoundly ambivalent relation with their African past, an affect evident even more fully in their attitudes toward the America of their present.

In Mengestu's novel, the trauma-scarred migrants are only partial occupants of the United States. They are melancholically suspended in a strange geography. For Sepha, in particular, Washington keeps shape-shifting into Addis Ababa. He not only has family in both cities and distributes holiday gifts in both but also reads the signs and actions of each city in terms of the other. A mural of Frederick Douglass recalls portraits of the former Ethiopian emperor Haile Selassie (176), and passing motorcades function the same way in both cities, reinforcing the sense that "someone of great import is passing, and that we are fulfilling our role as observers" (92). Sepha can recall the "most fearful awe that came when [he] saw each building" of Washington for the first time, and he links that emotion to the claims that his parents made about the effect of viewing Selassie—especially their sense of being overwhelmed at the spectacle of "power embodied, as it were, in a single man" (46). Inhabiting both cities and empires simultaneously, Sepha hangs between the Addis of his youth and the Washington of his adulthood, very much as he feels himself caught between the upwardly mobile immigrant's plan to acquire education, wealth, and consumer purchasing power and the Ethiopian enclave's rejection of American values. For Sepha and the others, a melancholic retreat from their initial manic enthusiasm for the symbolism encoded in the Lincoln Memorial, the White House, and the Washington Monument is the status quo. "It's been years since either of them has gone near those buildings," Sepha reflects of his friends, "and how could you blame them? Reality has settled in, and they're both still waiting to recover" (47).

During this waiting period, the African migrants maintain their fragile selves by means of media engagement. Mengestu's novel supplements many other scenes of media consumption in a number of other registers. Sepha is a dedicated highbrow reader who finds parallels with his own situation in the

stranded shopkeeper at the center of Naipaul's *A Bend in the River* (1979), for example, and he builds a bond with new neighbors by creating a new ritual in which he reads aloud in the store—with a special focus on the idealistic character of Alyosha in *The Brothers Karamazov*. In a version of bibliographic stalking, Sepha also tracks down references to Tocqueville and Emerson made by a scholarly neighbor. Each of these allusions deepens the novel thematically (especially its concern for the limits of commercialism), but at a second order of significance they also place Sepha in a community of readers and writers. In this mediated community, the academic literary canon is no more distinct from the mass media than Washington is separate from Addis Ababa.

This merging of media spheres becomes especially evident in the two passages that have provided the titles for this novel in the United States and Great Britain. The American title used here refers to a passage from Dante's *Inferno*, a passage that Joseph has been studying in his continuing education classes and that "he likes to declare . . . to be the most perfect lines of poetry ever written" (99). Joseph's enthusiasm is not merely aesthetic, however. With solemn irony, Sepha reports Joseph's assertion that "no one can understand that line like an African because that is what we lived through. Hell every day with only glimpses of heaven in between" (100). Joseph works with Dante's lines, attempting to produce a contemporary African *Inferno*. Although Mengestu associates revision with an overly rapid revolutionary process that repaints billboards and exchanges statues of one leader with those of another who is much the same, this politically compromised strategy remains the novel's own technique. In this title passage, writing as politically charged revision becomes a central motif of Mengestu's novel. Writing as revision opens the possibility of escaping melancholic repetition.

For Mengestu, however, revision is a media practice rather than a solitary aesthetic act, an idea stressed in the passage chosen for the title of the British edition of the novel: *Children of the Revolution*. Referring to the 1970s anthem by the English glam-rock band T. Rex, the title draws attention to the passage in which the three drunk friends sing along with a jukebox in a crowded bar. Not only is the crucial line from the refrain, "You won't fool the children of the revolution," reproduced twice in the text, but we are also told that it repeats "over and over, until the song ends, by which point we've all finished our drinks and are ready for another" (47). This repetition reinforces the original song's own strong ironies about the possibility (or, more likely, the impossibility) of setting aside revolutionary politics for pacific consumerism. These recent African migrants recognize themselves in an anthem to the faded glory of the European counterculture of an earlier generation. At the same time, they also feel the need for a breakthrough—a release from post-traumatic repetition, from singing the same old song.

Mengestu's novel not only points out the need to leave trauma behind but also describes that process, showing new forms of writing about to emerge. The events that bring Sepha to the conclusion that he has "dangled and been suspended long enough" (228) exceed private ritualized confession, turning toward political speech. Sepha gives up on a romance blossoming between himself and a neighbor but joins a community meeting advertised by a "hand-written, misspelled" flyer proclaiming "PROTECT OUR NEIGHBROHOOD [sic] /NO MORE EVICTIONS" (194). The misspelled syllable "BRO" on the locally produced flyer rhymes with the racially inflected us–versus-them rhetoric of the ensuing meeting and, by implication, catapults a silent brick through the white neighbor's car windshield. This brick is then reinterpreted by the community: "By noon the brick had moved from Judith's car to her living room. By midafternoon, there was a note attached to it. By four or five in the afternoon, the note had been deciphered. It said: *Get out.* Or: *Move out.* Somehow the event had been transformed. It had grown in weight and stature. It had become political" (209).

In the end, Mengestu's restrained, elegantly composed novel extracts its central characters from a situation characterized by static immigrant melancholia and hopeless relationships and sets them on the horizon of political events by means of a system of community-forming media rewritings. Forms of media from the imagined note to the studied classics contain the possibility of new social bonds as well as routine repetitions of old affiliations. From this community of re-readers, in Mengestu's novel, arises the potential for a new kind of political event, albeit one that does not yet articulate a clear message. Sepha, our guide to the racial and class politics of gentrifying Washington, D.C., is here anti-ideological, although finally pro-political. He places himself on neither side of the Cold War situation in Ethiopia—viewing Selassie as "a tyrant, not a god" (118), while still mourning his father's death at the hands of the Leninists who overthrew the emperor. However, opening with Sepha's exhaustion with a less-than inclusive United States and establishing such regular parallels between the lackluster glories of Addis and Washington, the novel clearly does not equate a refusal of ideology with a middle-of-the-road liberal compromise either. Instead, Mengestu uses the motif of mediated revisions to open, without answering, the question of the political purpose of the twenty-first-century migration novel.

Many of the same themes arise in Mengestu's second novel, *How to Read the Air* (2010), another multilayered meditation on migration. Traversed by several journeys, this two-stranded novel sets the failing marriage and teaching career of Jonas Woldemariam, a second-generation Ethiopian American, in counterpoint to his parents' relationship. The most important itinerary in the novel is a short would-be honeymoon to Tennessee that Jonas's father has planned for his estranged wife after they reunite in Illinois. Jonas pieces together some events of this trip from his mother's stories, fills in other moments with his own imagination, and deduces still other elements from his own cultural knowledge. He uses, in short, the skills he has developed working in a legal aid center for immigrants, a job in which his main responsibility is to embellish the truncated narratives furnished to him by applicants for asylum and other permission to stay in the United States. "I took half-page statements of a coarse and often brutal nature and supplied them with the details that made them real for the immigration officer who would someday be sitting opposite them," he explains (24). At first, Jonas considers this rewriting ethically questionable, justifiable only because it stirs up conventional sympathies for the migrant, but he later comes—especially when he almost involuntarily begins a multi-week and largely fictional narration of his father's escape from Ethiopia in a shipping crate—to embrace his storytelling gift. In Mengestu's second novel, to narrate is not necessarily to heal, as it may be in a fully psychoanalytically informed narrative; it is, however, a way to continue the enormously brave and dangerous act of walking away from horror and toward something new, an act associated in this novel with both of the narrator's parents, but especially the mother.

While *How to Read the Air* handles figures of the media very tactfully (omitting references to specific communication devices, for instance), the treatment of storytelling as a continual process of inventing and anchoring social relationships owes a great deal to the tropes of the digital migrant. Mengestu's writing—like Díaz's, Hemon's, and Chabon's—makes liberal use of the multi-stranded narrative, quickly establishing an echo chamber of associations in which any single moment or experience bounces off several others, redirecting forward-moving action toward hidden, secondary narratives or phantasmagoric spaces in a manner that some readers take to be distinctively digital.[50] The tiny New York apartment that Jonas shares with his wife, for example, recalls the crate in which his father secretly departs from Sudan as well as the Spartan room at the YMCA where, suffering from dementia, the same man later dies. Examining the storied crate, Jonas's father (or so

Jonas imagines) "considered its angles and its depth and then imagined all the ways in which he could and could not move inside it. . . . He crawled in on his knees, which was not how he would have liked to enter. . . . He had just enough time to arrange himself properly before the man sealed the entrance shut with a wooden door that was resting nearby" (288). Migration into a new space is as confusing as marriage in the novel; both involve a calculated compression of the titular air. This dense but silent atmosphere then produces intangible data that the narrator as son and husband learns to read. Like the urban allegories in *Beautiful Things*, the fractured, silent spaces in *How to Read the Air* rely on the mobile sensibility of a receptive, multitasking narrator who pulls them together in a migrant narrative influenced, but not contained, by trauma.

A related tone of readerly contemplation, maintained against a backdrop of possibly invented horror about which the migrant refuses to provide salacious detail, characterizes Teju Cole's masterful debut novel, *Open City*. As the title suggests, this novel shares Mengestu's concern with interurban echoes—taking Manhattan as an analogue for Brussels and Lagos primarily, with occasional detours to Berlin, Kigali, and Marrakesh. The openness, however, is more ironic. Cole's novel sinks gracefully from the initial surface-level self-presentation of its narrator, Julius, a psychiatry resident, into the lower reaches of his psyche. Early on, he describes his alienation from his white German mother and slowly reveals the troubling impact of his Nigerian father's death a dozen years earlier. Similarly, this precisely plotted novel moves from the manifest aesthetic pleasures offered by Mahler and Proust through a world of concerts, bookstores, and picnics in Central Park. While enjoying these activities, Julius broods about a scholarly patient whose research into the brutal history of Native Americans has touched him, and this literary empathy eventually reveals other important losses—the death of a beloved Japanese American literature professor (a former internee in a relocation camp during World War II), his own beating and mugging at the hands of young African American men with whom he had briefly imagined sharing a moment of "quick solidarity" (212), and, most surprisingly, his own rape of a teenage acquaintance at the party following his father's funeral. Framing this involuntary revelation with an insistence that a self may continue to be virtuous despite having committed certain despicable acts, the narrator avoids further justification—psychological or otherwise—of his own behavior. Repressions as well as therapeutic confessions appear necessary to the functioning of the adult self as Cole imagines it, and this important closing insight leaves the reader to reconsider many of the motifs and moments presented earlier by his finally unreliable narrator. Opening or—in Mengestu's trope—reading the city of the narrator's psyche becomes an active, not a passive, task. The pre-migration life of the narrator turns out to have far more weight than his exceptionally successful integration into the institutions of American culture and power might suggest.

One of the most important recurring features of *Open City* that the reader circles back to reinterpret in Cole's more temporal take on the multi-stranded narrative is the rejection of race-based solidarity. Both the mugging that Julius suffers and, behind that, the death of his black father seem to have scarred him in important ways, making it very difficult for him to admit any sense of identification with or connection to other black men. He refuses to be hailed as a "brother" or a fellow African by cabdrivers, museum guards, or any of the other black men he meets in his daily life. Only on a vacation to Brussels (ostensibly in search of his estranged German grandmother) does he befriend an intellectually inclined Moroccan employee in an Internet café. Instead of personal, face-to-face experiences of solidarity, Julius opts for aesthetic and intellectual identifications, finding echoes of himself in photographs of "three African boys running into the surf in Liberia" (152), as well as in African American literature (to a lesser extent) and news stories about the discovery of the African Burial Ground lying beneath the financial district near Wall Street. In person, when an old man in Harlem suddenly appears to Julius to be "someone I surely knew, or once knew, or had seen before," he immediately fears that "the speed of these mental dissociations might knock [him] off [his] stride" (18). The face-to-face engagement with other black men endangers the narrator, potentially engulfing him in personal loss as well as in a tide of African political and social upheaval that he is anxious to avoid contemplating. He is somewhat more receptive during his European journey to empathy with others—imagining, for example, that another visitor to a Belgian church may be seeking not only "refuge from the demands of family life" but also "a hiding place from what she might have seen in the Cameroons or in the Congo or maybe even in Rwanda," but he does not directly engage with this woman any more than he converses with the disturbing Harlem specter (140). This avoidance comes to seem, in light of the final passages of the novel, not so much the well-worn figure of the intellectual as asocial observer as an ironic meditation on the migration experience. Cole's narrator displays a shattered, dissociated consciousness that acts as a symptom of the losses that propelled him into migration and prevents him from recognizing a public collective narrative of this movement. This African migrant has not yet developed the kind of public awareness of his condition that is enjoyed (if that is the right word) by Native Americans or even the Japanese American internees described in the novel. In this way, Cole eloquently illustrates the silences and absences surrounding African history and populations in the United States, managing to make these gaps singular and collective simultaneously. Cole remakes the traumatic narrative of migration, repackaging its drive toward the revelation of horror in a complex, ironic narrative frame that requires a full exploration of the narrator's ambivalent complicity in several industries (psychiatry, heritage tourism, museums, churches, and even the stock exchange) built on the necessary forgetting of traumatic histories.

Similarly long detours through a culture industry that markets traumas that are geographically distant but psychologically potent appear in Chris Abani's *Virgin of Flames*. A short and intense imagist experiment, with its East Los Angeles setting, *Virgin* begins a few steps farther from a direct depiction of migration than do Cole's and Mengestu's first novels; its protagonist, a painter named Black, inhabits a multicultural artists' community where artifacts from around the world intermingle with domestic arts and crafts. Organized around a performance venue called the Ugly Store, this punkish community is not sufficiently intimate to serve the needs of this shattered son of quarreling Nigerian parents, and much of the novel depicts Black's quest for a more compelling and transcendent ritual environment. He helps to paint enormous graffiti images of the Virgin of Guadalupe in the urban wasteland and develops a routine for personal transformation, dressing himself in an altered wedding gown (with "ectoplasmic sadness oozing everywhere"), a blonde wig, and white make-up in order to become his own model for an enormous mural. Black yearns to fly away in the model of a spaceship that he uses as a hiding place and meditation retreat before giving it to a friend. At the novel's climax, he dons his virgin costume and occupies the spaceship, inspiring visitations from the city's legions of the faithful.

Abani's images for travel and the migrant's self-transformation are far more freely rendered in *The Virgin of Flames* than in Cole's and Mengestu's sparer prose (or, for that matter, in his own more squarely realist novel of Lagos, *Graceland* [2004]), but he shares with his contemporaries a quite definite sense that the migrant's wounds and scars are modulated by a complex media economy. The writer-artist figure is a crucial linchpin in this system, anchoring the potentially unspeakable or perhaps simply unknown experiences of the African traveler's pre-migration universe to an American landscape that—no matter how elegant or desolate it may be—is quite thoroughly mapped.

Abani may be more directly concerned with the ghetto and the slum than are Mengestu and Cole, but all three share the quite definite sense that rather than document "African" horrors from scratch (a process that too often involves the burden of overturning and correcting American stereotypes of African poverty, disease, primitivism, and other ills),[51] they will repurpose urban scenes, multiplying, layering, and dissolving them until they reach toward a new kind of global consciousness focused on the creative potential of the cosmopolitan African-origin subject. Their narratives focus on the migrant's conflicted present, rather than insisting exclusively on the wounds that may have set him flowing.

SOUTH ASIAN TRAVELERS: HARI KUNZRU AND MOHSIN HAMID

If the position of any particular author on a spectrum of twenty-first-century migration narratives has largely to do with the degree to which he or she has chosen to process a traumatic history and has wrestled with regional literary predecessors, that suggests that a retrospective historical consciousness defines immigration fiction, and, certainly, many of these narratives do employ a historical framework that involves some grappling with the culture or conditions of origin. That said, many twenty-first-century narratives also rely on a set of new figures—often forward-looking, grounded in post-migration realities, and attentive to the media landscape that links past and present. Rather than focusing exclusively on the treatment of past traumas, accounts of the genre should also consider the degree to which any particular author seizes hold of the multidirectional nature of migration, the layered urban spaces of the wired globe, the dispersed family network, and the figure of the author herself as a router or switching point—that is, the degree to which she embraces distinctly contemporary images. For any number of reasons, some of which seem to be related to the specific institutional advantages that some writers enjoy (such as an active regional publishing industry[52] and the mobility provided by British Commonwealth passports), several of the authors who most vigorously embrace the contemporary address South Asian migration.

That is not to say that Indian writing, in particular, has dispelled the aura of Victoriana with which it is so often associated. Marriage sagas, from Vikram Seth's *A Suitable Boy* (1993) to Bharati Mukherjee's *Desirable Daughters* (2003), continue to have a readership, and domestic novels that explore the psychic conflicts of traditionally minded, middle-class professionals remain crucial to the canon of Indian American immigrant literature, as Jhumpa Lahiri's widely discussed *The Interpreter of Maladies* (1999) might suggest. The pleasures and dangers of postcolonial nostalgia for the plots, if not the social institutions, provided by Victorian colonialism are also crucial to Kiran Desai's Booker Prize–winning tale *The Inheritance of Loss* (2006).

Nonetheless, a distinctly contemporary, media-savvy cosmopolitanism also has a presence in South Asian migration writing—a strain that takes a sharp turn into satire and hipsterism, often by way of migration to the United States rather than the United Kingdom. Directly addressing the global-culture industry, some South Asian authors add a clearly digital component to the twenty-first-century migration novel. *Transmission* (2004), by the British author Hari Kunzru, is a case in point. Following its benighted hero from his nerdy Calcutta bedroom to an aborted career as a programmer in Silicon Valley, with a brief swerve to swinging 1990s London, only to land finally at a Scottish film set, Kunzru's novel directly concerns the interface of digital and cultural codes in a system disrupted by mobile computer viruses. *Transmission* ultimately allows the Bollywood actress with whom both its programmer-hero and an English public-relations executive are obsessed to upstage both of her admirers. In personal, careerist, and virtual forms, Leela becomes the signal of a new, even more aggressive culture of capitalism in formation, and in this respect Kunzru's novel joins Douglas Coupland's *Microserfs* (1995), Chuck Palahniuk's *Fight Club* (1996), Brett Easton Ellis's *Glamorama* (1998), and Joshua Ferris's *Then We Came to the End* (2007) in laying the groundwork for a new kind of corporate satire for the wired age. After a very compelling contemplation of contemporary European radicalism in *My Revolutions* (discussed in passing in chapter 4), Kunzru returns in his fourth, more uneven novel, *Gods Without Men* (2011), to some of the questions about the interdependence of American and South Asian systems of capital and expertise. However, for a compelling—almost perfect—novel centrally dedicated to this question, we must turn to Mohsin Hamid's Jamesian novella, *The Reluctant Fundamentalist* (2007).

Like Kunzru, the Pakistani-born, Princeton- and Harvard-educated, British citizen Hamid is interested in triangulations and restless mobility. In a piece published in the *Guardian* in 2008, Hamid describes his own migration to London by way of the United States as part of "a giant circle of human motion and potential motion," a circle that is completed by the nearly simultaneous emigration of "pink skinned" British citizens to Goa, New York, and beyond.[53]

What distinguishes Hamid's concerns from more historically minded treatments of migration, however, is the pointed attention he pays to the economic disparities that channel human circulation. Even Hamid's short essay in the *Guardian* concludes with a meditation on housing prices in London and their frustrating impact on would-be migrants, such as himself, who aspire to metropolitan domesticity.

A preoccupation with economic, rather than psychological or political, motives for migration is even more carefully explored in Hamid's second novel, which was shortlisted for the Booker Prize. Arguably an emigration narrative as well as an ironically conceived immigration novel, *The Reluctant Fundamentalist* takes place over a single evening in early twenty-first-century Lahore; its narrator, Changez, explains to an unnamed, cell phone–bearing American auditor with military bearing how he left a lucrative career on Wall Street to become a university lecturer beloved by radical students in Pakistan. The story of Changez's aborted migration to the United States is entangled with a love triangle in which boundaries are regularly violated. Changez is fascinated with the symbolically nostalgic and depressive WASPy Upper East Sider, Erica, who is, in turn, preoccupied with her dead boyfriend, Chris. This love affair crosses social, national, and biological boundaries, holding up as its ideal "a process of osmosis" by which a Pakistani Muslim whose name recalls that of the Mongolian invader-hero Changez Khan hopes to "penetrate the membrane" of the psyche of Chris(tian) (Am)Erica (141). Hamid's love story, in brief, does not salve the wounds inflicted by a competitive world economy; his triangle is instead an allegorical microcosm that mirrors and extends into interior life a version of the dynamics of the geopolitical scene.

This allegorical tendency characterizes the spatial logic of Hamid's narrative as well. In contrast to Desai's messy map of the Himalayas in *The Inheritance of Loss*, Hamid provides a remarkably clear and directional system. The action of his embedded narrative moves occurs on four journeys, each of which serves as a turning point. Changez first encounters Erica while on a thrilling postgraduation jaunt to Greece; the twin towers of the World Trade Center fall while Changez is on a business trip to Manila; he grows a beard symbolizing his Pakistani roots during a visit to family in Lahore; and he finally comes to understand himself as a janissary (that is, a captive serving a hostile system) during a final business trip to Valparaíso.

One effect of these journeys is to layer each city on the other. Manhattan recalls Lahore: "[M]oving to New York felt—so unexpectedly—like coming home" (32). And so, for different reasons, did Valparaíso: "I was reminded of Lahore and of that saying, so evocative in our language: *the ruins proclaim the building was beautiful*" (144). While "unlike anything I had seen in Pakistan," the slums of Manila also recall "a poorer version of the 1940s America depicted in such films as *Grease*" (64). Changez finds something he recognizes everywhere. He even experiences déja vu on his first visit to Erica's home: "[P]erhaps it was because a spacious bedroom in a prestigious apartment on the Upper East Side was, in American terms, the socio-economic equivalent of a spacious bedroom in a prestigious house in Gulberg, such as the one in which I had grown up" (50–51). As a hyper-mobile, transitory migrant, Changez inhabits not a particular nation or situation but a multinational urban space.

These layered urban spaces, beautiful in their ruins, are also crucial to the novel's refusal of the long temporality of historical trauma. Hamid presents Changez's work as a Wall Street analyst as a ruthless and "constant striving to realize a financial future," and he sets this obsession with the future against "the critical personal and political issues that affect one's emotional present" (145). Nostalgia for the past is no more salutary; it is figured first through Erica's presumably suicidal preoccupation with her dead lover and then through Changez's adoption of the same pattern after his return to Pakistan. In his clearest moments, however, the narrator experiences a "sudden broadening of [his] arc of vision" that shifts him away from these temporal terms and toward a spatial or, better, geographical vision with a political base (141).

This shift to a bracing geopolitical present is duplicated on the narrative level by the framing of the work as a whole, as well as each chapter, by Changez's simultaneously sensual and dangerous encounter with his American auditor. Pulling the narrator and the narrative toward a present entanglement whose uncertain character (an assassination attempt? a business meeting? a friendship?) is decided by "a glint of metal," *The Reluctant Fundamentalist* closes with an appeal to a new mode of perception. "Let us, like the bats, exercise our other senses," Changez invites his auditor, once the capacities of their eyes and ears—the organs of space and time—have been exhausted (76).

That the organ Changez exhorts his auditor and dining companion to employ is the tongue—the organ of both taste and speech—should come as no surprise in such a carefully composed and self-reflective work. After all, the magic of speech is invoked in the first paragraph of the novel, where

Changez presents himself as "a speaker of your language," and much of the charm of the work involves the narrator's knowing use of both formal South Asian diction and idiomatic departures from standard American English.[54] At a deeper level, however, the novel not only presents itself as a meditation on urban forms and First versus Third World economies of space but is fundamentally concerned with writing as the trace of speech—that is, with lost or unused tongues.

To reinforce this imaginative treatment of an arguably new form of geopolitical space, *The Reluctant Fundamentalist* makes use of the languages of mass media, beginning with brief, intentionally overly serious references. Early in the novel, Changez fends off a pseudo-bohemian rival for Erica's affection by naming the dated Bryan Adams song that the rival plays rather badly on his guitar, and he summarizes his beloved's particular erotic appeal to his auditor by asserting that "she belonged more to the camp of Paltrow than to that of Spears" (22). Moving from inhabiting this territory to reflecting on it, Changez later describes a fellow financial analyst, an Afro-Caribbean, as being rather too fond of quoting from "popular cinema"—*Star Wars*, *Top Gun*—before moving on to an explicit discussion of the *Gatsby*-esque elements of this appropriately Princeton-based narrative. Blending Fitzgerald's interest in shams, social dislocation, and complex narration with a Jamesian concern for the faded glory of aristocrats observing the nouveaux riches and, later, a passage on Washington Irving's headless horseman, Hamid endows his narrator with an American university–level literary sensibility continuous with his media consciousness. Together with the second-order plot, concerning the valuations of different elements of the media industry—from the Filipino recording labels and Argentine independent publishing house that Changez assesses to Erica's easily published novella—this recurring pattern suggests that the novel understands itself as part of a system of triangulations in which American fiction serves as yet another rival, akin to Erica's *Tintin*-copying deceased boyfriend. That is, filtering the relationship in the present between Changez, the voluble and potentially deceptive narrator, and his unnamed, text-messaging auditor, is an English-language and largely American literary history concerned with improper and/or dangerous aliens and migrants. Feeling finally "rather like a Kurtz waiting for his Marlowe," Changez highlights not only the situation of his pursuit—that is, the inverted migration by which the American travels to his home territory—but also the by-now necessarily ironic literary clichés that shape the depictions of both his own migration (and supposed fundamentalism) and that of the American abroad. Both of these evacuated narratives potentially implode in the novel's final "glint of metal," a moment that releases bats and new senses and sensations. In the end, Hamid's self-negating novella closes in on itself, eliminating the traumatic, historical, and phantasmagoric versions of the migration novel one by one and leaving only a small space in which another kind of post-national narrative of migration might emerge.

2 THE ANXIOUS AMERICAN

Political Thrillers and the Peace Corps Fugue

Things have really fallen apart in the white man's head.
Ikhide R. Ikheloa, "Whiteman: The Heart of Our Darkness"

I F THE CONTEMPORARY migration novel has moved away from personal trauma, the same cannot be said of the out-migration narrative. Since the turn of the millennium, dozens of novels by young Americans have explored the theme of international travel, especially in the developing world, and many of these works turn on the protagonist's discovery of his or her profound sense of dislocation abroad. In these "heat-mosquitoes-and-brown-people" novels,[1] an encounter with other cultures, physical environments, and economic conditions profoundly disturbs the middle-class American protagonist's psyche. Commenting on this tendency in entries for *Granta's* issue "Best of Young American Novelists 2," Edmund White called this kind of writing the "Peace Corps novel" and remarked, not entirely enthusiastically, on its focus on "the young privileged American" encountering the developing world for the first time.[2]

White hints that young authors might be better off sketching others, rather than reproducing portraits of their own alienation against a new background. However, ethnographic objectivity—even in its more reflexive, postmodern mood—turns out to be rare in contemporary U.S. fiction devoted to international travel. Although, as chapter 3 demonstrates, novels set entirely outside the United States and narrated by non-U.S. citizens tend to be more assertive in their recasting of the national allegory, the story of a young, usually white American's travel from the United States to other locations remains largely preoccupied with the dissociated psychology of culture shock.

This trend is particularly pronounced in literal Peace Corps novels—that is, those numerous works written by Returned Peace Corps Volunteers (RPCVs).

Founded in 1961 with a congressional mandate to "promote world peace and friendship,"[3] the Peace Corps has grown rapidly from its first group of roughly 100 volunteers operating in a handful of countries. The twenty-first-century Peace Corps has an annual budget of nearly $400 million and sends thousands of Americans each year to dozens of nations around the world. In the words of one of the organization's founders and longtime leaders, Sargent Shriver, these volunteers "are a new type of overseas American"; rather than delivering direct foreign aid, collecting intelligence, or serving military functions, early volunteers were urged to work toward "social development" and "revolution" in the nations in which they were posted.[4] The Peace Corps volunteer's goal since the 1960s has been to lay the groundwork for economic development and liberal democracy through culture change.[5] In the organization's early years, this plan for cultural intervention not infrequently involved a direct attempt to remake local family structures, gender relations, agricultural practices, and standards of medical care.

This focus on cultural revolution has influenced the training of volunteers. Although participants with technical expertise in fields such as nursing and engineering have consistently been sought by host countries, throughout the organization's history, a high percentage of Peace Corps volunteers have been liberal arts majors engaged in a more open-ended educational mission; Harris Wofford, another founder, characterized the attitude of some of these volunteers as "bringing light to darkness."[6] Although not particularly desirable for the purpose of cultivating political goodwill, this posture of charitable virtue has been associated with the Peace Corps since its inception, and it has triggered a good deal of internal and external scrutiny.[7] As historians and participants alike have recognized, this attitude assumes that civilized, modern volunteers enter and necessarily improve backward, dependent host nations. Although individual volunteers or administrators do not always personally share this view, the institution itself was premised on the kind of universalizing liberal globalism that identifies technological development and secular egalitarianism with modernity and uplift.

These ideals have, however, been regularly tested in practice. Because several of the founders of the Peace Corps had a strong commitment to the civil rights struggles of the 1960s and took pride in promoting integration within the ranks of the volunteers,[8] a good deal of the scrutiny devoted to this landmark institution of the Kennedy administration has concerned its racial logic. Sensitive to the racial overtones of sending white volunteers with a modernizing mission to newly independent nations in Africa in particular,

Peace Corps leaders made major but largely unsuccessful efforts to recruit African American volunteers. Several black volunteers who did serve offered scathing criticisms of the institution's assumptions, especially those revealed during training sessions. White liberal and middle-class attitudes about the alien behavior of black people were apparently the norm during these sessions for many years, and African American volunteers bristled at the patronizing, sometimes pathologizing accounts of black populations that were presented as cross-cultural knowledge, especially during the institution's first decade. These veterans of the program felt the training sessions assumed that the ideal volunteer was ignorant of poverty and the realities of racial discrimination in his own country as well as the organization of everyday life in the developing world.[9] The training was pitched toward volunteers who were well-intentioned and well-off white Americans, and the institution as a whole was based on the idea that their mere presence in remote locations would promote international peace and friendship. Naïve volunteers were expected to extend the principles of Enlightenment humanism to far-off villagers entrapped by more fatalistic worldviews—such as "the idea that man is incompetent or incapable of shaping his own destiny," as Shriver put it.[10] However frequently volunteers were praised for the cross-cultural knowledge acquired during their service, the commitment to disseminating American universalistic creeds remained fundamental to the Peace Corps mission.

In short, the Peace Corps rests squarely in a tradition of liberalism defined not by the left-hand side of a domestic liberal–conservative dyad but by the more foundational commitment to Enlightenment values. This system prioritizes personal liberty over tradition, technological innovation over labor-intensive collaboration, market "forces" over state intervention, civil rights over economic ones, and universalist rather than relativist assertions about the proper shape for political organization.[11] Codified in the so-called American Creed, this bipartisan liberalism has a long association with volunteerism, advocacy, and civil society in the United States.[12]

These influential principles of the Peace Corps, especially those shared with other institutions of American government, have been carefully inspected in the RPCVs' fiction. This body of writing examines the Kennedy-era liberal's self-concept and explores the depths of this subject's commitment to changing the culture of the other. Many of the most recent Peace Corps novels find that subject's confidence in her own virtue to be seriously eroded. Although little evidence suggests that the emergence of this internal critique of liberal universalism has altered the day-to-day operation of the Peace Corps, the existence of this position indicates some of the conceptual and ideological challenges that devoted liberals face in the twenty-first century.

The body of literature expressing this self-critical version of liberal globalism is sizable. Of the more than 200,000 Americans who have served in the Peace Corps since 1961, at least 1,000 have published at least one book that reflects in part or whole on the experience, and some estimates run even higher.[13] A majority of these publications are first-person memoirs or other nonfictional accounts of Peace Corps service, but such a significant number are novels that the RPCVs have established their own annual literary prize, the Maria Thomas Award, to honor the best fiction published by a member of their group. Named in memory of Roberta Worrick, a former volunteer in Ethiopia who published a lively novel and two volumes of short stories under this pseudonym before dying in a plane crash in 1989, the award establishes a canon of successful out-migration narratives.[14] In this corpus, many works do adhere to the formula identified by White and his fellow judges at *Granta*. The vast majority of the Maria Thomas Award recipients ignore the genre of the ethnographic sketch almost entirely, preferring to focus on the psychological crisis experienced by the First World traveler. While expressed in personal terms, this crisis reflects the volunteer's values and the institutions that foster or contradict them.

This political framework is underscored by the genre choices of these authors. Inspired perhaps by the example of the most successful RPCV, travel writer Paul Theroux,[15] but also that of one of the premiere works of Vietnam War–era ambivalence, Graham Greene's *Quiet American*, Peace Corps fiction routinely models itself on the political thriller. As a genre, the thriller has a long and interesting association with anxious, disassociated narrators, and it has often tackled geopolitical questions—from Cold War spy rings to global environmental crises. Both form and content make the thriller uniquely well suited to the expression of the modern American liberal's disappointment. The Peace Corps thriller, in particular, explores the often naïve protagonist's psychological state in order to express its sense that the political unconscious of American development policy is riddled with disturbing repressed elements.

THE POLITICS OF THE THRILLER

The thriller works so well as a genre expressing liberal disappointment in part because it consistently unsettles the deliberative and possessive individualism of twentieth-century detective fiction. If, following Tzvetan Todorov, we understand the detective story to be defined by its double plot—crime followed by investigation—then the thriller is the version of the detective story that places emphasis on the uncertainties and forward movement of the investigation.[16] As opposed to a "whodunit," which emphasizes the discovery of carefully placed clues about prior events, the thriller sustains the reader's anxious curiosity about the plot's unfolding future. The thriller plunges the reader into an unstable institutional context by withholding diegetic explanation and shifting the locus of investigation from the "personal crime" of passion typical of the whodunit to the "professional crime" perpetrated by knowledge workers in the course of their employment.

The thriller, in other words, turns not on moral uncertainty but on the protagonist's susceptibility to misinformation.[17] The thriller stages the explanatory failure of an investigator's default ideology, rather than successfully applying it (as in the whodunit), releasing subjects from thinking altogether and plunging them into vertiginous sensation (as in the purest form of the suspense novel), or wandering the psychic and moral desert of the noir. Its closest cousin is certainly the hard-boiled detective novel, but its definitive preoccupation with institutional and professional questions ultimately differentiates it from the gumshoe narrative's specific concern with culpability and masculine vulnerability.[18]

Over the course of the twentieth century, the types of professional knowledge examined in the thriller shifted. John Buchan's stories of civil service imperialism gave way during the Depression to more melodramatic police plots, which, in turn, were succeeded by the existential thrillers of the 1940s and 1950s.[19] The mid-century heroes of Eric Ambler's and Graham Greene's fiction frequently strip away the sentimental clichés of the period to reveal an eternal bloodlust percolating beneath the surface of banal business culture.[20] This anti-ideological tendency was further developed in Cold War espionage thrillers (for example, John Le Carré's magnificent early work and Ian Fleming's James Bond parodies), in which official statesmen are typically revealed to be deceivers or pawns, while a hidden network of knowledge workers holds the real keys to power.[21] In the Cold War thriller's version of *Realpolitik*, massive bureaucracies enable disruptive activities at odds with their stated intentions, regardless of ideology.

This form of the thriller reached its pinnacle in Greene's prescient novel, *The Quiet American* (1955). The narrator is a British expatriate in Vietnam who observes a newly arrived and idealistic American official. The American disappears, and during the subsequent inquiry the expatriate's horror at the presumed victim's own activities grows exponentially. Greene's narrator exposes the American's naïve faith in technology, freedom, and military might, before finally assessing his own limited prospects once this Kennedy-era liberalism disintegrates under the weight of its own ill effects. Most often, Greene's vertiginous novel is understood as creating "an open space in which it was both possible and necessary to ask fundamental questions" about ethics and religion.[22] For the Peace Corps thriller, however, Greene's neo-Catholic values have been less influential than the dialectic he establishes between expatriate and official. It is precisely this dyad that collapses into a single un-stable protagonist in the volunteer's narrative. This uneasy subject exports the terror-ridden sensibility learned from recent versions of the thriller into the culture-contact scenarios of travel writing.

The RPCV's Fugue

Although political critiques of the effectiveness of the Peace Corps often fo-cus on the limitations of technology transfer or the contradictory effects of the Green Revolution,[23] these subjects play a minor role in fiction associated with the organization. They are present in one of the Peace Corps thriller's predecessor texts, William J. Lederer and Eugene Burdick's quasi–roman à clef *The Ugly American* (1958). Their hero is an "ugly" American oddball who renounces the perquisites of the diplomatic lifestyle in order to manu-facture bicycle-powered pumps and learn local languages. "What we need," he concludes, "is a small force of well-trained, well-chosen, hard-working and dedicated professionals. They must be willing to risk their comforts and—in some lands—their health . . . to apply a positive policy promulgated by a clear-thinking government" (239). Largely rejecting this pragmatic focus, however, the RPCVs' fiction tends to concentrate on the inner life; their heroes are less professional, rational, and effective. They take a psychological approach to the thriller, internalizing the institutional and (to a lesser extent) economic landscape of contemporary geopolitics, and ultimately testing the durability of the Kennedy-era liberal's map of the world.

More specifically, the psychology of the Peace Corps thriller explores the fugue state. The genre's disconcerted protagonists awake from a period of amnesia to discover that they have traveled. Like late-nineteenth- and early-twentieth-century *fugueurs*, they often repress memories of the experience of travel as well as events that may have instigated travel. Despite these losses, the protagonists commonly exhibit a high level of competence in their post-travel environments. They retain their ability to decode, make decisions about, and

The Political Thriller Versus the Peace Corps Fugue

	POLITICAL THRILLER	PEACE CORPS FUGUE
HERO	Mid-level functionary	Volunteer abroad
VILLAIN	High-level bureaucrats, behind-the-scenes power brokers	Impersonal, zealous bureaucracy
ENVIRONMENT	International, interlinked offices with no specific boundary	Little known foreign country, rural areas, hard-to-decipher language
CONFLICT	Which ideological system, if any, explains current crisis?	Who am I in this strange place? How do I relate to my past?
RESOLUTION	Scapegoat or symbolic villain punished, many lingering uncertainties	Disenchanted liberal returns home

actually shape their immediate surroundings. They dissociate from their pre-travel selves and become highly aware of their own reactions to new environments. Sometimes pre- and post-travel selves eventually fuse into a narrative of self-discovery. Equally often, however, this resolution does not occur, and the protagonist is left with multiple, unreconciled identities. It is this sense of the multiplying variations that gives the fugue state its name; in music, a fugue repeats a basic theme in several voices.

In clinical psychology, the fugue state is uncommon, having been largely supplanted by neighboring conditions such as post-traumatic stress and multiple identity disorders.[24] In the nineteenth century, French clinicians hypothesized that involuntary or amnesiac travel was a hereditary illness (characteristic, for example, of the Wandering Jew) or a side effect of battle fatigue or epilepsy.[25] Sigmund Freud referred to fugue states only briefly in his discussion of repression as a defense against traumatic memories in *Studies on Hysteria* (1895),[26] and "by the early years of the twentieth century," writes Carl Elliott, "the fugue state as a medical diagnosis had all but disappeared."[27] Recent discussions of recovered memories in victims of sexual abuse have drawn attention to the related phenomenon of dissociation, although often stirring up questions about the veracity of repressed memories. Whatever the status of the *fugueur*'s memory, though, the dissociative splitting of the self recalls the process that Freud called the economy of the drives—that is, the survival impulse of the psyche. Self-forgetfulness on this account is a healthy and sustaining reaction; it can even approach the loss of self-consciousness experienced in highly creative "flow" situations.[28] Perhaps for this reason, diagnostic criteria for the fugue state now affiliate it with the voluntary dissociative trance reported by practitioners of Vodun, Sufism, or other ecstatic religions.

It is in this last, most culturally relative, sense that the fugue state usually appears in literature. The protagonist of a fugue can retrospectively discover an earlier self (possibly refusing to integrate with it) while also moving forward through the journey in a new locale. In Peace Corps fiction and elsewhere, the literary *fugueur*'s sanity is rarely in question; instead, this figure's amnesia motivates the exploration of a shattered, disintegrated world.[29] *Fugueurs* travel a landscape from which they feel detached. Their journeys typically reach a second crisis point when the institutional mechanisms on which they rely, however skeptically, prove dysfunctional. To resolve this crisis, the *fugueur* has four options:

- Return to the homeland where traumatic disappointment or betrayal initially occurred and face the source
- Attempt to upgrade the rickety apparatus of liberal uplift (and the American self at the helm) to make it adequate to complete the mission that it has so far failed to achieve
- Remain abroad in an ongoing peripatetic state of refusal, anxiety, and protest
- "Go native," adopting the post-travel self as the primary identity

In the last option, amnesia about the pre-travel self may become permanent, or pre-travel memories may be recovered without being attached to the newly acculturated subject.

In most of these variations, the *fugueur* must learn to inhabit multiple geographical spaces. While the Cold War espionage thriller's rejection of ideology arguably brought its protagonists to a standstill on the edge of an existential abyss, the late-twentieth- and early-twenty-first-century Peace Corps thriller occupies a more fully mapped world. The new thriller's wrestling match with the ideology of liberal progress extracts the hero from a strictly national sense of personal identity and pulls the fugue into a less panicky, but still highly conflict-ridden, geopolitical universe.

Variations on the Peace Corps Fugue

In the double plot of the thriller, the investigator provides the hinge— recovering the past by reinterpreting the present and linking the worlds of crime and punishment by making himself vulnerable to risk. The specific thrills of the thriller, then, arise when apparent fixities are released from their moorings and a conceptual or cultural vertigo ensues. In the Peace Corps thriller. in particular, the most destabilizing thrill derives from the implosion of the liberal progress narrative itself as it encounters geopolitical contradictions and the many irrationalities of the global economy. These developments endanger the protagonist physically and politically. In the unsteady ideological situation that results, the stability of narrative formulas sometimes proves useful.

Some Peace Corps thrillers report the literal violence faced by and the physical vulnerability felt by volunteers during their service. Since the organization's beginning, volunteers have regularly died or experienced violent crime, and considerable official attention has been devoted to this challenge.[30] This kind of experience is vividly conveyed by works such as Phillip Weiss's *American Taboo: A Murder in the Peace Corps* (2004). The result of several years of scrupulous investigative journalism, *American Taboo* examines the situation leading up to and following the murder of Deb Gardner by fellow volunteer Dennis Priven during their service in Tonga in the mid-1970s. Despite clear evidence establishing Priven's guilt, Peace Corps country directors, with support from the higher ranks of the organization, arranged an insanity defense for the killer and had him transported back to the United States, where he was released and went on to work for more than twenty years in the offices of Social Security in New York City. Weiss's scandalized narrative of these events begins with a mildly satiric sketch of the volunteers—describing the future victim, for example, as "half Cherokee, half Pepsodent" (13). As in fictional works devoted to similar material, his focus rarely drifts to the Tongans themselves. Its real subject is the Peace Corps bureaucracy. In his account of Mary, the born-again country director for the Tonga program, and John Dellenbeck, a devout Christian working at Peace Corps headquarters in Washington, D.C., Weiss also figuratively links the project of the Peace Corps to that of missionaries seeking to convert the natives. Like Herman Melville's excoriating narrator in *Typee* (1846), Weiss is profoundly skeptical about what he regards as missionary zeal. "They had covered the case up," Weiss concludes, "to preserve their own careers, to preserve the American presence in the south Pacific, to preserve the churchly image of the Peace Corps. In so doing, they had also served the interests of a murderous criminal" (346). For Weiss, the Peace Corps' need for self-preservation not only sets the organization against the free-spirited and idealistic volunteers but also arises directly from its disturbingly pious aims.[31] Its particular vision of a globally portable virtue—a universal liberal creed—leads it to shelter a murderer.

The handling of the Gardner case was apparently not unique. Bob Shacochis, an RPCV who wrote the novel *Swimming in the Volcano* (1993), a finalist for the National Book Award that was based in part on his experiences as a volunteer in the Caribbean, has outlined his experiences with the Peace Corps' handling of attacks on volunteers. After testifying in court about being knifed, he began his own journalistic investigation into similar situations. Shacochis reports being blocked in his quest for information about the hundreds of volunteers who have died and the thousands more who have been assaulted during their service since 1961.[32] For Shacochis, "[T]he bigger concern . . . is who controls the story of the Peace Corps, who controls the story of Deb Gardner, and to what purpose. The Peace Corps, always, was really about us, what sort of people we Americans would be, who we were not just at home but in the world."[33] Censorship of stories about violence against volunteers amounts, for Shacochis, to the wrong sort of control, for the wrong purpose, and for the wrong ideals. Rather than promoting a culture of cosmopolitan engagement and honestly assessing the bodily and emotional risks that Americans experience in a world that does not always welcome their presence, the Peace Corps, Shacochis suggests, vigorously promotes and protects an uncomplicated liberalism according to which assaults never happen because "the world" is already actually or potentially so similar to the volunteers' American "home." The story of the cover-up cuts directly to the heart of the Peace Corps' mission and geopolitical vision for both Shacochis and Weiss, because it suggests a refusal to engage in the institutional self-questioning required by their less universalizing political ideals.

While journalistic accounts of this sort of violence can encounter vexing paper trails of unexplained data, the fictional approach reverses course. Peace Corps thrillers based in part or whole on events resembling the murder of Deb Gardner typically present the linear story of the actions taken by a self-regarding *fugueur*. The fugue is a method of inquiry, then, not institutional obfuscation.

The resulting patterns have been readily apparent to readers, several of whom have made the case for thinking of Peace Corps writing as a group. Laura Miller, for example, describes

> a category of [debut novels] written by earnest young men who have done stints with the Peace Corps or other NGOs [nongovernmental organiza-

tions] working in developing nations. The hero is a young man with the Peace Corps or other NGO working in a developing nation. He arrives in a village, filled with idealism if also warily infused with postcolonial reservations. He will fall into doomed love with the local tragic beauty, a girl who personifies the battered yet invincible yet ultimately unknowable spirit of the land. The hero will often also befriend a young man who will, over the course of the novel, get more and more involved with the political opposition to the presiding dictator, until he is killed in a riot or fighting with an insurgent group. Then the hero will, by the very skin of his teeth, escape the war-torn nation, thinking disconsolately on the plane during the flight home that he has just had the most real and important experiences of his life, and now they are behind him.[34]

For Miller, these stories of "earnest young men" are essentially romantic quest narratives. She treats their reliance on action-movie tropes as a negative attribute that underscores the originality of those few works that challenge these norms.

Novelist P. F. Kluge, who served in the Peace Corps in Micronesia, agrees, although he emphasizes a slightly different set of defining features. Kluge provides "the recipe, or at least the ingredients, of Peace Corps narratives" that he has seen:

> There were two currents of thought and feeling that inevitably converged. First, there was a stream of nostalgia, the recollection of heart-felt engagements, struggles and small victories in obscure places; embarrassments and epiphanies that lingered in the mind forever. But there was a darker second current, intimations of being on a children's crusade that combined naivete and arrogance, of being shrugged off and exploited by host country nationals, of being manipulated and patronized by Peace Corps staff.[35]

While Miller stresses the forward movement of the hero's all-too-conventional *Bildung*, Kluge is more interested in the ambivalent inner life of the Peace Corps hero, emphasizing the oscillation between motives and effects, local and institutional values, psychic and social life. Kluge treats as central precisely those elements of "round" characterization that Miller suggests are lacking in the Peace Corps narrative. However, both critics stress that the hallmark of this genre is its preoccupation with the American hero-protagonist. "Things have really fallen apart," writes Ikhide R. Ikheloa in much the same context, "in the white man's head."[36] Rather than reading this formula as the result of a persistent aesthetic failure, though, we can understand it as a signal of the author's involvement with a legitimate ideological problem: the unmooring of 1960s-era universalizing liberalism from its domestic base.

At least this approach can help explain why Carter Coleman's novel *The Volunteer* (1998) follows the conventions of the Peace Corps thriller so faithfully, even though Coleman was not himself a volunteer.[37] Set mainly in rural Tanzania, where Rutledge Jordan, a southern lawyer, has been posted, *The Volunteer* opens with Jordan rescuing an eagle chick endangered by habitat loss. Although officially tasked with teaching villagers to raise fish for market, Jordan becomes far more invested in caring for the chick in his makeshift home, and the bird quickly provides a metonymic link to Zanifa, an attractive "mulatto" girl promised in marriage to a local "sultan" and therefore scheduled to undergo female circumcision. Jordan spends time attempting to befriend the worldly and informative sultan, but he is unable to persuade this local potentate to abandon the circumcision ritual. Ultimately, Jordan rescues Zanifa by spiriting her across the border to Kenya on his motorbike and enrolling her in a girls' school. On the final page of the novel, men employed by the sultan take revenge by mutilating him, and the novel resolves with this concretization of the emotional wound that led Jordan to sign up for the Peace Corps in the first place—his loss of the virtuous belle to whom he had been engaged back home.

The plot of Coleman's novel thus follows quite faithfully the pattern outlined by Miller—from Jordan's "doomed love" to his friendship with a politically enlightened peer to his final, world-weary escape. At the same time, frequent flashbacks to the dissolute life that the hero led in the United States, as well as his skepticism about Peace Corps projects and the white expatriate community in Tanzania, reinforce the oscillating subjectivity sketched by Kluge. The attitudes expressed by the protagonist are linked to the stance of the author by the attention to craft on display in the novel. The protagonist sketches the eagle chick daily to mark its growth, and this provides a correlative for the rather mechanical inclusion of a great deal of Swahili vocabulary in the novel's dialogue. These exercises in self-discipline balance the high level of risk and even paranoia that the narrator insists Jordan experiences in a world whose logic he does not grasp. After all, even though equally irrational American and Tanzanian sexual ethics are the manifest subject of the novel, the protagonist is not simply rescuing a vulnerable virgin from sexual damage. He is also extracting himself from a situation in which he feels physically threatened by crowds of menacing others. Simply being present in Tanzania feels perilous to Jordan, since acting on the sexual desires, comforts, and speeds he takes as his birthright constantly expose him to irrational punishment.

Coleman's fugue also follows genre formulas in its treatment of memory. His hero is propelled into wandering by the traumatic loss of his beloved. Tormented by guilt, Jordan elects to forget the episode, leaving behind an empty self incapable of mourning. This renders him capable of identifying with others only through their potential wounds—damage he feels solely responsible for preventing, as he projects his own extreme ego vulnerability onto others. Only his final heroic rescue of Zanifa fully animates this listless hero. In *The Volunteer*, no drama is provided by the tedium of daily labor or the struggle to wrest a livelihood from a damaged habitat in what is called throughout the novel the "turd world." The developing world is excrementitious for Coleman's supposedly ironic protagonist because he has experienced an ego-shattering loss that makes him feel that his own life has been wasted. Like the post–Civil War South, where Jordan grew up, this environment is failed and degraded, providing little sustenance for his lingering faith in his own and the world's inherent virtue. Finally, *The Volunteer* leaves its hero shaken and blind in one eye, returning home without even a default ideology to aid him.

Although Coleman's depiction of cultural difference as essentially horrific violates the premises of contemporary cultural relativism, *The Volunteer* remains a novel whose thrill derives from its commitment to an endangered American creed. Much the same can be said for a less typical but more celebrated Peace Corps thriller—Richard Dooling's *White Man's Grave* (1994). Like Mark Jacobs's lesser-known *Stone Cowboy* (1997), Dooling's narrative takes culture rather than poverty as its central subject. However, Dooling's tartly satiric novel enters the culture wars even farther to the right than Coleman's, not only presenting African sexuality as terrifying and alien but also placing active witchcraft at the heart of African identity.

Like Coleman, Dooling wrote a Peace Corps novel without having served as a volunteer. A lawyer, novelist, and screenwriter, Dooling traveled from Nebraska to Sierra Leone to visit his former college roommate Michael O'Neill, a volunteer (1978–1982) who was captured by rebels during his service.[38] In this, his first and reportedly favorite novel to date, Dooling's protagonist, Boone Westfall, tracks down his friend Michael Killigan, a volunteer who has lost contact with his friends and family in Indianapolis. The novel follows

Westfall's journey from the "Land of the TV and the Home of the Airwaves" to West Africa (23). His first sight in Freetown is an impressive tree that his taxi driver tells him will reveal its hanging witch capes if he looks at it with four eyes—that is, with a witch in his belly. Even before we arrive at the witch bird tree, however, the need for a radically transformed vision has been firmly established. The missing volunteer's father has received a mysterious bundle in the mail, accompanied by the information that his son has taken "the shape of a bush devil hungry for the souls of the witchmen who killed him" (22). A multitude of objects, stories, and phenomena alien to midwestern business culture launch Dooling's multidirectional satire.

While a purely Conradian quest narrative might endorse the horrified father's response, taking readers deeper into the "bush" to hunt down the devil that his too-acculturated son has become, Dooling chose a different approach. *White Man's Grave* knowingly invokes a tradition of imperialist writing on West Africa, borrowing its title from British travel narratives stressing the dangers to European soldiers serving in the tropics.[39] Admittedly, the conclusion of Westfall's search for his friend does recall Conrad (via Francis Ford Coppola), bringing him to the rebel soldiers' den where, "able to see the whole room with eyes that had grown accustomed to the dimness," he discovers his captured friend across "a table strewn with human skulls spray-painted in neon colors and adorned with sunglasses and caps" (340). However, the novel arrives at this climax only after insisting on the portability of magical objects. By this point in the story, the witchery that emboldens the rebel captors has also arrived in the Land of the TV, and the novel insists that readers reverse their gaze, casting an equally anthropological eye on the rituals and brutality of Middle America.

For example, for help with the bundle that he has received (which turns out to include a live fruit bat), Michael's father, Randall Killigan, invokes his own fetishes: medicine, the law, and religion. Ridden with anxiety, he has himself tested for "some metabolic disorder, or an imbalance in brain chemistry, an electrical disturbance or a freak seizure" (71). Nothing concrete appears, although the doctor does inform him that the law (Randall's profession and most stable frame of reference) "consisted mostly of incantations and time-honored spells" (74). Driven to extreme measures, this hypercompetitive bankruptcy lawyer even attends Mass. "His own perceptions had so terrified him that he had sought shelter in the refuge of the weak. He was regressing to an earlier stage of psychological development," he reflects (235). With the pages of his holy books—the bankruptcy code, *Forbes*, the *Wall*

Street Journal, and the *New York Times*—all shredded and illegible, he desperately needs that drastically transformed mode of vision available to his son.

Well in advance of his father's crisis, Michael has been described as veering "from enchantment with Africa into disenchantment with America" (31). His rejection of rationalism allows for the possibility of magic. Even though Michael's later captivity highlights the risks faced by and vulnerability of the traveler who goes, in a sense, too far in his cross-identifications, and even though the full-blown physical transformations experienced by dangerously solitary witches are presented in Dooling's novel as disturbing hallucinatory experiences, only travelers between worlds—those open to multiple realities and willing to use four eyes—survive his satirist's knife. Dooling dissects a returning anthropologist's revulsion at the obscene wealth, waste, and self-serving hypochondria in the United States just as succinctly as he mocks the paranoia, graft, and brutality observed in Sierra Leone. In this novel, it is necessary to see and take seriously the magic invoked in both home and host cultures—not simply to travel in search of romantic wish fulfillment like the African American tour groups that "come over here wearing their kente cloths and clutching a copy of *Roots*" (101). Striking out from the capital and taking the physical and epistemological risks involved in encountering a world at odds with one's preconceptions is the task validated in this novel. That encounter, the novel concludes in its searing final portrait of the lawyer, includes the possibility of discovering that the evils one observes ultimately emanate from oneself.

In short, Dooling's novel begins as a satire of Peace Corps volunteers' idealism but quickly broadens its mission. It vigorously rattles the foundations of liberal faith in technology and the rule of law and unsettles any static notion of cultural difference, placing the United States and Sierra Leone on a single plane of physical endangerment potentially governed by absolute evil. The volunteer as witch retains some authority in this post-liberal universe, but professional expertise is held in this novel by anthropologists, witch finders, and death-worshipping soldiers rather than doctors, lawyers, and priests.[40] The so-called helping professions are of little use in Dooling's world, as the common denominator of all persons in a cross-cultural encounter turns out to be the grave. In Dooling's more libertarian interpretation of Greene's themes,[41] the outcome of a fully post-liberal cultural relativism must be an encounter with this mortal void.

Although the political implications of Dooling's satire probably have been exaggerated by reviewers for publications such as *National Review,*[42]

White Man's Grave does illustrate the malleability of the genre of the Peace Corps thriller. The novel demonstrates that the genre's basic elements can be organized in a manner that exposes the cracks in the "American Creed" and allows glimpses of a supposedly terrifying abyss of freedom lying below. However, this nihilist interpretation of the genre can also be played in quieter tones, as Mark Jacobs's very accomplished and "vastly underappreciated" *Stone Cowboy* reveals.[43]

During his Peace Corps service (1978–1980), Jacobs was stationed in Paraguay. However, his career in the Foreign Service soon took him to Bolivia, where *Stone Cowboy* is set. The titular cowboy, Roger, is an American expatriate who has just been released from a Bolivian prison. In the capital, he meets a schoolmarmish American searching for her brother. The brother turns out to be a magician working for a Bolivian drug lord, and their quest to find him takes the pair to the coca-producing highlands. Along the way, they cross paths with a number of other Americans and Europeans seeking release from industrial materialism through some combination of drug use, erotic experimentation, and physical labor. Through sexual abuse subplots, Jacobs locates a primal violence at the root of these hippie idealisms; however, the novel does not endorse the values that these Carlos Castaneda–inspired would-be visionaries are fleeing. Roger hails, after all, from Flint, Michigan—the postindustrial manufacturing city that had recently become an emblem of the specific vulnerability associated with working-class immobility in Michael Moore's documentary *Roger and Me* (1989). Instead, in this novel, mobile and politically minded realists of both the left-wing Sandinista variety and the Drug Enforcement Agency are equally invasive. Jacobs's hero is no more sympathetic to these geopolitical actors than he is to the "trolls," his private term of abuse for indigenous Bolivians.

Throughout *Stone Cowboy*, in short, it is not national, regional, or cultural differences that distinguish people. Hippies and Vietnam vets are as mutually dependent as North and South: "Yin and yang. Ponytail and brush cut, round and square. For a long time they went back and forth, and it was clear to Roger that they were two halves of the same strange character who didn't fit in any of the U.S. of North America anymore so they had to come out here to the Bolivian jungle to play out the weird family drama they couldn't act out at home" (213). The only distinctions that actually matter are those between the nomads and the residents.[44] The latter are defined by their often involuntary fixity in a mobile universe. For the dead-pan *fugueur* sensibility at the heart of this novel, detached nomadic wandering is the only way to escape from "el

Panóptico," the prison. "If you ran far enough without taking a bullet in the back," Roger reflects, "eventually you would have to come to a place where the woods ended, and there was no coca, no dope, nothing lethal. There was such a thing as a safe place. They ran. There had to be that kind of a place. Running" (140). Nomadism is the only substantial alternative this novel presents to drug-induced or poverty-enforced dependence, although it, too, ultimately runs up against the death drive. The novel reaches its climax with the gringo magician's death, a scene that recalls the famous slow-motion massacre that closes Arthur Penn's *Bonnie and Clyde* (1967), a film mentioned earlier in the novel. With this gory spectacle, Jacobs arrives at the same limit as Dooling. Both *Stone Cowboy* and *White Man's Grave* make the spiritual death of the most deluded American a launching point for a still restless *fugueur*.

Dooling, however, presents Michael Killigan's revelation that "Africa's misery was . . . a direct consequence of America's comparative wealth and the cunning of white 'big men'" (31) as something of a naïve understatement, given the centrality of merciless bankruptcy prosecution to the plot. Dooling's young men are left fully adrift, unable to discern any logic beneath their discarded liberal ideals. Jacobs's hero, by contrast, bases his moments of amnesia and revelation on a different kind of social knowledge. Rejuvenating himself in a fancy hotel before the final confrontation, he reflects that

> what got to him, watching the women's buttery rich asses and the men's cocky cool, was the way they totally tuned out everybody around them. They had their own planet, and no room for ugly people on it. Actually it wasn't a bad place to visit if you had plenty of money and could appreciate what it did to the women: the way they talked, the way they dressed, the confident way they came at the men. But next to them, behind them, under them, all those waiters and workers, people with tools and brooms and hoses in their hands: invisible, as in ghosts. They had their own planet, too, but it wasn't a place tourists were dying to get to. What you needed to do if you were going to be a rich person in a place like Bolivia was learn how not to see certain things. You fixed your eyes on the easy pretty, the pretty easy. (259)

To "learn how not to see certain things"—that is, to forget the invisible planet of the poor and to focus instead on superficial elegance—does not solve an existential crisis for the stone cowboy. To the contrary, in the context of his desire to tune out his own origins so he can talk to God, that discipline grounds him in a contradictory material world. His detachment replicates aspects of the "cocky cool" of Bolivian upper-class men, and his quest for release into pure nomadism knowingly reveals its compromise with a class-specific amnesia.

This approach to the *fugueur* finally has different political implications than Dooling's satire. Jacobs's Peace Corps thriller renounces both left-wing and neoconservative languages of virtue in favor of a vision of cultural revolution. "More likely than any sort of radical politics," Jacobs later wrote in *Counterpunch*, "and more likely to succeed with foreign audiences, is the emergence of what could be called a new progressive center, speaking by means of books, not TV."[45] Advocating the "soft" power of literary culture over the "hard" logic of military conquest, Jacobs anchors Peace Corps liberalism in media practice.

Both Dooling's and Jacobs' variations on the Peace Corps fugue measure American ideals of the 1960s against the geopolitical conditions of the 1990s. In the twenty-first century, however, the war on terror has arguably triggered a further transformation of the genre of the thriller, as Cold War ideological oppositions are recast along civilizational lines.[46] Robert Rosenberg's *This Is Not Civilization* (2004) and Tony D'Souza's *Whiteman* (2007) explore the meaning of these changes for the Peace Corps thriller in particular. Both of these winners of the Maria Thomas Award suggest a new consciousness of the syntax of this genre while retaining their focus on the contradictions of the "American Creed." For a start, both of these versions of "American literature with an internationalist bent" make the genre's conventional earnest young man somewhat more self-aware.[47] Rosenberg and D'Souza limit the *fugueur*'s narcissism and anxiety by focusing on civilizational dilemmas and on the self as perceived by others, respectively. Both novels depict world culture as a matrix, as a set of networked nodes, rather than staging a self that responds to crisis by seeking contact with a magical, horrible void. The primitivist themes explored by Dooling and Jacobs have not entirely disappeared, but the central preoccupation of the twenty-first-century Peace Corps thriller shifts from spatially distinct modern and primitive worlds to globally overlapping systems of urbanization and racial difference.

Rosenberg's Peace Corps service took him to Kyrgyzstan (1994–1996), but his novel ranges more widely. *This Is Not Civilization* pulls together four characters from East and West: Anarbek and Nazira of Kyrgyzstan; Adam, an Apache teenager; and Jeff, a white Peace Corps volunteer. All the strands of narrative meet in Jeff's apartment in Istanbul, and that city's famous Bosporus Bridge, which links Asia and Europe, becomes the novel's central symbol.

Crossing the bridge in a taxi, Adam "contemplated the open heights, the dark waters below, and tried to imagine a nomadic people journeying across straights like this—across the ice, from the farthest tip of Asia, into North America—and making their slow way along the coast and farther down into the deserts, until they had populated the lands, and all great migrations had come to an end" (279). The bridge stands at the heart of a city that stands at the heart of a world populated by nomads. The geographical metaphor of the land bridge becomes a figure for all kinds of migration and for the fragility of interpersonal relations among people of different backgrounds in this migratory world. During his visit to Istanbul, for example, Adam discovers parallels between his life and Nazira's in Kyrgyzstan; from distant continents, both have struggled with domineering traditional fathers, faltering traditions, and corruption in the desperately marginal village economy. The fleeting attraction they develop thanks to Jeff's largely unconscious mediation dissipates, however, when they return to their similarly crumbling villages on opposite sides of the planet.

As this romance suggests, Rosenberg's fugue distributes the *fugueur*'s amnesia among several characters. All the central characters are displaced in Istanbul, drifting and collapsing like the hot-air balloon that Jeff observes at a Kyrgyz festival. None is quick enough to outpace the logic of the market: Nazira escapes a forced marriage in her village, for example, only to risk debt slavery in Turkey's underground economy, peddling leather jackets on commission. Adam inevitably returns to the reservation, still hoping for a basketball scholarship that may never come his way, and Nazira's countryman Anarbek is crushed by a refrigerator in a horrific earthquake at the novel's turning point. A drifter himself, the former volunteer Jeff unwillingly becomes an agent of border bureaucracy and ineffective NGOs. His expatriate tendencies are literally nothing to write home about, as a passage from Adam's point of view concludes. "Suddenly it disgraced him to imagine what they would think of his living in a foreign country, as if he were too good for the reservation," he discovers, "as if he were after some kind of white folk's glory" (163). Jeff's disinterest in "massive wealthy modern America, waiting resolutely for his return" is considerable, as is Adam's second-order doubt about the moral authority of this disaffected stance (103). Neither of these points of view, it turns out, provides a stable foundation for a civilization.

Instead, Rosenberg's novel uses the figure of the earthquake to reveal the shakiness of an entire international system. This unstable structure is best observed in Turkey because Istanbul "lay at the center of the world," reflects Jeff:

An ancient earthquake had chiseled out these straits, and the ensuing flood had divided the continents. These roiling currents had swept the cold waters of the Black Sea down to the Aegean and the warm waters of the Mediterranean up to Russia. For over two millennia, from this very point, the city's empires had spread east and west. Its emperors and sultans had ruled from that mighty-walled peninsula. Their gray palaces still loomed over the sea; their domed mosques still peered from the crowns of flowered hills toward Mecca.

But on every hilltop now the concrete had grown outward and over the great peninsula. The vast empire had retreated upon itself. Its peoples left their inherited farms and war-ravaged nations. They fled distant mountain villages and the rusting ports of four different seas. They arrived with oversized bundles, crowded in burnt-out apartment buildings, collected in neighborhoods of shoddy cement structures and crouching cardboard houses. (285–286)

Jeff envisions a world peopled by refugees who inhabit the shells of fallen empires. While usefully correcting the overly shiny portrait of capitalist progress circulated by Peace Corps bureaucrats in the novel, this downbeat sensibility also undercuts the thriller as a genre. Jeff's catastrophic vision results in world of foregone conclusions, not a thrillingly unstable one. It recalls, perhaps intentionally, Jack Kerouac's account of the *fellahin*, the "basic primitive, wailing humanity that stretches in a belt around the equatorial belly of the world."[48] And it suggests that, like the Beats, the twenty-first-century *fugueur* risks projecting onto others his own disidentification with national ideals. In Rosenberg's novel, Kyrgyz and American experiments with dislocation end up much the same.

Rosenberg's deflated, almost Spenglerian perspective updates Dooling's pessimism about the prospects for liberal reform in a corrupt and evil world. He locates the destructive potential at Earth's core itself, rather than in the human soul, and he shifts the locus of concern to twenty-first-century versions of East–West relations, but the results are finally quite similar. We remain in the terrain of the Oedipal struggle, because the RPCV's loss of faith in the "American Creed" is still the dominant narrative.

By contrast, D'Souza's *Whiteman* revolves around a maternal legacy. A second-generation Peace Corps volunteer, D'Souza served in Côte d'Ivoire in part because he wished to "honor his mother," a volunteer in India in the 1960s.[49] His novel reflects the insights derived from both generations of service and shows that, like Rosenberg, D'Souza knows the conventions of the Peace Corps thriller well enough to reject and adapt some of them. For both literary and political reasons, however, his novel centers on a fictional aid organization, Potable Water International.[50] Despite the name change, as well as D'Souza's effort to diversify his depiction of Côte d'Ivoire by including ethnically Lebanese and Chinese characters, so many of the elements of the Peace Corps novel appear that *Whiteman* still recalls the genre.

For starters, D'Souza's hero, Jack Diaz, is clearly a beleaguered *fugueur*. Mourning, among other things, the death of his father, he experiences several forms of physical endangerment—most notably during the siege of an aid workers' compound in Abidjan. Jack begins and ends the novel in "a place [he] did not belong, and more than that, a place where they would not let [him] belong" (16). He loses his American identity so thoroughly that he is renamed several times—first as Diomonde Adama and later as Sergio, after a soap-opera star. But, most generically, he is the titular white man whose strangeness to the place is remarked by all. He does begin to recover, as the narrative proceeds, from this initial anonymity and disorientation—largely by means of a fugue within the fugue. Forgetting his isolation on hunting trips, Diaz/Adama enters a forest where "all is as though upside down" (73). When hunting francolins, "America and my life there felt as far away as they really were" (79). Developing new competences, such as hunting, alongside those he already enjoys as a protected volunteer, D'Souza's hero reinvents himself by getting lost.

This two-step process is repeated at several levels of the novel. Diaz repeatedly reevaluates his well-intentioned goals after realizing that he has misunderstood their effects. He reconsiders his effort to teach in the village school when his presence interrupts a black market in food aid. He discovers that he has been duped by the whores with whom he thought he had forged an intense bond, and he learns that his courtship of Cathy, his attractive supervisor in the NGO, has been preempted by her relationship with her Peul houseboy. All the protagonist's revelations, in short, turn on his realization that others have understood him better than he understood them. His self-discovery reveals his own blinders and a partial awakening to the judgments of others, rather than a solitary recovery of his former self and its shattered world. In this manner, D'Souza's novel telegraphs its reversal of the most formulaic versions of the Peace Corps fugue.

Some of D'Souza's other efforts to achieve the same effect—for example, the appearance in the framing chapters of a monkey and then a dog named Africa—are not quite as successful because they rely heavily on ironic renderings of racist tropes. Reviewers also considered some of D'Souza's images for contact and intimacy with a new culture too familiar and found its political insights predictable.[51] They noted how *Whiteman* reproduces the limits of its genre and suggested that the novel rattles the virtuous American liberal's self-concept without fully redefining that figure. By the time the novel closes with the phrase "It's Africa," for example, this proper name has devolved into jokey references to a dog that "wants" to talk to the hero on the telephone (279). This joke prevents the human voice of Africa from speaking. D'Souza's irony about this monologue never quite reaches the bite of Greene's bitter cosmopolitanism, and the author finally returns his protagonist to a depopulated urban universe and abandons the apparently pre-technological village. The narrator's sympathy (like Rosenberg's) with Muslims signals his antipathy to the post–September 11 jingoism mentioned in the novel,[52] but it no more disturbs his preoccupation with American-style universalizing liberalism than his sojourn in Africa makes him a black man.

In Rosenberg's and D'Souza's contributions to the Peace Corps genre, then, we notice some tonal shifts. Some of the existential grandeur of earlier versions has lessened as contributors to the genre have questioned its formulas. The intensity of the protagonist's propelling loss, the duration and depth of his amnesia, and the intensity of his endangerment have diminished as well. To varying degrees, the association with the detective story has also been downgraded, moving the genre from confrontations with specific crimes to diagnoses of global conditions. The protagonist's task has ballooned while his capacity for accomplishing it has shrunk. In the twenty-first-century Peace Corps novel, the protagonist begins with a less passionate commitment to the ideals of organization in which he serves, so he has a shorter distance to fall as disillusionment sets in, and his discovery of the limitations of bureaucratic liberalism comes as less of a shock. With the stabilization of the thriller's inherent vertigo, however, comes the possible loss of another important element of the genre: its sometimes obsessive dedication to documenting bureaucratic abuses and betrayal. The more low-key fugue of the Peace Corps thriller in the twenty-first century prompts us to ask how these post-liberal fictions imagine the institution that unifies them.

The Institutional Imaginary of Peace Corps Fiction

Most commonly, Peace Corps narratives are anchored in an individual protagonist's point of view as he or she explores the rural world of the posting and comes to terms with psychological dilemmas of the past. This focus on the subjective experience of coming-of-age or political awakening tends to push into the background accounts of the institutions that brought the volunteer to this new world. Training sessions rarely attract more than a passing mention in Peace Corps fiction, and the application and selection process that volunteers undergo hardly figures at all.[53] To the extent that the Peace Corps as an institution appears directly in these novels, it is usually represented by out-of-touch supervisors, the occasional irrelevant directive, or a failed emergency protocol. In Rosenberg's *This Is Not Civilization*, for instance, Jeff's Kyrgyz plot focuses on his discovery that the cheese collective in the village where he is serving is really a scam for attracting government and embassy grants; officials, including Peace Corps administrators, are totally unaware of this deception and urge him to involve locals in a complex loan program to support the nonexistent dairy farms. Similarly, in D'Souza's *Whiteman*, the Peace Corps higher-ups based in the capital so misunderstand the situation of the so-called mud hut volunteers that they inadvertently endanger them by waiting too long to call them into town during periods of violent unrest. In these works, institutions operate primarily as antagonists, as systems of rules that fail to embody or support the idealistic goals of the individual volunteers.

As figures of rigidity and stasis, the Peace Corps and other aid organizations provide the external "reality" that the skeptical protagonists test as they struggle to recover their lost identities. In Erik Erikson's classic formulation of the adolescent identity crisis, the developmental task of youth is to test the ideological coherence of the social world, probing its adequacy to personal psychic and physical needs. The specific shape of identity crises varies over time, Erikson asserts, because "the nature of the identity conflict depends on the latent panic pervading a historical period."[54] During periods when new facts at odds with established ideologies arise, when the decay of existing ideologies produces symbolic dangers, or when the breakdown of social authority triggers profound existential malaise, identity crises of youth may prove particularly intense, and adults' resolutions of their own earlier crises may prove insufficient. For Erikson, writing in the 1970s, reflections on youth struggles provided access to the deep structure of social relations. In this spirit, then, we might posit that in the Peace Corps novel, the young volunteer's psychic disorder is an index of an institutional problem. The institutional preconditions for travel are not so much ignored in these narratives as they are repressed in order to allow a purportedly more authentic vision of self and other to emerge. The subjective stance of the Peace Corps fugue produces an indirect knowledge of social conditions if we understand that apparently rigid institution itself as a psychically necessary imaginary resolution to historically specific dilemmas experienced by the American liberal self at the end of the twentieth century and the beginning of the twenty-first.

Appropriately, the prototype for this depiction of institutions appears in the work of Maria Thomas, the author memorialized by the RPCV's literary prize. *Antonia Saw the Oryx First* (1987) is not Thomas's first book, nor does it demonstrate all the elements of the more formulaic Peace Corps fugues, but it does represent institutions as signs of social rigidity.[55] The novel is set in post-independence Tanzania in the period leading up to the closing of borders and expulsion of foreigners in the late 1970s, a context that recalls the fugue's preoccupation with the volunteer's endangerment. However, Thomas chooses as the first of her paired protagonists Antonia Redmond, a white doctor born and raised in Dar es Salaam, and her characterization attends from the outset to the ambivalence of that position. "Like an African, the white doctor came to work on foot" (1), the novel begins—drawing attention to the role of color consciousness as the doctor moves through crowded streets as well as to her own and others' incomplete sense of her being properly African, let alone Tanzanian. Culture shock, then, does not play a major role in this character's world; she has little to do with dissolute white expatriates and diplomats. Her primary attachments are to her black African lover, Paul Luenga, and the barely functioning hospital where she works.

The hospital links Antonia to Esther Moro, the novel's second protagonist. The daughter of a traditional healer, Esther makes her way from an unsatisfactory village marriage to a would-be nursing career in the city. She ultimately emerges as the more effective of the two caretakers in the novel's mountaintop climax. During an escalating political crisis, the two women find themselves at the Lawns, a tourist hotel established in the ruins of a colonial sisal plantation; they attempt to revive the heroic South African freedom fighter Sam Nkosi, one of the novel's voices of political instruction. Although Nkosi later dies and the novel closes with Antonia's vision of "a second wave of colonialists back to repair the ruins or finish it off like vultures on a corpse," it is Esther's willingness to open herself to shamanic trances and her temporary transformation into a living embodiment of the famous Makonde sculptures mentioned multiple times in the novel that keeps another alternative alive (296).[56] Esther's vision of herself as a figure "made of black wood, the core of a tree," offers an enduring and solid complement to Antonia's titular childhood memory of catching sight of the elusive oryx (286). Both of these identity-confirming visions, however, are set in opposition to the novel's depiction of the crumbling and dysfunctional architecture of colonial and postcolonial governmental institutions.

Even thriving, durable institutions, such as Harvard University—where Antonia first meets her future lover, fellow doctor Paul—function in the narrative as negative ground. The two African exiles discover and cling to each other in order to survive the frigid New England climate, before returning to Tanzania, where Paul becomes a hospital bureaucrat. Paul soon gives up his efforts at writing poetry to read Marx and Lenin; this leads to his "turning everything into a political event" and claiming that Antonia's "so-called efforts on his country's behalf" are "a wayward form of ego" (48–49). Ultimately spurned when her lover returns to his village wife and allows her to be expelled from the nation, Antonia, like Esther, defines herself against the rigidity of masculine institutions.

In the end, then, Thomas's novel presents a feminized aestheticism as a more valid and purportedly anti-ideological point of access to authentic African identity than the bureaucratic socialism adopted by critics of liberal do-gooders. Thomas criticizes institutional stagnation in order to authorize something like the direct service ethic of the Peace Corps. It is the treatment of the institution as a symbol, however, rather than the specific political stance of the novel, that makes *Antonia Saw the Oryx First* the ideal Peace Corps fugue, well deserving of its status as the symbol of the genre. After all, many of the other contributors to the genre have, as discussed in the previous section, used the same figure of the static uninformed institutional backdrop to somewhat different political ends.

Although Thomas's depiction of the static institution is a recurring figure in the Peace Corps thriller, other variations create more room for their heroes to maneuver. Without exactly embracing bureaucratic reason, novels by Mischa Berlinski, Peter Orner, Richard Wiley, and Paul Eggers depict the institution as a more manageable space.[57] Their tonally varied works explore the interior of helping organizations, making their flexibility or baroque logic nearly as significant as the protagonist's psychological crisis. In these novels, too, some of the expectations of ethnographic illumination held by readers schooled by didactic detective narratives such as Tony Hillerman's Navajo series and Alexander McCall Smith's Botswana novels are fulfilled. However, despite the occasional pause for researched explanations of local customs, the object of the ethnographic gaze for Berlinski, Orner, Wiley, and Eggers is most commonly the do-gooding organization itself, rather than the intended recipients of this would-be good.

The most artistically ambitious novel of this group, Mischa Berlinski's *Fieldwork* (2007), addresses the institution of ethnography quite explicitly, as the title suggests. The novel maps the intricate relations of three Americans in Thailand: the journalist-narrator, Mischa, who accompanies his Peace Corps volunteer girlfriend to Thailand; Martiya van der Leun, a Berkeley graduate student in anthropology whose imprisonment Mischa decides to investigate; and David Walker, the Dead Head missionary whom she has murdered. This fictional account of the relationship between the author-figure and the missionaries he intended to study is mediated by the anthropologist. Mischa's journalistic investigation begins with curiosity about the now-dead anthropologist's crime but ultimately backtracks through her entanglements with the missionary family and their mutual involvement with an invented ethnic group, the Dyalo. Martiya is studying the Dyalo, while the Walkers are hoping to convert them, and the violence that prompts the investigation turns out to be, from the journalist's perspective, a sacrifice that Martiya has made in order to preserve her personal and collective beloveds from Christian interference. Mischa's narrative, in other words, follows the path of the thriller in discovering the motives for a crime, but it does so in a distinctly ethnographic fashion by reconstructing the life story and sensibility of the anthropologist and using them to explain her actions. In this spirit, in a lengthy, self-conscious digression on Bronislaw Malinowski, the narrator asks what drives a passionate investigator, concluding that "Martiya was hardly better suited to her self-appointed task of understanding the Dyalo when the Curiosity took her; but of course I was hardly better suited to my self-appointed task of understanding Martiya" (236).

Here, the narrator compares both himself and Martiya with Malinowski (and earlier to book collectors), on the grounds that all of them have entered a cycle of exchanges of mysterious objects. As travelers inhabiting a fugue state, they are themselves rather mysterious. Their metaphysical rootlessness aligns them with the more literal dissociations described in passages devoted to the journalist's recreational activities—smoking opium in a trekker's hut, swimming from houseboats, standing in the rain in Chaing Mai. *Fieldwork*, in short, treats the fugue as a formal device rather than a psychological state, and it is similarly free with the problem of representing institutional hierarchy— shifting that issue to scenes depicting the Dyalo.

Highly elaborate, restrictive, and remote, the customs of the Dyalo are, naturally, a subject of great interest to the anthropologist, but the plot of the thriller also turns on them. After all, it is precisely because the missionaries accept the reality of the metaphysical bureaucracy of spirits that guide Dyalo life that they are able to function successfully in Thailand. Because they believe in the threats posed by that pagan bureaucracy, the missionaries seek to convert the Dyalo, and thus, in the view of the anthropologist, they endanger both her most intense erotic relationship and her career. To defend the complex institutions of the Dyalo, Martiya kills first David and then herself in a Thai prison. While the more conventional Peace Corps thriller places the blame for the volunteer's intense sensation of vulnerability on the short arm of the organization that he expected to protect him, Berlinski's sophisticated adaptation of the genre turns a version of the *fugueur* into a defender of bureaucracy and a hostile critic of missionizing uplift. The revelation of the novel turns on bureaucratic principles, and the thrill of its investigation derives from the vertigo produced by first swapping out the narrator's relatively secular Jewish backpacker stance[58] for the missionaries' zeal and then exchanging the missionaries' point of view for the anthropologist's professional expertise, before finally converting the anthropologist's scientific approach to the Dyalos' worldview. Shuttling among these options, Berlinski's narrative makes a virtue of institutional and formal logic—preferring them to the visionary authenticity and discovery of one's own identity so dominant in more formulaic interpretations of the Peace Corps thriller.

A more conventional but still appealing treatment of institutional logic features in Peter Orner's humane novel *The Second Coming of Mavala Shikongo* (2006), which is set in a boys' school in the Namibian desert. Orner's narrator, who—like the author—serves as a volunteer English teacher,[59] tracks not only his own lustful appreciation for the title character, a female soldier, but also the balance of power between teachers and administrators in the school. Much of the gentle comedy of Orner's episodes follows from the incongruity between the teachers' private desires and the goals of their instruction. This theme can emerge because the volunteer in *Second Coming* is, rather uniquely in Peace Corps fiction, described as largely in sympathy with his similarly educated Namibian colleagues. Despite its attention to the presumably seasoned soldier, though, Orner's novel does not ultimately become a full-blown thriller. The institution in which he works does not in any fundamental way alter the narrator's condition, nor does he learn a great deal about its inner logic while functioning comfortably within it.

Richard Wiley's *Ahmed's Revenge* (1998), however, comes much closer to the thriller—featuring, as it does, a detective, a crime, and a clear explanation of events.[60] Set approximately ten years after Kenya achieved independence, the novel directly invokes white settler literature, such as Isak Dinesen's. It begins "I had a farm in Africa, too" (1), and asks what sort of violent retribution for colonization the children of colonists should expect. The widowed white protagonist learns that her husband and her father, the former Minister of Wildlife, had for years been smuggling elephant tusks, but the real insult for which the titular revenge is taken is the persistent assertion of white privilege. "Though you were twelve years old, your father's life, the examples he set, taught you not to care, that's all. He taught you not to notice ordinary Africans," the protagonist is told (125), and her awakening to her continuing blindness to racism reveals that she had grown up in a state of colonial amnesia. Her emergence from the collective fugue state over the course of the novel allows reparation to substitute for revenge. In hopes of compensating for her father and husband's duplicitous smuggling, the protagonist restores authentic ivory tusks to Ahmed, an enormous elephant skeleton housed in the national museum that symbolizes Kenya's precolonial glory. Filling in for the well-intentioned volunteer, she takes it on herself to settle the score for generations of colonization single-handedly.

In *Ahmed's Revenge*, the illicit organization of smugglers and the official institution of the museum frame the action. As in *Antonia Saw the Oryx First*, these fraternities tend to downshift into metaphors for the presumed problems of colonial and postcolonial rule. The nearly total ignorance of the museum staff manipulated by the protagonist and a Kenyan detective as she inserts her vital piece into the rickety elephant skeleton easily illustrates the institutional stolidity necessary for Wiley's tale of heroic individuals. Despite this conventional treatment of the institution, Wiley's focus on the modes of circulation—elephant tusks rather than Malinowski's objects of unknown function—does add a new element.

For a fully fledged treatment of the Peace Corps as a dynamic institution, though, the best place to turn is Paul Eggers's *Saviors* (1998). From the title forward, this debut novel signals its debt to Graham Greene's skeptical cosmopolitanism and deadpan assault on idealism. Perhaps Greene is such an inescapable predecessor for Eggers because his novel also concerns Vietnam. Set in and around Bidong Island, a Malaysian facility where Vietnamese boat people were interned, *Saviors* has as its main characters two former Peace Corps volunteers who stay on after their service to work in the camp. The plot begins with their movement from the mainland, where the office of the United Nations High Commission on Refugees offices is located, to the island; they learn how official and unofficial power operates on the island before witnessing the effects of a major change in Malaysian policy toward the boat people. A story that might have devolved into a piece of descriptive reportage turns toward the thriller, however, with the unexplained death of Nguyan van Trinh. In the prologue, this character's point of view establishes the human suffering at stake as a result of the refugee crisis, and a complex subplot emerges around the paperwork necessary to document Nguyan's demise, as well as a more local dispute over control of a plank with his name inscribed on it. The plank reappears at several key points in the action—as a table for the aid workers, a monument where a crucial confrontation occurs, a raft for armed insurrectionists, and a memento that washes up on shore shortly before the two former volunteers' departure. As a figure for the dead, the plank also becomes a recurring sign of the guilt that threatens to unhinge some of the aid workers. In particular, this possibility looms for Reuben Gil, a brashly unconventional figure who fights the camp bureaucracy.

In this novel, though, a radical individualist such as Gil is only partially virtuous. Always unstable and surreal, Gil is described as very large, heavy, red-headed, and hairy—all features that lead the Vietnamese to consider him a demon and give him names such as jungle junkie, red monkey, white bastard, and biting tree. He and his more temperate female sidekick, Porkpie, clearly inhabit a fugue state; both are dissociated from themselves, largely unable to cope with injuries, and incapable of writing to family and friends at home. The novel stages their revelations (for example, "It's not about love. It's about power" [258]) and wires them together to oppose Malaysian troopers who try to displace the refugees. But, ultimately, Eggers does not endow this pair with any insight greater than that of the organizations whose corruption and ineptitude they deride. A great deal of commentary is devoted to explicating these travesties—black-market profiteering in supplies, excessive control exercised by police forces, and petty personal and racial politics—and this thread of the novel seems to have prompted the publisher's blurbs comparing *Saviors* with *Catch-22* (1961). Although tonally *Saviors* more closely resembles Greene's reserved irony, the allusion to Joseph Heller is appropriate. Eggers's novel reproduces Heller's attention to imprisonment as the effect of organized heroism as well as his concern with the sleaziness of relations between the island and the mainland and his desire to magnify the irrational hilarity that the whole situation invokes in selected inhabitants. Furthermore, an early scene in *Saviors* involving the mild-mannered administrative head of the camp invites comparison with Heller's Major Major, since both characters are so clearly overwhelmed by the impossibility of their tasks and so desperately looking to escape responsibility for executing wildly unreasonable orders.

The fact, however, that Heller's novel found a still-devoted readership while Eggers's well-executed novel, despite strong reviews and the Maria Thomas Award, drifted off into relative obscurity may be chalked up to the different historical contexts each faced. By the turn of the millennium, Vietnamese refugees hardly seemed the most pressing issue to many American readers (who have tended to be more excited by soldiers' accounts than by narratives about those displaced by military action), even though the inhumane treatment of these and other refugees was arguably one of the foremost crisis issues of the decade.[61] The factors that Erikson called the psycho-historical elements of crisis had shifted. Although the demonstrable illogic of innumerable international institutions purporting to do good has, for many observers, grown ever more inescapable,[62] the still decaying ideologies of liberal institutions did not seem to generate the same sense of symbolic danger in 1998 that they had in 1961. The assault on institutional absurdity that Heller launched resonated with a widespread identity crisis among American adolescents. His novel spoke to the fear of conscription into military service, which became an important danger in the 1960s, perhaps because it expressed the potential for harm to others and oneself that such service might require one to endure.

By contrast, in the early twenty-first century, there has been a major reorganization of the symbols of danger in the United States, as the nation's official geopolitical imagination shifted from the threat of Communism to that of radical Islam. In theory, this reorganization has required a certain amount of redefinition of the liberalism of the "American Creed" facing that danger — shifting the propaganda focus from explicitly economic topics, such as the merits of private property, to a different set of civil and political rights. As Slavoj Žižek argues, however, the production of a fundamentalist other seems ultimately to shore up rather than destabilize the logic of liberal democracy. For a full-blown contradiction (or, in the terms that Žižek borrows from Kant, an "infinite judgment") on liberal democracy, a double negation is required: "a radically anti-capitalist movement (the refusal of integration into the world market) coupled to a systematic dissolution of all traditional hierarchical social links, beginning with the family."[63] For Žižek, the anticapitalist aspects of Islamic fundamentalism are offset by its adherence to traditional ideologies of the family and other social forms. Sharing fundamental premises with liberal democracy, then, this new symbolic danger fails to trigger a more widespread identity crisis that may recognize and draw attention to the continuing problems of capitalist liberalism.

In other words, the impact of twenty-first-century Peace Corps novels may be limited, if Žižek's diagnosis is correct, by the psychohistorical situation that they confront. To more fully overcome that situation, these narratives of disappointed liberals who feel abandoned by institutions that no longer function, if they ever did, in accordance with the volunteers' principles would have to resolve a contemporary conflict, not just restage it. Indicting the institutions of liberalism for failing to be paternalistic or protective enough, however, simply asks for more of the same. Like Islamic fundamentalism (on Žižek's account), the Peace Corps thriller may not do enough to contradict the institution it opposes, and so it may not go far enough to resolve youthful identity crises in the present. For a bolder and more thorough experiment with the fugue state, the representation of liberal institutions, and the novel of political ideas itself, we will finally have to start elsewhere.

NORMAN RUSH'S BOTSWANA

Born in 1933, Norman Rush is the better part of a generation older than Richard Dooling and Mark Jacobs. After a five-year stint as a country director for the Peace Corps in Botswana (1978–1983), Rush published *Whites*, the volume of short stories that initiated his Botswana trilogy. It was followed by *Mating*, his first and lengthy National Book Award–winning novel,[64] and its even bulkier companion, *Mortals* (2003). As many reviewers have noted, these fruits of Rush's late middle age clearly benefit from the decades of reading and observing that preceded them. Rush's powerful, unruly writing is saturated with allusions to African politics and literary history—especially the Anglo-American moderns. The joyful logorrhea of his work calls to mind the maximalist projects of Gaddis, Beckett, and Joyce, and these favorites are joined by allusions to Eliot and Conrad; at the same time, Rush's writing is also often and favorably compared with that of contemporary American writers of the big political satire: David Foster Wallace, Jonathan Franzen, Don DeLillo, and Leslie Marmon Silko.[65] As many readers recognize, Rush's writing is characterized by a literary ambition and seriousness not fully in evidence in other Peace Corps novels. However, one of the less appreciated elements of Rush's literary output is his thorough overhaul of the crisis of liberal idealism. This feature of Rush's writing makes a profound contribution to the contemporary American novel of ideas.

Of Rush's three Botswana books, *Mortals* most directly addresses the genre of the thriller. At 715 densely allusive pages, its plot is extremely detailed and complex, interlinking academic and military institutions of intelligence, official assaults on rural development schemes, culturally variable concepts of property and sanity, and many other topics. What matters for this discussion, however, is the impressive way that Rush reaches past the blockages of the conventional Peace Corps thriller, bringing the genre to a more fully realized form. While the stories in *Whites* tackle the various forms of bad faith exhibited by expatriates in Botswana, and *Mating* takes its anthropologist narrator on a wildly paradoxical journey to a matriarchal utopia in the Kalahari Desert, *Mortals* fuses the concerns of its two predecessors. Its third-person narrator, Ray Finch, is a CIA agent who serves officially as an English professor at an Anglican school in the capital, Gaborone. A specialist in Milton, the politically disenchanted Ray loves etymology, mourns the diminution of English vocabulary, and labors intently on the "profiles" of suspicious people he compiles for his disturbingly illiterate superiors. Ray is something of a Miltonic fallen angel, trapped in a bureaucracy whose logic he is not able to manipulate, and as the novel proceeds he is sent to the mouth of hell. Caught up in a soon-to-be-squelched rural insurgency movement,[66] Ray is handed over, at his boss's request, to Boer mercenaries and torturers before escaping into exile in South Africa. As this hasty summary should indicate, *Mortals*, set in the early 1990s, in the immediate aftermath of the Cold War (that is, in the transition from the period Rush calls the *Zweikampf* [duel] to a condition of "leftlessness"),[67] is concerned with political failure and the prospects for Africa in the rapidly changing geopolitical scene. By making the initially rather unappealing CIA agent his hero, Rush displaces the question of idealism from the naïve volunteer, presenting his readers with a far more knowingly compromised middle-aged bureaucrat on the verge of renouncing his affiliations.[68] It does not come as any particular shock to the hero of *Mortals* that the CIA betrays and endangers him; his particular form of American exceptionalist liberalism has long burned off its most naïve scaffolding in favor of a more pragmatic appreciation for tangible reform. Rather than adolescent reality testing, this hero's task involves discovering whatever modest room for love and education he can locate in a crisis situation. He has, in the words of the novel's final chapter, "learned to be circumspect" (709) and reserves his energies for modest daily tasks: "The seedlings had to be ordered from

Cape Town. . . . And then there were two locals, potential teachers, to be interviewed" (712).

This quiet resolution follows, however, a thorough anatomy of disruptive political passions. The sexual thrills of idealist extremism are central to Rush's study of feminism and pacifism in *Mating*, and in *Mortals*, Rush again makes his most puritanically and idealistic character the object of a torturous erotic attraction. The other man in Ray's marriage to a much younger woman is Davis Morel, a biracial doctor from Cambridge, Massachusetts, who arrives in Botswana with suitcases stuffed with atheist propaganda. In addition to practicing psychotherapy, Morel begins a campaign designed to eradicate what he regards as the deleterious effects of Christianity in Africa, and both his zeal and his polymathy make him irresistible to Iris, Ray's wife. Morel's speeches—such as the learned discourse on the Christian appropriation of Jewish symbolism in chapter 21—add a great deal of intellectual interest to the novel, even though the protagonist feels "remote from Morel's arguments, completely," and too tired to go "down, down into the foundations of life . . . X-raying the historical accidents that had led to a world not completely satisfactory" (278). His own attention first as a spy and finally as a participant is more fully engaged by the program of Samuel Kerekang, a British-educated agricultural researcher whose quiet experiments with water conservation and Tennyson-reading communalism inadvertently trigger the insurgency movement. Against his own tastes, though, Ray is misled by sexual jealousy into overestimating the significance of Morel's activities, and his misjudgments endanger him physically and cost him his marriage. Similarly, his fundamental insecurity about not having published a book and his feelings of sibling rivalry make Ray an exceptionally close reader of his dying brother's experimental manuscript. The narrative center of *Mortals* is, in short, a conflicted bureaucrat who is drawn to idealisms that he can no longer either fully renounce or wholeheartedly advocate.

Rush's novel employs the fundamentals of the thriller genre (especially its emphasis on the mid-level bureaucrat swept up in a post-ideological universe that he never masters or entirely decodes). However, his dedication to the enlivening effects of intellectual pleasure transforms the genre. Rush moves the more reactive aspects of the fugue-state narrator to one side in order to clear room for a densely populated mental landscape. Rush's characters think. They read. They have emotional lives that precede their experiences as travelers, and they continue to learn and reflect as they move through geographic space. The languages, cultures, history, and natural environment of Botswana engage them and contribute a great deal to the texture of the novel, as does the remarkable literary erudition of Rush's narrator.

In the long interlude preceding Ray's capture and torture at the hands of the Boer mercenaries, for example, he travels with a driver through the Kalahari Desert. He is officially an inspector of resource management, and his undercover CIA task involves investigating Kerekang's movement, but his personal project is reading. Each evening at nightfall, Ray crouches on a camp stool surrounded by mosquito netting hung from an umbrella and studies his texts before burning them. He first makes his way through his notes on Kerekang's movement, then intently and paranoically studies the copy of *Madame Bovary* that his wife packed for him, before turning his attention to a manuscript composed of epigrams and bravely mediocre short stories written by his brother. His thoughts wander as he reads. His anxiety about cuckoldry figures the political uprising, and vice versa, while anxiety about how to edit his brother's work reminds him of his uncertainty about his cover story as well as moments from their childhood together. These flexible interpretation skills come to fruition when Ray is confronted by Uno, a Boer mercenary. At this moment, Ray begins "seeing something in the shape of events that he had missed before" (429). He reevaluates the geopolitical situation, but since "he had no power," it is not his own ability to "sort everything out" that matters (430). It is instead his ability to shuttle between observation and reflection that is invoked. This moment of crisis, like the novel as a whole, concludes with a string of short paragraphs. Ray observes Uno trotting past and "clutching to his chest the consolidated . . . manuscript"; then he meditates for a moment on "Sol Invictus, the Roman name for the sun," and the absence of storks before Uno returns, "trotting again, carrying a blindfold and plastic handcuffs" (431). In this scene, as in many others, Rush uses Ray's fluctuating mental processes, not his abstract grasp of "the geopolitical mind" (429), to convey the terror of the situation. That escalating terror becomes the meaning of this encounter.

In short, *Mortals* certainly is not, as Sheldon Weeks disappointedly re-marked of *Mating*, an informative work of travel writing any more than it is an unprocessed expression of youthful angst.[69] Instead, Rush's is a world in which "alien politics" matter.[70] He plunges his readers into a world where they are always sifting through layers of data. In his fiction, it is the narrator's present in the developing world, not an American past, that has been lost to amnesia. Rush gambles that deep engagement with his expatriates' moral and political calculus will engage his readers' curiosity and carry them along with him on a far-reaching journey toward that forgotten world. In so doing, he creates a new task for the Peace Corps novel—shifting its energy away from tests administered to the self and institutions of American liberalism and toward the emergence of a more worldly and immediate political sensibility.

3   NEOLIBERAL ALLEGORIES

The Space of Home in Contemporary International Fiction

The apartment had been my home for only half a year but now that I was
leaving it came to embody every Berlin home I'd ever had, each its own
repository of reverie and melancholy and downtrodden expectation, a little
cave of solitude.
Chloe Aridjis, *Book of Clouds*

Slums, however deadly and insecure, have a brilliant future.
Mike Davis, *Planet of Slums*

S INCE THE LATE 1980s, the national allegory has been the subject of intense debate. According to Fredric Jameson's canonical essay, "Third-
World Literature in the Era of Multinational Capitalism," two processes define this genre:[1]

1. Psychological conflicts within the individual represent conflicts within
   the nation.
2. Collective (usually national) types multiply and collide within a multinational world system.

Jameson argues that the impact of both phases of allegory is particularly strong
in what he calls "third-world literature." For Jameson, the "third world" is a
geopolitical, not a geographic category; it refers to a representational strategy
that takes uneven economic development seriously and downplays the largely
psychological and libidinal concerns of First World artists.

As Jameson argues in his roughly contemporaneous essay on postmodernism,[2] however, cultural production in the First World also expresses a political
attitude toward late capitalism, albeit unconsciously. So-called Third World
literature is not unique for Jameson in expressing its material circumstances;
it simply has forms for doing so that make this political aspect more directly
apparent than those styles most in vogue at the time in the First World.
Jameson's use of the concept of the national allegory thus aims to awaken
readers enmeshed in a largely internalizing, personal aesthetic matrix to the

continuing vitality of political—especially geopolitical—writing that more directly addresses the circumstances of its own production.

Jameson took as his main examples of national allegory works by the early-twentieth-century Chinese author Lu Hsun and the Senegalese novelist and filmmaker Ousmane Sembène (most active during the 1960s). Few have denied the political aims of authors like these who explore periods of revolutionary upheaval. Controversy has focused instead on the applicability of the concept of the national allegory to contemporary postcolonial culture and domestic realism.

For roughly ten years, the most influential critique of Jameson's argument was Aijaz Ahmad's.[3] Arguing that First and Third World literatures should be situated on a single plane, Ahmad emphasizes an element of self-critique in Third World literature, focusing on South Asia, his own sphere of expertise. He also points out the often public or "national" concerns of some First World literature; he gestures, rather sweepingly, to the entirety of African Americans' and women's writing as examples. Ahmad shares Jameson's desire for a dialectical and materialist criticism of contemporary culture, but his objection to representations of collectivity leads him to conclude that the concept of the national allegory is compromised by its spatial imaginary. In particular, he worries the category of the Third World, on the assumption that it is both spatial and determinant. Deciding that the spatial logic of national allegory is absurdly self-contradictory, Ahmad urges a focus instead on works that escape a division between the First and the Third World and whose stylistic variety recalls the multiplicity of capitalist formations and socialist resistances to them. He proposes, in short, a turn away from any allegorical reading that takes either the nation or the collectivity as the horizon of interpretation and turns toward a one-world model of cosmopolitan hybridity. There can be no geopolitics of the national allegory in Ahmad's analysis, because there is no Third World.

As Ahmad urged, cosmopolitan narratives tracking the fortunes of migrants and mobile subjects received a great deal of attention in and out of the academy during the 1990s. The most celebrated writer of this moment of academic micropolitics[4] was, of course, the pre-fatwa Salman Rushdie; his playful involutions of Indian and Pakistani narratives of the birth of the nation in *Midnight's Children* (1981) and *Shame* (1983), respectively, became touchstones. However, this cosmopolitan turn did not solve the problem of the national allegory so much as displace it. The second, crucial layer of the national allegory—its figuration of a geopolitical scene—remains a live issue for global studies, and national types continue to retain their utility. After all, as we will see, many twenty-first-century novelists continue to invent flat second-ary characters that represent the foreigner—often an American. These minor characters often serve as auditors, and they can have a significant impact on the central narrative, disturbing the maturation process of more rounded in-digenous protagonists, for example. This reversion to the logic of types is one signal of the continued influence of national allegory as a default genre for encoding a particular geopolitical situation in the national novel; it provides an opening for reflecting on American power and ignorance in particular. As a number of critics recognize, no matter its faults or limitations, national allegory as a concept continues to provide certain useful literary tools for a wide range of contemporary authors.[5] Novels from Canada, France, Japan, Kenya, Palestine, Ukraine, and the United States—as well as work in such neighboring genres as the Oriental tale, prison diary, short story, and even urban-planning discourse[6]—arguably make use of elements of the national allegory. Consequently, scholars have revived interest in national allegory as a highly mutable, flexible genre and have explored the resources it offers for investigating emerging ideologies of the global scene.

Approaching national allegory as a problematic rather than a stale set of generic prescriptions allows us to understand this form as an American genre reinvented in the twenty-first century—that is, to see how national allegory has been recast as neoliberal allegory. This thesis builds on the insight of Joseph Slaughter and others who have asserted that national allegory is really always "international allegory."[7] The form ponders the results of a collision between the Western subject's fantasy of nationhood and the raw material of the colonial/postcolonial situation. Works in this vein often reflect on the in-ternational circulation of misinformation and fantasy about foreign locations, offering themselves as remedial geography lessons for audiences that famously know too little about the "rest of the world."[8] From this angle, the national al-legory also reveals something about that readership's collective fantasies about collectivity. Thought of in this sense, the national or international allegory re-veals the "pragmatics" of genre; the use that readers make of the genre circles back to inform the object itself.[9] When new uses arise, Tzvetan Todorov ar-gues, genres can appear to transform retrospectively; they posthumously grow new arms and legs. The pragmatics of a genre influence the sense of its ontol-ogy, much as Slaughter maintains that the nation as a category can be recast as the effect of a discourse that, in fact, assumes it as a cause.

Bearing in mind this sense of a belated or posthumous redefinition, then, this chapter explores the pragmatics of national allegory. Whatever the spatial illogic underlying the concept of Third World literature as national allegory, American readers have (with the avid assistance of the publishing industry and reviewing apparatus) received a large subset of contemporary fiction set outside the United States as contributions to this genre. These readers have contributed to the pragmatic resuscitation of the national allegory in the twenty-first century. For this reason, the genre arguably participates in the institution of U.S. fiction.

The novels examined in this chapter have, after all, been routinely recommended to their potential readers because they add up to "to much more than appears on the surface" and presumably reveal tensions between groups, nations, parties, and periods.[10] Reviewers consistently praise the way these novels, for example, "display a manageable cross-section of contemporary urban Indian life, including class and religious frictions," or offer a "savage yet hilarious anatomy of a society."[11] These writings are thought to reveal how "modern Pakistan's beauty commingles with its brutality," or they illustrate the "wacky hybridity of contemporary Filipino culture, a culture laden with vestiges of Spanish and US colonialism and thus replete with bizarre contradictions."[12] A special vitality is often attributed to this fiction, suggesting that readers would have trouble supplying the living social context surrounding the story. Chimamanda Ngozi Adichie "vividly brings to life the political and cultural crises that beset post-independence Nigeria," one commentator notes, while Ken Kalfus paints "a vivid picture of Russian life."[13] According to innumerable reviewers and book-jacket blurbers, encountering this newly animated foreign world alters American readers in some way, perhaps simply by becoming continuous with their own experience. Authors of national allegories are repeatedly celebrated for digging "deep into the collective history of international conflict and current strife to bring us the harsh reality shown here, engaging us both as readers and as global citizens."[14] A long parade of reviews, blurbs, promotional pieces, and literary samplers, in short, encourages American readers to receive a range of contemporary fiction as politically significant national allegories—that is, as guides to "current strife" and "collective history."

Reviews and marketing materials definitely reproduce this discourse, but they do not generate their categories out of thin air. The novels described as guides to national conditions usually do employ some elements associated with national allegory, such as representative types, the alignment of personal and social crises, or orientation toward an international audience. It can be difficult to decide whether this use of a set of genre conventions finally results from the demands of the marketplace, the citizenship or location of the authors, or a specifically literary desire to test the capacities of a genre. Surely, many factors are in play. What is clear, however, is the active revival of a set of genre norms associated with the national allegory. For better or worse, the national allegory is an operative form in contemporary fiction.

While twentieth-century variants on the national allegory—from Sembène's village novels to Rushdie's magical adaptations—may be understood as testing the limits of nationalism as a specific ideology for envisioning collectivity, many twenty-first-century fictions set the problem in a different matrix. With some significant regional variations, twenty-first-century novels received in the United States as national allegories turn at least some of their attention to the specific insecurities and vertiginous sense of placelessness associated with economic neoliberalism. This partial shift toward economic rather than political ideology introduces a new set of dilemmas for representing collectivity, dilemmas that regularly find spatial figures (especially the multifamily dwelling) more productive than the psychology of a representative and conflicted individual. This spatial rather than psychological figure enables authors exploring the paradox of imagining collectivity in the context of neoliberal assaults on the state to raise new questions: Where is wealth, and how does it circulate? How can and should goods be shared? The neoliberal allegory wants to know where the filters, accelerants, and/or barriers to the global flow of capital are located and how compelling local narratives might be in the face of foreign imperatives. Its most burning question, though, concerns the conditions of our common life—how we live together. These questions bring a new set of central figures to the national allegory, rendering it fresh but still recognizable in the twenty-first century. The mutability of the genre—its availability for a new pragmatics—suggests both its coherence in the geopolitical context and the transformative power exerted by some distinctly contemporary concerns.

NEOLIBERALISM AND AMERICAN FICTION

If economic neoliberalism has swept the globe like a "tidal wave," then this wave has carried in its wake not only a massive reduction of state power in favor of entrepreneurial freedom but also a consolidation of the class power of domestic elites and a reconfiguration of the global imperial order.[15] Worldwide, under the slogan of a new liberalization or freedom from state regulation, private businesses have seized control of resources formerly held in common, launching the so-called second enclosure movement. In response, usually at the urging of major lenders, states have imposed austerity measures that reduce spending on health, education, and social welfare while leaving military budgets and corporate subsidies largely intact. This dismantling of state programs has left a vacuum that consumerist ideals and institutions have often rushed to fill.[16] Some associate the resulting turn toward consumer society with a rise in egalitarian ideals and urban liberties; however, in developed and developing economies alike, it is also linked to the growth of inequality and the increasing concentration of elite ownership of wealth, combined with the erosion of middle-class purchasing power. In this contradictory situation, currencies fluctuate wildly, many regions experience food insecurity, and new patterns of global migration and citizenship emerge.[17] Neoliberal anti-statism clearly has several faces and presents a complex challenge for narration.

Perhaps for this reason, the cultural expression of these multifaceted structural changes tends to be oblique. Situations of rapid social transformation, the anthropologists Jean and John Comaroff argue, tend to convert "once legible processes" into "opaque, even spectral" forms for their participants; as a result, popular expressive culture will rarely dive right into the heart of the new phenomena. Instead, it looks for ways to connect older, better known narratives to the uncertainties of a rapidly changing present.[18] In their analysis of post-revolutionary and postcolonial cultures, the Comaroffs describe a wide range of cultural practices—sometimes occult in character—as the indirect expressions of anxieties about neoliberalism.[19] Following the shock of their sudden entry into a volatile and unevenly developed neoliberal economy, they suggest, global subjects seize hold of narratives of modernization and redirect them toward other ends—usually by fusing them with more resolutely local, antimodern form and content.

In twenty-first-century fiction, the same basic processes occur. Well-known but dated genres such as the national allegory combine with local forms and content.[20] The resulting generic hybrids track the downward spiral of national ambitions against the strange possibilities offered by replacement narratives. These emerging neoliberal allegories rarely provide direct descriptions of the relocation of sites of production, the mechanics of a newly mobile labor market, or the volatility of the exchange relation. In their widespread efforts to update the national allegory, however, they indirectly express these conditions.

The neoliberal allegory takes different forms in different locations, despite its engagement with homogenizing tendencies in American publishing and reviewing institutions. For example, this genre began to appear in the United

States much later than in Latin America. That belatedness may be partially explained by the fact that the Washington Consensus (a multinational initiative that sponsors aggressive neoliberal reform) made the implementation of its policies a condition for lending in Latin America at least twenty years before essentially the same policies went into effect in the American manufacturing sector. However, the different time lines for public discussion of neoliberalism also reflect the uneven development of political opposition to it. In many nations with recent experience of colonialism and/or revolutionary upheaval, neoliberal imperatives sponsored by the International Monetary Fund faced active local movements that relied on well-established political and cultural narratives to interpret this intervention. In some cases, such movements authorized popular and literary experiments with "magical" alternatives to the supposed inevitabilities of the neoliberal assault.[21] This cycle of economic, political, and aesthetic reorganization arguably played itself out well before the cultural effects of neoliberalism began to be widely discussed in the United States.

In the absence of a widespread popular resistance to neoliberalism in the United States, until recently fewer American authors experimented with the neoliberal allegory, despite experiencing many of the same initiatives aimed at shrinking the state and redistributing property and income upward and despite the ready availability of literary models from Latin America and elsewhere. American Rust Belt narratives, for example, often mournfully document the demise of small-town integrity and chronicle the effects of outsourcing on dominant conceptions of masculinity, drawing quite directly on the melancholia of the western and the closing of the frontier. There is outstanding writing in this vein, ranging from the well-known "dirty realism" of the 1980s and early 1990s to the more experimental writings of George Saunders and Ben Marcus.[22] Tellingly, though, a great deal of this writing is almost obsessively local and domestic. Its working-class characters are predominantly white and rural and tend to experience movement toward the closest metropolis as violently traumatic; the possibility of international migration rarely figures at all—even as a Beat-inspired dream of escaping into mythic Mexico. The figure of the financier (discussed a little more in chapter 5) offers another opportunity for American narratives of neoliberalism, but even superlative work in this vein, such as Adam Haslett's *Union Atlantic* (2009), projects a workplace culture largely contained by the nation. A similar localism can be observed in U.S. fiction devoted to middle managers (for example, workplace satires such as Joshua Ferris's *Then We Came to the End* [2007], a novel that is geographically much more static than Hari Kunzru's multinational triangulations in *Transmission* [2005]). In all these works, international locations register mainly as playing fields for American interests. Without this exterior scene, economic novels have a problem with motivation. When no collision of national types is allowed and class antagonisms remain inexpressible, the panoramic social novel of the 1930s and 1960s shrinks down to the size of the village, and effects without causes are all that can be documented. The horizon of the global economy as well as any figures enforcing its new rules become nearly invisible in this kind of American writing, even when it is manifestly concerned with exploring neoliberal economic transformation.

International fiction, by contrast, finds numerous figures for neoliberal processes. Some of these are familiar (for example, a revival of certain formulas of the family romance or domestic realism), while others are florid and attention grabbing (for instance, satiric depictions of obesity and overconsumption). The most fundamental operation of the neoliberal allegory, though, is the relocation of the figure of the national "home" from the telos of the narrative to the ground. In other words, if the national allegory makes the establishment of a national home the final resolution of domestic conflicts, the neoliberal allegory begins inside the conflicted home and routinely compromises the borders of any visionary dwelling held in the offing. For related reasons, it also prefers paired or multiple heroes to singletons. In the neoliberal allegory, conflict is experienced externally between versions of the hero. A splitting function bisects and trisects any potentially representative type almost immediately, and as a consequence spatial figures replace psychological processes as signs of the collectivity. The neoliberal allegory tends to be organized as an exploratory, episodic narrative—not entirely picaresque in its open-endedness, but not so heavily ordered by forward-driving movement as is the bildungsroman. In this wandering plot, crisis is triggered by collective vertigo rather than a one-on-one confrontation between self and other. If the national allegory in its pure form heads toward a denouement when the protagonist alters his stance toward the collectivity (for example, by conversion to nationalist ideology), the neoliberal allegory transitions into its later phases by means of catastrophic events originating outside the immediate frame of reference. These events (invasion, mass uprisings, world war) change the landscape for all, allow no immediately perceptible villain, and require a reconsideration of local ritual and convention in light of the increased exposure to an exterior world. The neoliberal allegory, in short, retains the figures of the hero-nation and multinational system, which are

The National Versus the Neoliberal Allegory

	NATIONAL ALLEGORY	NEOLIBERAL ALLEGORY
SCENE	Groups in conflict	Divided home is damaged but not destroyed
HERO	Representative individual	Collection of types
ORGANIZING ACTION	Travel, education, political commitment	Mapping, contrasting scenes, multiple episodic threads
CRISIS	Individual maturation, birth of nation	External, collective events destabilize range of characters
RESOLUTION	Individual develops new perception of social whole; wedding or birth promises new future and new national home	Brief recovery from aftershock, nonreproductive reunions

so vital to the national allegory, but on the whole its politics express a deep anxiety about individual and collective positions in a world system more often than they trigger a utopian vision organized around a coherent national project, as shown in the table.

These recurring generic modifications occur in many different moods and tones: lyrical, grim, apocalyptic, archly postmodern, scandalized, nostalgic, chick-littish, and so on. Fully cognizant of the limitations of one-size-fits-all nationalisms, authors of the twenty-first-century neoliberal allegory routinely think through local variations and needs at the same time that they pragmatically keep an eye on their international readership. The resulting regional variations keep the emerging form of the neoliberal allegory fresh and pliable without sacrificing the vital questions that bind readers, writers, and their subjects to one another. Precisely because of its many "local" qualities, the neoliberal allegory demonstrates its suitability to the project of asking how global subjects can and do live together.

THE ROMANCE OF CONTEMPORARY SOUTH ASIA

Perhaps the best place to begin a consideration of the twenty-first-century national allegory is contemporary English-language fiction about South Asia. Since the 1980s, Indian fiction in English, in particular, has attracted a major international readership, especially in the United States—where a number of prominent Indian-born authors live, work, and publish.[23] This cluster of reading and writing practices is accompanied by a lively critical discourse that often challenges norms taken for granted in the American publishing industry.

In critical discussions of the English-language Indian fiction read in the United States, the reputation of the national allegory has been largely negative. Many commentators regard the national allegory as an outmoded form that should be replaced by writing in a more cosmopolitan vein. Arguing that "Indian writers whose faces are so resolutely turned toward the West" almost inevitably produce "bad books" when they attempt to educate their Western audiences, reviewers have documented the clichés that they find in the national allegory.[24] The literary historian Menakshi Mukherjee, for example, contends that an overweening concern with an international readership, together with the practice of writing in English rather than in one of the many South Asian languages with a much longer literary history on the subcontinent, leads too many authors toward a necessarily banal treatment of "pan-Indian" concerns, such as the situation of women or conflicts between faith and reason, tradition and modernity, or postcolonial solidarity and national difference.[25] Writing focused on national themes and operating on an allegorical register, Mukherjee and others assert, necessarily sacrifices personal expression and formal experimentation to the empty abstractions of social commitment.

This aesthetic critique of the national novel is compatible with at least two political attitudes. Some consider the social concerns associated with national allegory as inherently illiberal, opposed to the prioritization of personal freedom so vital to liberal democratic political theory, while others argue that the genteel clichés of national fiction produced for an uninformed Western audience are cloying precisely because they reject a newer leftist literary practice that directly engages community organizing.[26] In this context, smoking out traces of the national allegory or even nostalgia for the form in works by authors reputed to have more cosmopolitan sensibilities becomes a vital critical task. These revisionist readings do not always rebuke the national sensibility entirely; moments of formal experimentation and fertile political imagination are on occasion attributed to sub-rosa appearances of the national allegory.[27] However, critical accounts of Indian fiction in English mainly treat a preoccupation with the nation as an American imperative best subverted by South Asian readers and writers in favor of more varied, multilingual, authentic, and/or contemporary approaches. While agreeing with Dirk Wiemann that "national allegories abound in the cultural production of postcolonial India" and noting their enormous international appeal,[28] many literary critics decry that situation and agitate for its transformation.

Writers have apparently been listening. In the subset of Indian fiction written in English and widely read in the United States in the twenty-first century, the genre of the national allegory has moved in the direction of the neoliberal allegory. Reviews in American publications such as *People* and *Booklist* may still read the work as illustrative of the condition of India as a whole, and this fiction may still spend more time explaining the social context and non-English vocabulary than fiction intended primarily for a regional audience might find necessary.[29] Yet, even while continuing to fulfill the pedagogical function that the American publishing industry so often demands of "foreign" authors, this new fiction also challenges other expectations of the national allegory.

In particular, it is not uncommon to find contemporary fiction on South Asian themes employing lightly fantastic and romantic elements that appeal to readers with a taste for late-model Orientalism—a taste well documented among American readers.[30] According to Srinivas Aravamudan, purportedly exotic genres such as the "Oriental tale" can serve the aims of the national allegory even better than more conventional forms of domestic realism.[31] Perhaps for this reason as well as audience concerns, a number of contemporary authors have mixed national allegory with features drawn from literary traditions of the subcontinent as well as English Romanticism to modulate the national allegory.[32]

Recent novels by Amitav Ghosh and Pankaj Mishra illustrate this tendency most directly. Although different in scope and tone, both Ghosh's *Glass Palace* (2000) and Mishra's *Romantics* (2000) take as their protagonists a detached, free-floating hero who values feeling above reason and order.[33] Ghosh's wide-ranging historical novel begins in Burma on the eve of the British invasion in 1885; it then follows the Burmese royal family into exile in India and swings out to Malaysian rubber plantations for several crucial transitions, before finally establishing its home base in an apartment house in Calcutta. This triangulated geography is crisscrossed by several parallel plotlines, but the life cycle of an initially penniless Indian boy, Rajkumar, frames and punctuates the narrative. Serving as a de facto hero-observer, Rajkumar takes readers deep into the Burmese forest to witness the wonders of the teak trade; his arrival at the exiled royal family's compound in Ratnigari triggers a sudden change in the household's composition; and the revelation of his enduring relationship, late in life, with his hostess in Calcutta brings the novel to closure on a sweet note. As a hero, Rajkumar does not instigate all the action or anchor global processes in local events. Instead, the distinguishing feature of this energetic entrepreneur is his lack of national feeling, his essential placelessness: "He was, in a way, a feral creature, unaware that in certain places there exist invisible bonds linking people to one another through personifications of their commonality. . . . Rajkumar recognized no loyalties no obligations and no limits on the compass of his right to provide for himself. . . . [T]hat there should exist a universe of loyalties that was unrelated to himself and his own immediate needs—this was very nearly incomprehensible" (47). Cast in this early passage as a proto-neoliberal who is subject only to exigent needs, Ghosh's Rajkumar remains mobile and romantically detached from his surroundings throughout the novel.

Rajkumar's anti-culturalism contrasts with the security initially experienced by Arjun, an Indian officer in the British Army during World War II. Required to serve in the segregated forces on behalf of an empire that recognizes neither his full citizenship nor India's desire for independence, Arjun suddenly finds his loyalties "unmoored." "How would one begin the work of re-creating the tissues that bound people to each other?" he asks himself; this "was a labour that would last not one year, not ten, not fifty—it was the work of centuries" (439–440). Arjun experiences the loss of culture as an exhausting defeat, while Rajkumar's framing perspective is more ecstatic. Many other characters in the novel are similarly dislocated (Burmese in India, Indians in New York, Americans in Malaysia, Malaysians heading to Singapore, Chinese in Burma, and so on) and reflect on their condition in terms that fall somewhere between these two extremes. Regardless of tone, though, a sense of rootlessness recurs throughout the novel, triggering dilemmas of the self for all the major characters. Ghosh's protagonists drift and wander, "lonely as a cloud" (to recall Wordsworth's famous phrase),[34] back and forth across the Bay of Bengal.

As Mishra's title indicates, his novel also examines romantic detachment, although for a smaller group of characters and a narrower time frame. Set in the late 1980s and early 1990s, *The Romantics* begins with the arrival of its hero, the bookish Samar, at a student hostels in Benares. Samar makes two groups of friends: one cluster of European and American "seekers" infatuated with Indian religion and music, and the other a political crowd of Brahmin students circulating around an older peer. Samar travels with a member of each group, and the erotic and social revelations he has on these journeys so unsettle him that he finally leaves Benares. He is drawn first to Pondicherry, where his father has retired to the Aurobindo ashram, and then finally to a remote Tibetan village in the Himalayas, where he lives quietly as an English teacher. Throughout his travels, Samar is haunted by figures from his reading of Flaubert, Chekhov, and Edmund Wilson. Samar's situation is directly compared several times with that of the provincials in Flaubert's *Sentimental Education* (1869), but even this literary anchor fails to tether our narrator. His displays of learnedness in European literature do not displace his Western friends' clichéd perception of India as "an exotic hotbed of illiteracy, poverty, and religion" (87), and he finally concludes that he was as naïve about the thuggish behavior of the politically active students as he was idealistic about his emotional attachment to a young French woman. The same process occurs at the figurative level where Samar's initial responses to nature—those "tingly mornings, tenderly azure skies, soft sun-caressed afternoons, and long, indigo twilights" (150)—ultimately give way to a disenchanted focus on the modern, commercial aspects of his environment (signage, traffic, prostitution, corrupt officials, and hotel lobbies).[35] Mishra's novel, in short, suggests that it is not only Western seekers who generate overly romantic and uninformed narratives about India, but also perhaps young domestic intellectuals ensnared by their own provincialism.

Although *The Romantics* tracks a single hero's path from elation to deflation, while *The Glass Palace* disperses those sensibilities among many characters, both novels take up the essential romantic task of charting their heroes' oscillating moods.[36] Moments of exhilarating sensory perceptions are routinely disrupted by aesthetically discordant elements in both works. Their heroes are usually, by definition, too narrowly focused on their inner lives to spot these disruptive alien forces on the horizon. Rajkumar's dreams of gathering enormous wealth derived from war profits are suddenly shattered when his eldest and favorite son is killed by elephants, and Samar is shocked to his core when the French woman with whom he is enamored severs ties with him in a curt note. Their stories progress through the accumulation of sensation and shifts in tone rather than through deliberate movement toward a goal; the narration emphasizes the fact that the heroes learn little, although they are able on occasion, perhaps utterly by chance, to feel something new.

This accumulative pattern also organizes two related novels: Manil Suri's *Death of Vishnu* (2001) and Romesh Gunesekera's *Heaven's Edge* (2002). The former's title announces the expiration of Suri's hero, the self-appointed guardian of a Bombay staircase, so its end is known. This frees the novel to explore Vishnu's flickering consciousness as he hovers on the edge of death and perhaps achieves reincarnation. These passages of sense memory are off-set by the more absurd impressions and situations of the inhabitants of the apartments connected by the staircase where Vishnu lies dying. "Even yesterday, he had barely stirred when she had filled his plastic cup," a rather self-important neighbor reflects, "and she had felt a flutter of resentment at not having received her usual salaam in return" (14). Steam from this cup of tea triggers sense memories for the immobile Vishnu: "his mother discarding all her used leaves . . . Padmini pressing her lips against the metal rim . . . Kavita trying to keep her dupatta from falling off as she bends down" (15). These variations on a theme interest Suri's novel more than any specific action that Vishnu or others can take to prevent his death.

Similarly, in Gunesekera's post-apocalyptic fantasy,[37] set on a strife-ridden island resembling the author's birthplace (Sri Lanka), the visiting tourist-hero seems to be headed inexorably toward the ground-zero location where some sort of nuclear device had exploded long before his arrival.[38] His progress toward that presumed goal diminishes in significance, however, as he moves through a string of small communities where he experiences periods of idyllic serenity punctuated by severe terror. Coordinated group action inevitably fails in Gunesekera's devastated landscape. The universe of *Heaven's Edge* is populated mainly by inarticulate sex slaves and dysfunctional machinery produced for another era and worldview. Like Ghosh's vast historical canvas, Mishra's interior monologue, and Suri's mosaic, Gunesekera's story is episodic—with scenes of vivid description joined together by slenderer threads of temporal or spatial transition.

Within individual scenes in these peripatetic works, visual elements become crucial figures for the social situation experienced by the drifting romantic hero.[39] The titular glass palace in Ghosh's novel, for example, refers initially to the largely unseen treasures of the Burmese monarchy, but is finally reclaimed as the name of a photography shop where aesthetically minded citizens protesting the subsequent dictatorship assemble. For Mishra's hero, too, photographs provide necessary clues to the past and a tool for interpreting social changes, because the unaided memories of both individuals and collectives are suspect. Set into motion as film, photography also reinforces a powerful drive toward romantic fantasy. Suri's novel introduces a film-obsessed young woman on the verge of eloping, while Vikram Chandra's masterful novel of suspense, *Sacred Games* (2006), develops a major subplot concerning a young Muslim woman's liaison with a gangster who finances the plastic surgery that allows her to emerge in full physical splendor as a ready-made

Bollywood icon. A similarly two-pronged investigation of the dirty realities that underlie lush film spectacles appears in Jessica Hagedorn's *Dream Jungle* (2003), a novel in which prostitution and neocolonial spoilage undercut the filmic illusion of a primitive Philippines. A flickering television screen creates much the same effect in the final tale in Daniyal Mueenuddin's brilliant collection of linked stories, *In Other Rooms, Other Wonders* (2009). Signaling an old man's financial success and triggering a major loss (his somewhat dim-witted young wife runs away, frightened by television images), the electrified image compresses into a single scene the deflationary trajectory experienced repeatedly by the volatile heroes of these fictions.

Other types of framed vision can also provide turning points in these impressionistic works. An important signal that a transition is coming in the life of the hero of Samrat Upadhyay's *Guru of Love* (2003), set in Nepal during the Maoist uprising of the 1980s, occurs when he looks down through his apartment window to the courtyard of his building and witnesses his neighbor molesting a girl. Similarly, the climax of Gunesekera's *Heaven's Edge* occurs when the idealized heroine clears away some undergrowth to reveal below it the aged pump mechanism that will irrigate the gardens of her final idyllic retreat. The window of the clerk's office to which Siddhartha Deb's hero—an aged father and former civil servant—must repeatedly return to plead for his pension in *The Point of Return* (2004) becomes yet another framed vantage point that functions as a site of shifting perceptions. As the reverse chronology of Deb's novel moves farther back in time with each succeeding chapter, the narrator's initially frustrated response to his pedantic father is reframed and deepened, until the narrator himself finally departs, accompanied by the closing credits of a film: "the last long walk, the music fading, dying out against the frame of the town dissolving slowly, the trees and house blurring into an outline, merging into the horizon running its cracked line against the smooth sky" (300). Rather than adopting the clerk's view of the father, the narrator has learned to reverse his gaze and peer into the heart of bureaucratic entanglements from the perspective of the brave young man he can now imagine his father to have been. This newfound empathy, here as so often, takes a cinematic form.

These visual frames signal the interest that many of these novels have in a technologically mediated version of the Romantic aesthetic of the picturesque.[40] Carefully composed scenes that refer to their own perimeters, often reinforcing framing devices, communicate a social tension that lies beyond the comprehension of the hero. These intensely visual passages usually occur at moments of narrative crisis. While a sentimental aesthetic might decode the allegorical significance of these turning points for the reader, romantic ambiguity is more characteristic of these twenty-first-century South Asian fictions written in English. Arguably correcting for the didacticism of the most conventional national allegories, these works take a more lyrical approach.

They still remain allegorical, however. Although representative heroes are rarely observed in these novels, and although domestic conflicts are rarely resolved by the marriage of warring ethnic types to each other in the final pages,[41] they continue to rely on other key elements of the national allegory. In particular, the representative status of the foreign traveler remains in place in these works. Nearly all Ghosh's characters are aliens in some sense; Mishra's seekers, Gunesekera's returned migrant, Hagedorn's filmmakers, Mueenuddin's trailing spouse, Upadhyay's dreamers of emigration to America, and many other similar characters underscore the genre's need for the figure of the incorporated other. These works read as "national" to the reviewers and publicists cited at the outset of this chapter because these aliens authorize an essentially touristic voyeurism. Pointedly marked as an outsider rather than a so-called native informant, the foreigner allows explanatory narratorial digressions on such topics as the organization of the teak trade (Ghosh), the timing of civil service exams (Mishra), the preferred tactics for military surveillance (Gunesekera), the financing of home ownership in Bombay slums (Chandra), and the division of domestic labor in an upper-class Filipino household (Hagedorn). These discourses may be informative or redundant for the reader, but either way their status confirms the allegorical work of the narrative. The foreign witness (or detective in Chandra's novel) translates the local scene for a readership abroad; the transparency and self-sufficiency of the South Asian setting are not taken for granted. These novels rely instead on instructive figures with international and allegorical significance.

They also make use of allegory at the level of plot, establishing parallel transitions and intertwined crises for the protagonist and the nation.[42] The heroes' lives are routinely entangled with public events and reflect on their relationships to the collectivity. The clearest example of this conflation appears in *The Guru of Love*; Upadhyay arranges for his hero, Ramchandra, to catch his penultimate glimpse of his lover in the middle of the turbulent public events that toppled Panchayat rule in Nepal. Across streets filled with militant protestors, Ramchandra watches his beloved lose her grip on her baby and "experienced a twisted knot of panic; he was only dimly aware that the government procession near him had broken into chaos. The prime minister and the other ministers were running back toward the New Road Gate. Someone shouted, 'They have their tails between their legs,' and people laughed" (238). The hero's helpless shame fades into the public scene, even as, through an odd reversal, the ministers' abrupt departure becomes a kind of figure for the left-leaning Ramchandra's personal defeat.

Although sometimes less obviously, a similar drive to align public and private crises appears in many of the other South Asian examples of the national allegory. In Ghosh's novel, the flight of refugees intersects with family narratives several times, and the drama of Partition, as well as the turmoil surrounding the emergence of Bangladesh from East Pakistan and the civil war in Sri Lanka, provide crucial turning points of a similar nature in Chandra's, Deb's, and Gunesekera's works, respectively. *The Romantics* more subtly sets the maturation of Mishra's hero against the backdrop of political events beginning in 1989 (especially the rise of Hindu fundamentalism), mainly in the subplots concerning student rioters. But it is perhaps Mueenuddin's novel that provides the most innovative treatment of this feature of the national allegory.

Mueenuddin links his artful tales of rural and urban Pakistan by means of a network of recurring characters, locales, and situations, such as the relationship between an older man and a much younger concubine or second wife. He also tells a larger, longer public story of the waning power of an old feudal class in the face of new industrial wealth.[43] Accordingly, *In Other Rooms* presents several characters who are representative of the feudal aristocracy—most notably, the elderly landowner K. K. Harouni—as well as several members of the nouveaux riches. We are offered only occasional glimpses of these types, however, and it is ultimately not their isolated narratives that reveal the big picture so much as the accumulated impressions of a slow, multi-stage transition evoked by the group of stories as a whole. Each individual story provides a point of access into a larger process that is visible only cumulatively. The dissolution of the landed gentry to which Harouni belongs and the shift of power to industrial farming must be inferred from the background of the interlinked stories; it is never an open subject of discussion or description.

Whether synecdochic, allusive, or fractal in their relation, however, individual and collective crises remain interdependent in these works, and this bimodal structure drives them toward reunion as a figure of closure. Although certainly also appropriate to the romantic formula, reunion advances the aims of national allegory.[44] The deferred meeting of couples or relatives separated by public events holds out the promise of a reformed collectivity at the close of the story—rather than, say, bringing the romantic hero's crisis of self-definition to a new level through his discovery of a vocation or initiation of a new voyage. If these reunions were marriages, as in earlier versions of the genre, we might, following Northrop Frye, consider them to be comic motifs and suspect that they ultimately endorse the status quo by resolving tension through the presumed birth of a new generation that will face much the same problems.[45] However, it is interesting to note that not a single work in this diverse set of South Asian novels concludes with a heterosexual marriage that promises reproduction. Ghosh closes *The Glass Palace* with a niece meeting her long-lost uncle and two elderly lovers; Mishra allows his hero only a brief reunion with his Western mentor before she departs for England. Suri returns the prodigal daughter to her parents after a failed elopement, much as Upadhyay returns the wandering husband to an aging wife turned seamstress, and Gunesekera reunites his hero and heroine, only to reveal that she has been rendered sterile. The inexorable pull of the father–son reunion in Deb's *Point of Return* finally releases its narrator into public life again. Finally, in what is perhaps the darkest reunion in this group, Chandra's detective finds himself once again at the door behind which his friend and prey, the gangster Ganesh, is dwelling, only to have the whole framework explode in a blaze of apocalyptic glory. In the neoliberal allegory, then, the reunion motif carries with it the weight of public events and a tangled history that must be confronted rather than comically dissolved. It returns protagonists to their collective past in order to launch them into a future they have yet to create.

The shape of that future is suggested by the final, massively overdetermined figure of the national allegory: the home. In the prototype of the national allegory, the figure of the home commonly operates as a powerful—even magical—force for closure by anchoring central characters to a private world that compensates for public upheaval and hypothetically resolves any internal conflict through reproductive futurity (a new family in a new space).[46] These functions are shared by American suburban realism and narratives of exile; from Thomas Wolfe's *You Can't Go Home Again* (1940) to Jonathan Franzen's *Corrections* (2001), innumerable American narratives imagine the home as a site of reconciliation. In the neoliberal allegory, however, the home is in jeopardy at the outset, and its security is rarely fully reestablished in the closing passages. Ramchandra's building of a two-room house in a middle-class neighborhood of Kathmandu in the final chapter of *The Guru of Love* is the exception rather than the rule. Far more typical are Upadhyay's preceding scenes of many families living together in compound housing that creates a high level of intimacy, surveillance, and commercial exchange. Something like the nineteenth-century European apartment house (rather than the American-style single-family dwelling) seems to be the default dwelling in these novels. If the apartment building created a sensation of unease as well as newly utopian forms of social engagement in London and Paris when it was a relative novelty in the late nineteenth century,[47] both of these effects have given way to a more realist sensibility in the twenty-first century. In contemporary South Asian fiction written in English (and well beyond, as we shall see), multifamily housing routinely serves as a microcosmic figure for a fractured but workable social collective. It is sometimes paired with a quest for bourgeois privacy, but far more often privacy itself as an ideal appears deeply compromised in the context of an unstable public life.[48] The neoliberal allegory explores a landscape in which home is already a social and collective space penetrated by capital and entangled with a low-functioning state.

Sometimes the compound housing is literally an apartment building, as in Upadhyay's *Guru of Love* and Suri's *Death of Vishnu*, a novel that moves from the ground floor to the roof. In *The Romantics*, Mishra treats the student hostel less comprehensively; readers visit only a few rooms in the busy dwelling. But it also appears in a more heavily built-up terrain; Mishra sets the hostel in relation to the intentionally collective space of the ashram and the isolated idyll of Samar's spartan house in the Himalayas. On Mishra's spectrum of architectural options, the hostel clearly serves a mediating function, planting it in the "real" world to which the romantically inclined narrator eventually awakes.

In many other neoliberal allegories, the modernist convention of rereading Victorian domestic space through an upstairs–downstairs narrative is observed. In *The Glass Palace*, Ghosh clearly invokes this tradition in his street-level account of the Burmese monarchy melting into the Indian upper classes, as does Hagedorn in the portions of *Dream Jungle* narrated from the point of view of a household maid and Gunesekera in the post-apocalyptic country-house scenes in *Heaven's Edge*. However, it is again Mueenuddin's stories that most dramatically blur the lines that separate servants and their employers. Not only do similar desires arise in characters in different sectors of the household (such as old men renewing their youth with younger wives and lovers), but relatives become servants, servants become mistresses, favorite sons become employees, and so on. Social roles shift with location in Harouni's widespread feudal household. The mutability and interdependence of the roles in the household are its virtues, and Mueenuddin's volume closes not with the crumbling of a large manor house (a move that might recall English sorrows over castles converted into tourist destinations), but with the museumification of a solitary dwelling. In "A Spoiled Man," the odd little mobile home fashioned by a mountain man separated from his family of origin survives him; it is an uncanny relic: "vividly alive, a motionless hirsute presence, the antenna, the flowers, the four massive legs, the pipe that drained the inside spittoon trailing into the grass as if drawing nourishment" (247). The magical power of this memorial quickly fades, however, as it—not the neighboring manor—crumbles into disrepair, its attributes being redistributed among the larger household's members until, finally, "the door of the little cabin hung open, the wind and blown rain scour it clean" (247). With these final words, we see Mueenuddin situating private-sphere domesticity within a longer, broader, busier narrative of collective dwelling.

Finally, Chandra's sprawling Bombay presents a city-wide image of compound housing in his vivid depiction of the slums inhabited by Bangladeshi migrants. In detailed opening scenes describing the domestic routines of small spaces, Chandra conveys the close entanglement of street and kitchen. In the world of one- and two-room *kholis* in the district of Navnagar, as Chandra describes it, home extends into the street and the shared aural space of the neighborhood, while the interiors are largely organized by the commercial activities of the residents. A police investigation in Navnagar quickly yields results, because the neighbors know one another's business and respond to threats of police power. This is a city where "the rich had some room, and the middle class had less, and the poor had none," Chandra's investigator reflects, and upward mobility and the luxury of more private space trigger nostalgia for "these tunnel-like streets . . . , these shakes that crept forward every year, each added-on room seizing ground and holding on" (75). These street–home hybrids are the living heart of Chandra's Bombay, while isolated homesteads such as the booby-trapped safe house where Ganesh, the gangster protagonist, finally discovers his beloved guru's secret and the even starker bomb shelter to which he ultimately retreats become figures of extreme terror. The crowded slums—no matter how smelly, trash strewn, or overwritten with commercial images they may be—represent prospects for common life in Chandra's novel, while the sterile white boxes of modernism, wealth, and spectatorial relations to the broader society in the end promise only earth-shattering explosions and fundamentalist violence. To live alone or solely with one's immediate family is, in *Sacred Games*, to align oneself spatially with xenophobic nationalism. Chandra's romantic populism celebrates instead the densely populated, intensely social, intergroup world of multifamily dwellings spread out laterally.

In these nine twenty-first-century South Asian novels written in English, in short, the ghostly occult space is most commonly the single-family dwelling. The family drama does not resolve in the establishment of a new private homestead, as in the national allegory; it is instead in the collective, commercial, vibrant spaces of compound dwellings that we find the flag of contemporary social life planted. Privatization as an economic and social logic associated with neoliberalism converts the "private" spaces of single-family dwellings into figures of uncanny or terrifying alterity, while the populous multitude is more commonly depicted as inhabiting sometimes sordid, sometimes comic compound arrangements. The details of commercial and erotic exchanges that link the many nodes of this multifamily housing generate many of the comic and ironic subplots in these works, but no matter what their tone, in the romantically inflected version of the neoliberal allegory common in South Asian Anglophone fiction, the centrality of the figure of collective housing is firmly established.

THE REALIST IMPULSE IN CONTEMPORARY NIGERIAN FICTION

If South Asian literature written in English has been dominated by India, the same might be said of Nigeria in relation to contemporary African fiction written in English. Even if we remove from the picture Chinua Achebe's *Things Fall Apart* (1958), easily the best-selling African novel of all time, Nigerian writers still have an outsize presence in the American literary marketplace. Only South Africa and Kenya come close in terms of the number of authors with a readership in the United States, and if we restrict ourselves to up-and-coming writers rather than the Nobel laureates of the previous generation (J. M. Coetzee, Doris Lessing, Nadine Gordimer, and Wole Soyinka), the impact of Nigerians on the American literary scene becomes even more evident. Writing from the perspective of engaged expatriates, Nigerian-born authors who live and/or publish in the United States include Helon Habila, Chimamanda Adichie, Uzodinma Iweala, Chris Abani, Adaobi Tricia Nwaubani, and Sefi Atta—all of whom have made important modifications to the national allegory in particular. Their work somewhat resembles that of Nigerians expatriated in Great Britain (Helen Oyeyemi and Segun Afolabi come to mind), but it also illuminates some aspects of the American reception of recent Anglophone writing from other parts of Africa—including that by Hisham Matar (Libya), Nuruddin Farah (Somalia), Moses Isegawa (Uganda), Zakes Mda (South Africa), and Zoë Wicomb (South Africa). The works of these writers share some techniques and suggest that a few commonalities can be observed across a multinational African literary field, even though the writers certainly also work in importantly distinct locations and literary traditions.

Critics of the contemporary African novel written in English agree that political fiction oriented toward the problem of the nation dominated the literary scene from the late 1950s through the early 1980s. "It is a truism that the modern African novel comes into its own with nationalism," Catherine Kroll asserts.[49] Whether they break down the national novel into subgenres (like Simon Gikandi), trace its emergence and sources (like Ernest Emenyonu), or periodize the postindependence period by decade (like Derek Wright), major Africanists agree that the writings of Achebe, Ousmane Sembène, and Ngugi wa Thiong'o established an inescapable precedent by placing the problems of neocolonialism and nation formation at the heart of their fiction.[50] The realist style and narratives of political struggle adopted by these writers of the 1960s/1970s generation were crucial to their confrontation with European literature on Africa, especially the Conradian strain focused on exploration and the supposed primitiveness of colonial subjects. By the late 1980s and the 1990s, however, a climate of disillusionment with the postindependence state had developed in many locations, and some writers began to test the power of fabulation—exploring the magical, mythic, and fantastic as resources for African fiction. This international and interlinguistic trend[51] helped authors such as Ben Okri, Kojo Laing, Syl Cheney-Coker, and T. Obinkaram Echewa find an international audience. Their experiments with orature, polyphonic narration, and postmodern reflexivity have, however, since become the target of a new wave of critique launched by the intellectuals of the so-called third generation. Arguing, for example, that "orature, which is only a part of the totality of precolonial African culture, has replaced the whole," Wole Ogundele has made a case for a less mythic and more actively historical form of the novel.[52] Invoking the precedents of Wole Soyinka and Dennis Brutus, Ogundele calls for a critical realist literature that utilizes the creative power of myth while recognizing the human capacity to act on the long history of Africa before, during, and after colonization. Some find evidence that this new approach to the problem of the nation-state appears in twenty-first-century Nigerian fiction. In Adélékè Adéèkó's assessment, third-generation writing on the "nation state has no charming myths, no great heroes, no legendary saviors";[53] it explores instead the overlap between banality and cruelty, rejecting both patriotic self-sacrifice and romantic nostalgia for the pacific village in favor of multinational, often urban scenes.

A number of African Anglophone authors have joined these critics in expressing their concern about magical realism; they argue that this style can reinforce an international readership's presumed tendency toward ethnographic fantasy. The Kenyan author Binyavanga Wainaina articulates this position most forcefully in his satirical list of pointers "How to Write About Africa." "Never have a picture of a well-adjusted African on the cover of your book, or in it, unless that African has won the Nobel Prize," Wainaina drily recommends. "An AK-47, prominent ribs, naked breasts: use these."[54] On his list of the most "taboo subjects" for stereotypical writing on Africa, Wainaina places "ordinary domestic scenes, love between Africans (unless a death is involved), references to African writers or intellectuals, mention of school-going children who are not suffering from yaws or Ebola fever or female genital mutilation." Exhausted by apparent do-gooders' continual rhetoric of crisis and that stance's twin, a persistently romanticized vision of a supposed African primitivism, in this widely read piece,[55] Wainaina expresses an interest in the "ordinary domestic scenes" of realism. One-size-fits-all magical realism has become, for Wainaina, as constraining as the national allegory that it replaced. Like other third-generation Anglophone African writers, he is interested in working in a full complement of genres. Wainaina's position affirms that African authors should not be confined to any single genre or style, since they have a long history of writing in many forms—from village novels, science fiction, satire, civil war–crisis stories, and crime fiction to the kinds of political novels that the sociologist Wendy Griswold calls "allegories of despair."[56]

Despite this generic range, African political fiction still attracts the largest audience in the United States. As with South Asian fiction, American reviewers of twenty-first-century Nigerian novels, as well as Anglophone African writing more generally, tend to emphasize continuities with the tradition of the national allegory, even when the authors involved are actively engaged in revising that genre. For Nigerian authors, however, romanticism is largely perceived as a problem. "[K]eep your descriptions romantic and evocative and unparticular," Wainaina satirically asserts. From the heroic white traveler to the child-like African beneficiary of international aid, and from indistinct yet harmonious nature to mythic history, tropes of contemporary romanticism too strongly recall colonial-era depictions of Africa or (still worse) *Out of Africa*–style nostalgia for colonialism.[57] Rejecting many, though not all, romantic modifications of the national allegory, a number of contemporary African authors, including those writing from abroad, have drawn instead on the motifs of domestic realism. Recent Nigerian Anglophone fiction, in particular, invokes the realist bildungsroman, a form open to historical themes and an international context. Writing from the point of view of intellectuals responsive to community needs and responsible for socially constructive representations of the community (a point of view arguably out of fashion in the United States at present), a number of expatriate Nigerian authors have developed a new realist "allegory" that aims to inform their multinational readership about the condition of the nation in the neoliberal economy of the twenty-first century.

The heroes of the new fiction illustrate this commitment to contemporary neorealism most directly. As Madeleine Hron has demonstrated, the child-hero has become a popular motif in new Nigerian writing.[58] Whether in the person of Uzodinma Iweala's child-soldier in *Beasts of No Nation* (2005), Chris Abani's slum-dwelling Elvis in *GraceLand* (2004), or Sefi Atta's rapidly maturing girls in *Everything Good Will Come* (2007), the point of view of the child awakening to the world allows the domestication of the figure of the romantic guide. From the child's limited perspective, the nature of social life can easily be portrayed as complex, even mysteriously lacking in detail, while remaining potentially comprehensible to others. The child's often confused point of view allows the reader's education in the logic of social life to occur, thus giving breathing space to the pedagogic impulse and even some traces of the ethnographic gaze demanded by foreign readers and/or publishers.[59] From young Elvis's perspective, for example, Abani can explain the workings of the Lagos lending libraries and village film culture, much as the reactions of a young houseboy recently arrived from the village introduces readers to 1960s-era university culture in Chimamanda Adichie's *Half of a Yellow Sun* (2006). At the same time, in Iweala's hallucinatory narrative, the child's sense of profound dislocation in a world that is responsive to adult motives beyond his immediate comprehension also keeps the allegorical impulse alive. Iweala's "no nation" remains as nameless as the leaders and the militias that conscript his hero; tutelage in horror orients the child-soldier regardless of his specific location. This initiation process is as central to Iweala's short debut novel as the comic education in the ways of the e-mail scammers (called 419ers in reference to the statute on fraud) is to Adaobi Tricia Nwaubani's hero in *I Do Not Come to You by Chance* (2009).

A maturation narrative also frames several more complex novels in which a child is not the central figure. Late in Adichie's novel, for example, we learn that the author figure is none other than Ugwu, the houseboy whose arrival in the regional capital of Nsukka launched the narrative. His perceptions move from an initially skeptical view of other people's disorientation ("Master was a little crazy" is the novel's first sentence) to a far more self-knowing doubt about his own capacities as an author: he "realized that he would never be able to capture that child on paper, never be able to describe well enough the fear that dulled the eyes of mothers in the refugee camp when the bomber planes charged out of the sky. He would never be able to depict the very bleakness of bombing hungry people. But he tried, and the more he wrote the less he dreamed" (498). This historical novel, set during the war in Biafra, results, we learn, from an adult's effort to put to rest the demons encountered by the child.

Helon Habila's *Measuring Time* (2007) traces its protagonist's development more simply and chronologically, retelling Mamo's childhood from an adult point of view. Rather than reserving that frame for a discovery late in the novel, as does Adichie, Habila repeatedly pulls it into the foreground. As his title signals, temporality and historical memory are central concerns of this novel, and Mamo's sickly childhood is recorded, examined, and retroactively explained in his adult writings. The distant, rather hagiographic narrator first reports that Mamo "would make a lengthy reference to [sickle-cell anemia] in his biography of his mother, explaining in detail the chemistry and the biology of the disease" before going on to quote at length from this imagined text (20). Habila's novel consists of a doubly mediated childhood—reshaped first by the adult Mamo and then by the narrator, who recounts Mamo's development as a writer.

Whatever the thickness or thinness of the frame separating the child's perceptions from the narration, though, the immature hero consistently has an anxious relation to the parents' generation, often fearing rather than craving the separation so vital to American adolescence narratives.[60] The child-hero is not particularly mobile—or, if mobile, does not experience that mobility as liberatory. For example, Habila's homebound protagonist, Mamo, has a twin named LaMamo who runs off to serve as a soldier; his infrequent letters describe the brutality he witnesses. Wartime chaos renders even Adichie's naïve Ugwu callous all too rapidly, as he participates in the rape of a bar girl. In these works, as in Iweala's *Beasts of No Nation* and, rather differently, in *Harare North* (2009), Brian Chikwava's novel of a Zimbabwean former soldier's relocation to a squat in Brixton, the soldiering life endangers the young and exceeds their comprehension. Home life is something to be desired and treasured in the context of this utterly un-romantic form of conscripted travel.

On the domestic scene, difficult fathers bear some responsibility for the young men in their care becoming caught up in unsavory activities. The political ambitions harbored by Mamo's father distract him for most of his sons' childhood, much as the intellectual and ideological discussions that take place in Ugwu's master's salon culminate in the war in which he serves. A well-intentioned father can be as dangerous as a negligent one, however, as Nwaubani's narrative suggests. It is, after all, her hero Kingsley's status as *opara* (eldest son) that makes him responsible for supporting his family and paying the staggering medical bills that follow the illness of his incorruptible father. Faced with this dilemma, Kingsley strays from the path that his father laid out for him in engineering, becoming instead a champion 419er. Whether largely absent (as in Iweala's *Beasts of No Nation*, Abani's *GraceLand*, and Chikwava's *Harare North*), virtuous and preoccupied (as in Adichie's *Half of a Yellow Sun*, Nwaubani's *I Do Not Come to You by Chance*, Moses Isegawa's layered Ugandan allegory, *Abyssinian Chronicles* [2000], and Hisham Matar's *In the Country of Men* [2006]), or actively malignant (as in Habila's *Measuring Time*, Zakes Mda's *Madonna of Excelsior* [2004], and, rather differently, Nuruddin Farah's *Links* [2003]), the father plays a vital role in narratives focalized through the child, especially the son.[61] Fathers and father-substitutes such as Iweala's military leaders and Isegawa's description of Idi Amin serve as essential links to the homes they anchor and thus, by implication, to the national histories they recall in these narratives. The child-heroes of these fictions operate in relation to fathers and other figures from earlier generations, rather than beginning life adrift and freely at sea as newly formed individuals. Even in novels, such as Matar's and Mda's, that are deeply sympathetic to the perspective of mothers,[62] the central question for the protagonist remains "Can you become a man without becoming your father?" (Matar 149). National, cultural, and economic legacies transmitted paternally serve as important constraints for the heroes of quite a few contemporary Anglophone fictions concerning Africa.

The question of the father's legacy arises with particular urgency in these novels because patterns of social reproduction are depicted as undergoing rapid transformation and disruption. External turmoil, unpredictable forces, and tumultuous events far beyond the control of the father–child duo threaten patterns of fidelity and individuation. In some novels written from exile, these external triggers acquire a recognizable national-political face, such as Qaddafi's police in Matar's *In the Country of Men*, the district judge in Mda's *Madonna of Excelsior*, and the cartel leader in Farah's *Links*. In recent Nigerian fiction, however, this convention is less often observed. The forces that political theorist Achille Mbembe has taught us to call "necro-political" for their almost gleeful extraction of power from the spectacle of mass death arrive indirectly in these neo-dictator novels.[63] Like the religious riots that suddenly sweep through Mamo's town in *Measuring Time* and the hysterical paralysis that one of Adichie's central figures experiences at the moment the Biafran state's secession is announced in *Half of a Yellow Sun*, crucial collective events are often depicted in these novels as ruptures, seizures, or periods of insanity whose etiology is too complex to isolate. Neither the sexual violence that punctuates Abani's *GraceLand* and Atta's *Everything Good* nor the wartime depravity of Iweala's *Beasts of No Nation* can be traced to a single perpetrator or attributed to a specific, preventable situation. Even Nwaubani's more comic environment in *I Do Not Come to You by Chance* ultimately makes the 419ers subject to the whims of ignorant foreigners who bite (or not) on the carefully composed e-mails soliciting their goodwill and cash. Consistently in these narratives, the course of father–child social reproduction threatens to veer wildly off course because of events arriving, like Habila's several returned and damaged soldiers, suddenly at their doorstep.

In an Achebe-era national allegory (or its best-selling American variation, Alex Haley's romantic *Roots* [1976]), these alien disturbances might have triggered nostalgia for the presumed purity of village tradition; however, this motif is less common in twenty-first-century Nigerian fiction read in the United States. Most of these novels are resolutely urban in setting (Adichie, Abani, Atta, and Nwaubani); quite a few describe middle-class social environments, especially the families of educators (Habila, Iweala, Adichie, Nwaubani, and Atta); and many imagine a move abroad, rather than a return to the rural heartland, as an avenue of possible escape from contemporary problems.[64] Increasing international contact and mobility, not isolation within the borders of the nation-state, sustain these narratives of neoliberal economic penetration and necro-political corruption. Although often resolving conflict by means of locational change, these narratives typically spend little time describing migration or flight itself; instead, they figure the presumed benefits of movement through "hermaphroditic landscapes" that interweave urban and rural elements.[65]

This spatial reorganization takes many literary forms. Nwaubani's hero, Kingsley, is deeply moved when his father's hospital bed is relocated to their family living room, for example; Habila's protagonist Mamo discovers exciting new prospects through the mail—not only when letters from his twin brother arrive but also when he learns that the alternative history of his town that he had penned in a period of intense inspiration was accepted for publication. The spatial disruptions and hybridizations represented by the oases of compounds run by nongovernmental organizations in military situations are as vital to Iweala's and Habila's narratives (and Farah's as well) as are the services immediately provided. These hybrid spaces sometimes also trigger psychological breakdown in those who are too inflexible to accommodate them. In the compelling surprise ending of *Harare North*, for example, Chikwava's hero not only expels white British hipsters from the squat he inherited from other Zimbabwean asylum seekers but also strips the squat down to its studs and floorboards in a fit of desperate discomfort with the ways in which his post-migration world has been contaminated by pre-migration anxieties.[66] An intermixed, multipolar environment is the norm, these narratives suggest, and rejecting it may bring a figure uncomfortably close to the disproportionate excesses and swerves of necro-political state rhetoric.[67] A realist accommodation to the multinational condition of exile and/or neoliberal penetration of the national space requires, instead, figures of renovation and transition.

The national household, in other words, appears in twenty-first-century Nigerian Anglophone fiction as an expansive form. It opens to welcome greater numbers into its multifamily compound space. Nwaubani's narrative, for example, concludes with an epilogue in which Kingsley has supplanted his murdered uncle, running 419 scams from his chain of Internet cafés. Employing relatives and impressing those "hordes from the diaspora [who] were shaking off their phobias and coming back home" (399), the new Kings Cafés allow the *opara* to marry well and maintain his mother and siblings in an elegant style. Although most definitely not following in his father's footsteps, Kingsley allows his mother to misread the books he has used as decorations in his office as signs of a paternal legacy. His new business empire sets her dreams of familial continuity alongside his own multinational scams. Habila's novel also concludes with the formation of a new household, when the pregnant widow of Mamo's twin comes into his care. The figure of an aid workers' compound provides closure for Iweala, Adichie, and Farah, each of whom hints at multifamily reunions on the horizon. Unlike the emphasis on disrupted father–child legacies, this motif has proved particularly portable. It also appears in the resolution to novels written by American authors that are set in Africa, such as Dave Eggers's *What Is the What* (2006), which concludes with Sudanese refugees organizing into new political/familial units in the United States, and Russell Banks's *The Darling* (2004), in which an

American returning to Liberia relocates her African in-laws and even reunites with favorite animals as well. The figure of the capacious house and expanding family recurs in many variations of the neoliberal allegory.

One of the strongest traces of the national allegory apparent in twenty-first-century African fiction written in English, in other words, is the insistence on the presence of collectivity well in excess of the couple or that group so many in the United States call the "immediate" family. Nigerian domestic realism here "occults," or makes strange, some elements of the broader conception of social life held over from the national allegories of the late twentieth century. Both forms find common ground in their resistance to a distinctly neoliberal social vertigo, and their combination in this fiction results in figures focused on compound housing in a multinational space.

Post-Soviet Satires

In marked contrast to the romantic and realist tendencies so readily apparent in recent South Asian and African fiction written in English, a great many twenty-first-century English-language novels describing the post-Soviet condition explore the resources of satire. This trend may partly reflect the influence of contemporary authors writing in Russian and other Slavic languages. After all, in comparison with the more limited accessibility of African and South Asian literature, Russian fiction has been widely available to Americans both in the original language and in translation for at least fifty years. The longer history of immigration by Slavic-language speakers to the United States as well as the relatively lavish funding provided to academic Slavicists during the Cold War reinforced this pattern.[68] A well-established scholarly apparatus also interprets Slavic-language literature for the American public. One result of these interlocking literary institutions is that fiction describing the post-Soviet transition economies can assume a fairly high level of literary and cultural background on the part of its English-speaking readers and thus avoid flat ethnographic types. This familiarity also aids satire, a form that is ideally suited to exploring the surreal or exaggerated features of out-of-place survivors from another era.

In addition to reflecting the institutional setting of Russophone writing, Anglophone post-Soviet satires are in conversation with the content and style of Russian literature written in Russian. Since 1989, not only has socialist realism largely disappeared, but some of the old warhorses of politically correct dissidence have been put out to pasture. The romantic nostalgia of Boris

Pasternak's *Doctor Zhivago* (1957) and the determined outrage of Aleksandr Solzhenitsyn's *Gulag Archipelago* (1973–1975) seem to have been less inspiring for Russian-language writers of the past two decades than the edgier dystopianism of Yevgeny Zamiatin, for example.[69] Satirical works, such as Mikhail Bulgakov's *Master and Margarita* (1967), that were published abroad or formerly available only in underground samizdat publications have also become major influences. A number of contemporary émigré and domestic authors have given free rein to their fascination with nineteenth-century classics, reviving and sometimes updating well-known types such as the holy fool, the superfluous man, the underground man, the righteous man, and so on.[70] Others have developed new relations with socialist realism—either recycling slogans or genre norms ironically, continuing (consciously or unconsciously) to use narrative patterns typical of the earlier style, or explicitly confronting the urbanizing, futurist impulses of the Soviet era with more nostalgic, sometimes chauvinistic impulses of the village novel or the dystopia.[71] Whether these investments in retooling predecessor narratives are described as postmodern, postrealist, or magical historicist,[72] they clearly reveal the wide variety of sources and the range of styles that contribute to contemporary Russian satiric writing. In a number of ways, popular younger writers such as Victor Pelevin, most famously, but also Dmitry Bykov, Vladimir Makanin, Sergei Dovlatov, Venedict Erofeev, and Evgeny Popov are critically reevaluating the available narrative options in light of new Russian social experiences.

Two of the recurring characters in Russian-language post-Soviet satires are the New Russian—half entrepreneur, half gangster—and the adherent of occult or sectarian religions.[73] Open discussion of forced migration during the de-Sovietization process has also brought greater attention to ethnic and religious minorities in the former Soviet Union, and questions concerning sex and the body frequently arise as well. Many of these figures also reappear in English-language fiction that depicts the post-Soviet scene—with one major exception. While, Rosalind Marsh argues, portrayals of Soviet-era leaders, especially Stalin, have constituted an important subgenre of contemporary Russian-language fiction,[74] twenty-first-century English-language fiction about post-Soviet life typically displays little interest in leaders. In line with an American Cold War emphasis on freedom of expression, this writing is almost exclusively concentrated on the daily life of intellectuals or would-be artists. If liberals have historically argued that the test of a society is its treatment of children, the elderly, or the infirm, in English-language fiction on the post-Soviet condition, the fate of the artist-intellectual becomes a vital sign of the health of the nation. Self-referential attention to the situation of the intellectual also reinforces the essentially satiric stance of these writings.

Tonally, the English-language satires of Russian life offered, for example, by Gary Shteyngart, Ken Kalfus, Gina Ochsner, Lara Kapnyar, Anya Ulinich, and Olga Grushin cover a range that stretches from wildly absurd to modestly ironic. While hints of melancholia can be detected in some post-Soviet fiction describing non-Russian locations (for example, Chloe Aridjis's Berlin in *Book of Clouds* [2009] and John Wray's memories of Ukraine in *The Right Hand of Sleep* [2001]), far more frequently English-language writing strikes a more triumphalist note. Neither Pauls Toutonghi's passages on Latvia in *Red Weather* (2007) nor Mary Helen Stefaniak's depictions of late Cold War Hungary in *The Turk and My Mother* (2004) are particularly mournful, and Brigid Pasulka's Poland is depicted from beginning to end in *A Long Long Time Ago and Essentially True* (2010) as an essentially comic ground where folkloristic anecdotes meet urban irony, much like Jonathan Safran Foer's Ukraine in *Everything Is Illuminated* (2002) if the Holocaust sequences were removed. Even in tonally more somber works such as Grushin's, the exile's bruised nostalgia takes a back seat to other sensations.

Instead of mourning a lost past, twenty-first-century Anglophone accounts of post-Soviet life attend to the disarray of the present. These writings convey a sense of vacancy and disorientation created by the implosion of social institutions; they consistently treat personal psychology as a national trait and experience.[75] The hero is usually a defeated, depressive man with artistic ambitions. Personalizing the situation of a beleaguered populace, this lost soul is assaulted on one side by the brutal machismo of the New Russian and on the other by a distant, difficult, or unavailable sexual partner symbolizing a failed ambition. Gary Shteyngart, for example, opens his lively *Absurdistan* (2006) with his hero Misha's description of himself as a "grossly overweight man with small, deeply set blue eyes, a pretty Jewish beak that brings to mind the most distinguished breed of parrot, and lips so delicate you would want to wipe them with the naked back of your hand" (3). Misha's identity as a Philip Roth–ish cliché of the oversexed Russian Jewish adolescent centers on his genitalia, especially the organ that resembles "an abused iguana" as the result of a botched bris (34). Many passages express Misha's longing to be reunited with the voluptuous Bronx girlfriend from whom he is being kept by authorities who have discovered his connection to the 1,238th richest man in Russia—his father. A rapacious overconsumer and would-be American devoted to rap, Misha finds himself trapped locally in "St. Leninsburg" and, more generally, in "Russia, a nation of busybody peasants thrust into an awkward modernity" (6).

Misha's initial situation as a beset Russian reappears in many other novels. Gina Ochsner's *Russian Dreambook of Color and Flight* (2010) populates contemporary Siberia with an entire cast of ambitious personalities constrained by humiliating circumstances—from Olga, a brilliant linguist who is reduced to massaging the news for a conservative military newspaper, to her son Yuri, a young soldier who has recently returned from an inglorious stint in Chechnya, and Tanya, an overweight would-be writer and flight attendant whose counterfeit icons fill the regional museum where she works in the coatroom. The heroes of Ken Kalfus's excellent collection *PU-239 and Other Russian Fantasies* (1999) are similarly besieged, with the main character in the title story, for example, leaving a secret plutonium-producing facility after exposure to life-threatening radiation. Like the narrator in Kalfus's concluding novella, Timofey attempts to work his few options but ultimately finds himself outmaneuvered by mobsters. The title character in Olga Grushin's *Dream Life of Sukhanov* (2006) initially seems more successful and serene than do Ochsner's and Kalfus's entrapped figures, yet the world of this conformist Moscow art critic swiftly crumbles around him, revealing his weak grasp of the motives of his family and peers.

Narratives that are set in other parts of the former Soviet bloc and/or deal with women also employ similarly hapless heroes who are similarly besieged. *A Long Long Time Ago and Essentially True*, Pasulka's fable of contemporary Poland, for example, centers on a young woman so unattractive that even her relatives call her Baba Yaga, after the fairy-tale witch. Following the deaths of her parents and grandparents, at the outset of the novel the bereft Baba Yaga leaves her village for Krakow, where she lives modestly in the corners of her aunt's crowded apartment, overshadowed by her more glamorous cousin. In Pasulka's novel, the social disorder that accompanies the transition to capitalism mainly effects Baba Yaga's age-mates, including the doomed cousin, but in Aridjis's *Book of Clouds*, the underemployed narrator is directly attacked by presumably neo-Nazi thugs, prompting her departure from Berlin and abandonment of a new love affair. Similarly, Wray's *Right Hand of Sleep*, although set in Austria during the late 1930s, includes some intriguing meditations on its hero's return from life on a collective farm in Ukraine; the depressed hero takes himself off to a small cottage to recover from the death of his common-law Ukrainian wife before he is assaulted by Nazis. Neither Aridjis's nor Wray's novel is fully engaged with Nazism or anti-Semitism in the full-throated manner of *The People's Act of Love* (2005), a skillful and complexly imagined rethinking of revolutionary ethics in Russia by the British foreign correspondent James Meek. In *The People's Act*, a mild-mannered Jewish captain inhabits an environment riddled by a casual anti-Semitism that has some bearing on the sectarian religious tendencies, sexual rejection, and extreme physical violence (including cannibalism) also explored in the novel.[76] In Aridjis's and Wray's novels, however, Nazism and anti-Semitism mainly provide analogies for the surge of thuggish nationalism that requires, in both cases, a flight from the post-Soviet scene.

Whether comic (as in the works by Shteyngart, Ochsner, Kalfus, and Pasulka) or leaning toward the more lyrical or ironic (as in the novels of Grushin, Aridjis, and Wray), the defeated protagonist, together with the emblems of lost love and extreme violence that flank him, is repeatedly placed in a delicate utopia too small to contain him.[77] Shteyngart's oversize Misha strains almost any accommodation, but as *Absurdistan* comes to a close on September 9 and 10, 2001, readers begin to suspect that world events will expel Misha from the "little paradise" of the Mountain Jews (325). Wray's and Meek's novels also position utopian communities (of nudists and castrati, respectively) as counterpoints to the terrifying upheaval of social transformation.[78] Although sources of fascination, neither of these communities shelters the protagonist beyond a brief dinner or conversation. Still more transitory and compromised utopian spaces appear in several of Kalfus's stories (a dacha in an artists' community, a sleeping place under the kitchen table). Pasulka has her heroine revisit and once again abandon an idyllic Polish village, and even Aridjis's damaged ghostly Berlin allows for travel by means of the gleaming, magical subway, much as Grushin's Sukhanov attains a temporary release through aesthetic bliss in a book-filled neighbor's room in the communal apartment he inhabited as a child.

All these scenes of failed or lost utopias miniaturize their ideal worlds in relation to the ill-at-ease hero and the rougher, more dynamic surrounding social life. These small spaces fail to fulfill their stated purpose of providing fixed identities—as a Jew, an artistic genius, a sanctified man, or a pure Polish national. Scenes of quashed utopias, in short, become sites for reflecting on the utopian projects (in the bad static sense) that underlie contemporary national and ethnic identities as well as moments for revisiting the utopian impulse (in the more mobile, laudatory sense) of the Soviet era.[79]

The miniaturism of utopias in the post-Soviet satire also contrasts with the uncontained hyperactivity of commercial exchange. Pasulka's Krakow, for example, includes several transitions straight from the cramped bar where Baba Yaga works into aesthetically confused crowd scenes in the city center: "[O]rphaned flower wreaths float at the edge of the water, waiting to be fished out by their rightful suitors. There's a stage set up opposite the castle, the scaffolding glowing red and orange, and a band sings covers of American songs. Apparently everyone in the city arranged to meet each other on the same bridge, and people press in on me from all sides, spilling beer and shouting conversations" (76). Similarly anxiety-ridden scenes of public life also appear in Ochsner's Siberia. Not only do sinkholes mysteriously open up in the courtyard of her main characters' housing block, but the building itself is ultimately swallowed up by mud, and enormous piles of useless objects (dentures and mismatched high-heel shoes, for example) accumulate in direct proportion to the rapid disappearance of the most desirable commodities from the kiosks and small marketplaces in surrounding streets. Aridjis's figure for the same sensation is the immense display of electronic billboards in Berlin's Alexanderplatz, a monument to commercialism ignored by the sensitive architectural historian who employs the narrator. Shteyngart's Misha is a hyperbolic emblem of the enormous and continual appetites of the new entrepreneurial class he partially represents. These complex exchanges are released in their fullest and most explosive form while Misha gorges on fast food in the Absurdi capital during an invasion by corporate-funded mercenaries.

In between these chaotic, anxious scenes of exchange in the present day and the constricted utopias of an earlier day lie the everyday worlds of our defeated heroes. All these novels of post-Soviet life spend time describing uncomfortably compressed living spaces. From the personal bitterness, ethnic hatred, and political betrayals that most of these authors associate with Soviet-era communal apartments, there is a direct line to the quasi-erotic physical shame of shared hotel rooms and offices; these narratives insist on the comic adversity resulting from sharing space with non–family members.[80] Unlike South Asian or African fiction, they also repeatedly stress the violation of domestic privacy. While Mishra's hero in *The Romantics* relishes the simplicity of his student hostel and enjoys the access it gives him to new people, for example, in the novels of Ochsner, Grushin, Pasulka, and Kalfus, metaphors of invasion predominate. The proximity of neighbors leads to involuntary exposure to sensory information—such as the inescapable smell of courtyard latrines in Ochsner's novel, the annoying sound of a neighbor's off-key singing in Grushin's narrative, or the erotically disconcerting vision of a young woman dancing in Kalfus's "Birobidzhan." Of the many treatments of this theme in post-Soviet fiction, though, perhaps the oddest is Aridjis's. Despite living alone in a spacious apartment with high ceilings, the heroine feels persecuted by the sounds and light that penetrate her sanctuary—to the point where this reclusive figure even joins a Dark Skies organization devoted to protesting the effects of artificial light. This almost paranoid obsession with the incursions of others on one's sleep—the ultimate private act—helps explain the recurring use of dreams in these novels.

In many of the post-Soviet novels, dreams undermine waking life—often to the point where the narrator's grip on reality becomes insecure. This is the central motif in *The Dream Life of Sukhanov*, which asks how and why life would be different if regrettable personal and political decisions had not been made. An unstable waking life also figures in *The Russian Dreambook*, where dreams reveal unfulfilled desires (whether for fish, toaster ovens, direct speech, or westward travel). Dream-like qualities also appear in Kalfus's "Fable" as well as in some of the more hallucinatory passages of nature writing in *The Right Hand of Sleep* and the recounting of village folklore in *A Long Long Time Ago*. Like the films that Baba Yaga adores, Pasulka's surreal folklore presents a redacted version of the characters' present, providing clues to their longings. Creating pivot points between village and city, oral history and literary realism, the folkloric dream symbols smooth the transition of Baba Yaga as she moves from naïve village girl to sophisticated documentary filmmaker.

Ultimately, these uneasy transitions suggest that the several competing narratives available in each of these works negate one another. Dreams finally serve the ends of satire, dissipating secure daytime ideals. Despite their range of tones and moods, all these novels unravel precedents and leave few options fully intact. Like the easily out-maneuvered protagonist of Kalfus's final novella, their depressive, defeated narrators often retain dreams of art making that seem increasingly implausible in the crowded commercial spaces they occupy; they juxtapose the gigantic and the tiny, the social and the utopian, and the vicious and the nostalgic. The national ambitions of these satires are clearly marked by their titles (Ochsner's *Russian Dreambook*, Kalfus's *PU-239 and Other Russian Fantasies*, Shteyngart's *Absurdistan*) and their representative heroes, just as their preoccupation with neoliberal ideologies and the market economy create unstable scenes and dangerous antagonists. The most distinctive features of this fiction devoted to the post-Soviet experience, however, is its commitment to satire, a commitment deriving from the authors' firm sense that no single style can properly capture this tremendous social transformation in one go.

TWO VIEWS OF PERU

South Asian, African, and post-Soviet versions of the national allegory demonstrate how variable the form can be when it responds to the tastes and traditions of different regions. The national allegory can also vary significantly *within* a region, as illustrated by two novels that address the recent history of Peru. Both Ann Patchett's *Bel Canto* (2001) and Daniel Alarcón's *Lost City Radio* (2007) make use of genre norms, but they pull them in different directions stylistically and politically.

Patchett's intentionally overblown, melodramatic novel explores the apparently unifying power of opera for the servants, houseguests, hosts, and insurgent captors who encounter one another during the siege of an elegant country house. Although references to Alberto Fujimori's controversial authoritarian rule in Peru (1990–2000) are clear enough in Patchett's passages describing Japanese influence in Latin America,[81] the novel's political themes are largely subordinated to aesthetic rapture. Even Patchett's guerrillas are swayed from their purpose by the grandeur of the country house. One young fighter muses:

> None of her family left behind in the mountains could have understood there was a house made of bricks and sealed glass windows that was never too hot or too cold. She could not have believed that somewhere in the world there was a vast expanse of carpet embroidered to look like a meadow of flowers, or that ceilings came tipped in gold, or that there could be pale marble women who stood on either side of a fireplace and balanced the mantelpiece on their heads. (156)

Simply observing the lushly appointed home compromises the guerrilla's political motives. "Would it be the worst thing if nothing happened at all," the guerrilla wonders, "if they stayed together in this generous house?" (156). Patchett imagines a world of violent conflict and social division provisionally healed by the visual consumption of the haute-bourgeois decor of the nineteenth century.

Alarcón, by contrast, sets his novel in an unnamed city and country strongly reminiscent of his hometown of Lima, Peru, some ten years after the conclusion of a dirty civil war. The inner lives of his rebels are less susceptible to omniscient narration, since the very existence, let alone the membership, of the so-called Illegitimate Legion is officially in question. Among the ordinary citizens populating *Lost City Radio*—an urban radio personality, a boy from the jungle who seeks her, the radio personality's vanished husband, and the boy's teacher—the memory of conflict is painfully fresh, and they have little hope that either art or ideology will heal their wounds. Far from offering gorgeous spectacles of restorative power, the houses in Alarcón's novel are unsettlingly open and vulnerable. Norma, the radio announcer, for example, habitually leaves her doors ajar, so that if her husband returns he will immediately see that she is sleeping alone. This anxious transparency is matched by the extreme vulnerability to fire of dwellings in *Lost City Radio*. Boyhood pranks, political concealment, and/or terrorist-inspired arson cause houses to disappear in this novel almost as easily as the inhabitants who are dragged off for interrogation in the state torture facility known as the Moon.[82] The officially nonexistent brutality of the Moon inverts the logic of the novel's other major figure—Norma's radio broadcasts, which aim to reunite separated family members. Although sharing with the prison a certain duplicity (faking reunions when persons are not actually found) and complying with the police to some degree (vetting their lists for suspects before reading them on the air), the radio station becomes Alarcón's most potent symbol for a spatial and political consciousness at odds with entrapment and imprisonment in the national home. Radiating through the airwaves, Norma's textured speaking voice brings a humane level of care to an environment where the names of towns have been officially reduced to mere numbers. This restorative warmth even enfolds Norma herself when, in the novel's penultimate scene, she hears the boy read the name of his missing father and her husband on the air. The bittersweet sensation of hearing one's enduring domestic loss publicly broadcast provides the final chord in *Lost City Radio*'s otherwise almost journalistically detached story.

In short, although both Patchett and Alarcón make images of the besieged home filled with unifying sound the centerpiece of their imagined Perus, the tone, mission, and effect of their novels diverge markedly. Both arise out of an allegorical impulse—the house as a microcosm in the case of Patchett, and the almost Orwellian use of fable in the case of Alarcón. Yet each offers a separate type of engagement with the form, turning it toward different ends and positioning the penetration of national space differently (as rescue, for Patchett, and as painful reminder of loss, for Alarcón). This pair of texts thus demonstrates how variable the allegory of collective life can be. The national allegory as a form does not restrict or control the political implications of the resulting work within a single region any more than it requires homogeneity of content or effect on a global scale.

Amid all these intra- and interregional variations, however, one element remains constant. The emerging genre of the neoliberal allegory does require as one of its fundamental elements some use of the figure of the dwelling place. Housing is ever-present in these novels as a preoccupation of characters, a motif for narrators, and a figure for the novel. This recurring feature may limit the content of the national allegory somewhat by suggesting that its proper concern is the domestic sphere, not the workplace. After all, few of the novels surveyed in this chapter stray into the labor market, and those that do (by Siddhartha Deb, Samrat Upadhyay, Olga Grushin, Gina Ochsner, and Daniel Alárcon, for example) almost exclusively describe the working life of bureaucrats, teachers, and writers—middle-class subjects whose largely self-directed and intellectual labors arguably have been among the least directly affected by the neoliberal revolution of the past thirty years. Even these subjects are rarely depicted as actually working. Most of the action takes place when the protagonists are taking breaks during the workday, recharging their physical and emotional batteries during rest periods at home, enjoying leisure time or holidays, or preparing for work at some point in the future. The dwelling places that these characters inhabit bring social relations to the forefront and, in many instances, provide compelling figures for social turmoil associated with economic change, but it is rare for even a modified police procedural such as Vikram Chandra's *Sacred Games* to ascribe narrative interest to "procedural" details of the economy. Even economic relations that occur inside the home—such as the domestic laborers in Daniyal Mueenuddin's stories—recede behind familial concerns. This tendency suggests that there may be space in twenty-first-century international fiction for a more politically charged version of the nanny novel—a version that perhaps moves beyond the conventional seduction plot to explore the workings of the remittance economy.[83] To date, however, the social significance of the dwelling place seems to have precluded treatment of it as a site of labor.

Although a properly geo-economic novel has yet to emerge, authors of the geopolitical novel have improvised in some important ways on the well-established figure of the house. Extra-literary homes and housing are, of course, highly symbolic, laden with culturally variable associations and

practices—from the relation of public to family-only space and the orientation of sites of labor to those of leisure, to their porosity (or not) to animals and
their orientation toward astronomic phenomena. Physical houses balance
competing symbolic claims as well as social relations, so literature reflecting
on the social symbolism of housing has many concerns to manage. Often,
fiction condenses multiple social dialectics instantiated in the house into one
or two simpler or more static elements, such as the replacement of the dead
Puritan with the living relative's sweetshop in Nathaniel Hawthorne's *House
of the Seven Gables* (1851) and the failure of the modern family to live up to
the more heroic sea-faring bravado of earlier generations in John Cheever's
Wapshot Chronicle (1957).[84]

Twenty-first-century fiction, however, allows a few new complications. In
particular, the novels discussed in this chapter reflect on some of the spatial
anxieties characteristic of the so-called planet of slums[85]—that is, a global
scene characterized by ultra-rapid urbanization and proletarianization on a
massive scale. The neoliberal allegory tends to reject suburban realism, building instead on the narratives of urban crisis that we might associate, in American literature, with African American writers such as John Edgar Wideman in
Philadelphia Fire (1990), Ralph Ellison in *Invisible Man* (1952), and Richard
Wright in *Native Son* (1940).[86] Like these authors, twenty-first-century national allegorists abandon the single-family house or cottage as an ideal.

The compound, collective housing they describe also updates the "apartment stories" that Sharon Marcus has memorably argued arose in late-
nineteenth-century European fiction.[87] Exploring the public and private
spaces of the urban café and boulevard, as well as civil society more broadly,
Marcus's apartment stories register the promise of metropolitan modernity.
In twenty-first-century postcolonial and/or post-Soviet settings, however, the
ideals of that modernity usually appear strained. In the geopolitical novel,
the visibility and frequent social interactions allowed by the apartment are
frequently linked to surveillance, and the doorway becomes a site of endangerment (as in post-Soviet narratives of the police knock on the door, but also
threshold moments in writings by Pankaj Mishra, Amitav Ghosh, Siddhartha
Deb, Vikram Chandra, and Chimamanda Adichie). Similarly, the promise
of sexual freedom that Marcus associates with the European apartment often
takes an unsavory turn in the neoliberal allegory. The financial transactions
supporting prostitution, mistresses and lovers tend to reduce their appeal dramatically (for the clearest examples, see Adaobi Tricia Nwaubani, Samrat
Upadhyay, Pankaj Mishra, and Brigid Pasulka). Nor is the sheer experience

of the crowd an exhilarating novelty in this writing; these are not the novels to turn to for accounts of the flaneur's delight in the novel juxtapositions of the urban social scene. Urbanization is not in and of itself liberatory for these twenty-first-century authors.

The neoliberal allegory is, instead, mainly a narrative of failed or compromised modernity. The prospects for social improvement that this form envisions tends to be indirect and symbolic — that is, occult. As a final example, consider the moment early in *Measuring Time*, when Helon Habila's twin protagonists, hoping for visions, kill a dog reputed to belong to a witch and smear its rheum in their own eyes. A thick crust forms, and when the boys awake from their nocturnal adventures, they fear that they have gone blind. Their aunt comes to check on them, and, sobbing, they throw themselves at her. Only then do their tears soften the secretions, allowing them to see the "morning sun rays behind her, bathing her as she stood on the threshold" (33). At this moment, Habila's heroes replace their childhood desire for magic with an even more revelatory vision of quotidian, familial power. They learn to cherish their aunt and their new relation to family and the home. Finally, it is not a magical escape into otherworldliness that allows Habila's novel or the genre of the neoliberal allegory to overcome some of its self-imposed limits. Instead, supercharged realism, satire, or romanticism brings the genre into a newly ecstatic relation to the expansively conceived national home.

4 IDEOLOGY, TERROR, AND APOCALYPSE

The New Novel of Revolution

Only armed prophets succeed in bringing lasting change.
Niccolò Machiavelli, *The Prince*

It is through revolt that subjectivity (not of great men but of whomever)
introduces itself into history and gives it the breath of life.
Michel Foucault, "Useless to Revolt?"

IN 1989, as the Soviet Union and its satellites began to unravel, Francis Fukuyama, a former Reagan and Bush–era State Department official, launched his "end of history" thesis. Fukuyama's triumphalist argument asserted that history as defined by ideologically charged struggle had come to a close. All remaining political rebellions, Fukuyama predicted, would involve struggles for recognition within (but not against) American- or European-style liberal democracy, since "the ideal of liberal democracy could not be improved on."[1]

In the more than two decades since the book version of *The End of History* was published, however, Fukuyama has reconsidered his position. Recognizing that revolution as a practice and an ideal has actually made something of a comeback in the twenty-first century, *America at the Crossroads* criticizes the anti-democratic and anti-revolutionary aspects of American foreign policy in Iraq and Afghanistan, and Fukuyama's most recent book, *The Origins of Political Power*, emphasizes the geopolitical role played by right-wing revolutionary movements, as well as the impact of states with a revolutionary pedigree, such as China.[2] A universal and peaceful embrace of liberal democracy—the process that Fukuyama calls "getting to Denmark"—appears far more conflicted, violent, and unlikely at the start of the second decade of the twenty-first century than it did (at least to Fukuyama) in the latter decades of the twentieth. One of the hardest cases for the end of history thesis has been the Arab Spring.

Described by some hopeful observers as secular and pro-democracy uprisings against decades of one-party nationalist dictatorships in Egypt, Tunisia,

Yemen, Syria, and Libya, the movements that are collectively known as the Arab Spring also pay tribute to the Islamic revolution in Iran and reflect on the neocolonial influence exercised by Western powers.[3] They have mobilized supporters across the political spectrum, and it remains to be seen who the beneficiaries of political upheaval in the region will be and what kind of social transformation, if any, will follow the ousting of aged leaders. Women's rights, for example, remain a subject of dispute. Social modernization and so-called liberalization are in no way guaranteed by the moments of ecstatic rupture that Michel Foucault, among others, associates with a revolutionary confrontation with entrenched state power.[4] Dramatic street protests and other spontaneous rebellions launched by coalitions unified only by their opposition to existing rulers create openings into which a great many possibly irreconcilable forces may rush.

Existing political theories do not provide complete explanations for these events. For classical liberalism, the main event that legitimates revolution is a sovereign's assault on the citizen's property.[5] However, property rights have not been major slogans in the Arab Spring or other contemporary anti-state movements (such as the struggles in Burma and Tibet). Other civil rights, such as the right to participate in the political process, have had greater significance, but many of the most active movements have focused on social issues—especially the relation between political and religious authority. Religious cries for social and political revolution offer a profound challenge to liberal political theory, since this tradition normally treats the separation of church and state as fundamental, consigning religious authority to private or at least non-state spheres. Classic leftist theories of revolution (for example, those of Lenin and Mao) usually agree. They divide revolution into two stages: first the political and then the social and/or cultural revolution, which might address religious and educational institutions or other divisive sites.[6] However, the recent events asserting a deep need for what Foucault called (in reference to the Iranian revolution) "political spirituality" parse the issue quite differently. In the revolutionary movements in North Africa and the Middle East since the 1970s, theological and social questions have often not been separate from the political, nor do they necessarily follow the lead of political authority; instead, social and cultural needs (expressed by religious bodies) have often driven political crises.

Rather than expressing the end of ideology, though, these movements seem to signal the beginning of "a new relation between the political movement and the level of the ideological," as Alain Badiou puts it; they point toward a fundamentally new experience of the political that is no more comprehensively explained by the liberal conception of the possessive individual publicly legitimated by property rights than it is by the orthodox leftist tradition of the party-organized masses (or, for that matter, the rightist politics of the great man).[7] These revolutionary events in culture are accompanied by the militarization of culture in the so-called war on terror. Together, they suggest an urgent need to rethink existing accounts of the origins, motives, and justifications for revolution, as well as associated visions of political process and social effects.

Twenty-first-century American novelists have tackled these questions directly. In a wealth of new fiction devoted to revolutionary movements in France, Haiti, Russia, Cuba, Iran, Bangladesh, Uruguay, and beyond, writers of the past decade have carefully scrutinized their narrative options. Mining and ultimately transforming the generic and political assumptions of existing traditions of the novel of revolution, twenty-first-century authors have (like revolutionaries themselves) opened up spaces in which "subjectivity . . . introduces itself into history," as Foucault would have it. More particularly, writing the twenty-first-century novel of revolution has led a host of authors to revise existing accounts of the revolutionary consciousness, the process by which revolutionary ideas are implemented, and the historical narrative itself. In genre terms, contemporary authors have found it necessary to rebuild the historical romance from the ground up, reversing the increasingly metafictional trajectory that led the concerns of Ernest Hemingway to mutate into those of Don DeLillo. Without entirely abandoning the critique of historical realism offered by metafictionists, writers of the past decade have supplemented its resources with elements drawn from narratives of the apocalypse.

The Literary History of Revolution

Contemporary authors seeking models for narratives of revolution have many options. From late-eighteenth- and early-nineteenth-century English Jacobin and anti-Jacobin fiction to the documentary narratives by American witnesses to the Russian Revolution, stories of expatriates' encounters with nationalist uprisings in the colonial context, and post-1960s fables of political disappointment, the Anglophone novel has surrounded revolutionary themes with a dense web of associations. All these choices, however, are framed by the larger problems of the historical novel. With very few exceptions, the controversial genres of radical fiction developed during periods of upheaval such as the

1890s and the 1930s—the panic novel, the proletarian novel, the strike novel, the so-called bottom-dogs novel, and so on[8]—have in the long run had much less impact on fictional representations of revolution in "mainstream" American political fiction than have the conventions of the historical romance.

A fundamental question for any historical fiction is the relationship it establishes between the narrating present and the narrated past. A novelist may choose to immerse readers in a past imagined as an open-ended and active struggle that ultimately turns dialectically toward the present; this is the strategy preferred by György Lukács in his landmark interpretation of the form, *The Historical Novel.*[9] Textbook examples of the immersive approach include John Reed's documentary of the October Revolution in Russia, *Ten Days That Shook the World* (1920), and Hemingway's novel of the Spanish Civil War, *For Whom the Bell Tolls* (1940). In both works, detailed descriptions of the adventures of minor and major figures propel narratives whose outcomes are well known in their broadest strokes. These passages suture the emergence of the hero's active political consciousness to the circumstances that constrain collective action. Reed, for example, shifts back and forth between the revolutionary council of the Soviets and the heavily policed fortress of the Duma, while Hemingway wrestles with the interpersonal and organizational obstacles that prevented the small Republican bands with which his hero sympathizes from defeating the Nationalist armies. In both works, a fundamentally realist encounter with social institutions and power politics encloses the more romantic strains of revolutionary zeal. Such narratives risk, however, devolving into overly glib or thinly imagined fiction if they are not fully enough engaged with the texture of unfolding events to make the reader forget the known outcome. They risk downplaying revolutionary novelty by making its dynamics appear inevitable. Another danger is that their preoccupation with limits to the revolutionary project can lead the genre to shade, perhaps against the author's intent, into counter-revolutionary parables about the impossibility of deep structural change, such as that offered by D. H. Lawrence in *The Plumed Serpent* (1926). Either way, the Lukácsian narrative explores the past in all its complexity in order to illuminate the present.

Fully apprised of the dangers of this developmental approach, a number of later twentieth-century authors of revolutionary fiction turned toward more reflexive habits designed to absolve themselves of any charges of oversimplifying historical narration. They preferred instead to shatter the illusion that the historical process can be known in its entirety. Devoting themselves to a full rendering of the writing and research processes involved in constructing the historical narrative, authors of "historiographic metafictions" on revolutionary subjects (in Linda Hutcheon's famous phrase) often gave as much airtime to author figures as to active revolutionaries.[10] Don DeLillo's *Libra* (1988), for example, oscillates not between Cuban and American forces during the Bay of Pigs invasion but between Lee Harvey Oswald's would-be revolutionary perspective during this period and that of the CIA handler researching his subject.

However exciting such experiments felt during the moment of their first proliferation in the 1970s and 1980s, this metafictional approach to the historical novel has hit some dead ends. In particular, it tends to devolve into a preoccupation with the procedures of the research, risking antiquarianism. Instead of the open-ended emergence of present from past, when taken to their logical limits, historiographic metafictions tend to sever past from present, an action that converts the historical details—such as Oswald's love of subways and relationship with his mother—into merely decorative motifs. These carefully researched details are notable for their oddity but do not significantly illuminate the present. Historical fiction in this vein tends to use the revolutionary event as simply one among many occasions to reflect on the absence, impossibility, and/or unknowability of the historical past. All historical episodes then reveal essentially the same, rather banal existential abyss.

A closely related subgenre of the research-procedural novel turns on the shattering of historical sequence—its dispersal into the frozen time that Walter Benjamin memorably described as the *Jetzt-zeit* (now-time).[11] All the fragments become impossible to assemble into any coherent narrative, stranding the would-be researcher in a perpetually crisis-ridden present. William Gaddis's final short novel, *Agapē Agape* (2002), for example, takes the form of an anxious, paranoid deathbed rush of verbiage produced by a scholar who is drowning in material for a voluminous study of the player piano but who is unable to summon the final burst of energy necessary to bring his vicious anti-technology rant to fruition. Although filled with passion, the crisis novel shares with the historiographic metafiction the mission of loosening the tie between past and present; it, too, makes a world either preceding or following the revolutionary moment impossible to comprehend. The themes of the historical novel as crisis writing turn out to encompass "not the emergence of the nation, but the ravages of empire; not progress as emancipation, but impending or consummated catastrophe," writes Perry Anderson.[12] A fixation on revolution as crisis, in other words, sacrifices the more pedestrian social narrative of those effects that Machiavelli called "lasting change" to the iciest and most wind-swept heights of apocalyptic prophecy. While, we will see, an apocalyptic strain definitely fortifies twenty-first-century revolutionary fiction, the full-blown prophetic stance—complete with joy at the imminence of rapture for the saved and ominous predictions of locusts and plagues for the damned—rarely characterizes this writing.[13] Entirely apocalyptic narratives ultimately abandon historical time in favor of the new temporality of the post-Judgment era, and a revolutionary novel committed to exploring and possibly explaining events in a particular time and place rarely makes such a final challenge to historiography.

Rather than treading the post-historical path, contemporary revolutionary fiction, as a subset of the historical novel, keeps alive many conventions of its master genre, relying on them well past the expiration date announced by late-twentieth-century metafictionists. Revolutionary fiction continues to interpret revolutionary events that precede and, arguably, determine the shape of the narrative. Well-known historical figures (usually political or military leaders) appear regularly in these novels, and the narrative generally describes a situation of turmoil or escalating crisis that comes to a climax in a public event. Invented characters, socially subordinate to the historical leaders, normally traverse this scene, coming into close proximity to the climactic events, although rarely comprehending them fully. The limited point of view provided by these small heroes is supplemented by external knowledge that is either provided directly by an intrusive narrator or alluded to by means of well-known "trigger-words" that direct the reader to a contemporary political lexicon.[14] Many of these narratives are organized into sections that use linear before–after sequences; within each section, however, a multiplicity of perspectives usually undercuts any overly simple account of the causes or effects of the revolution. By way of closure, as has been conventional since at least Stendahl, these narratives tend to leave the reader with bloody figures, shocked and/or damaged refugees, or quick leaps into the post-revolutionary future. In short, these novels maintain many of the default elements of the historical romance as invented by Walter Scott, even though they frequently make an effort to disturb Scott's complacency about the necessity of revolutionary violence and emphasize, like William Godwin, the scars left by history.[15]

While perpetuating this set of well-established narrative conventions for the revolutionary novel, twenty-first-century authors leave the significance of this tradition open. This open-endedness replicates academic debates that interrogate the relationship between political and cultural change. Some literary historians see revolution as the cause of cultural change; they point to literary evidence, such as the small place that English fiction granted to private epistles after the French Revolution and the rising prominence of neoclassical rhetoric and the plain public speech.[16] Some suggest that these priorities constricted opportunities for writing by women, while others argue that revolutionary situations release new literary-political emotions, such as righteous indignation in the Romantic era and a taste for the exaggerated forms of a "revolutionary grotesque" among Russian modernists.[17] Revisionists disagree, however, arguing that pre-revolutionary cultural conventions such as the aristocratic hero persist long after a period of upheaval.[18] They tend to regard political and social/cultural revolution as separate processes. A third thesis asserts that cultural (here, literary) change anticipates revolutionary upheaval.[19] Proponents of this approach treat the meaning of revolution as an unanswered question, something to be determined through struggle.

All these positions on the relationship of politics to culture have found novelistic expression. Authors of the contemporary revolutionary novel evaluate the effects of revolution quite differently, even though they share a set of literary conventions. They revive many elements of the historical romance in order to test the genre's visions of social life, and their innovations to the form update and multiply the meanings of the genre.

INNOVATIONS IN THE CONTEMPORARY NOVEL OF REVOLUTION

Innovations in revolutionary fiction began with the abandonment of several subgenres of the existing tradition. One of the first casualties was the frequently decried *roman à thèse*, or novel of political ideas, as well as novels that praise the revolutionary hero's sacrifices and utopian nationalism.[20] Both versions of the revolutionary novel are largely absent from contemporary U.S. literature—with the possible exception of light historical fiction that takes the American Revolution as a backdrop, such as Jeff Shaara's *Rise to Rebellion* (2001) and *The Glorious Cause* (2002). In general, geopolitical versions of the revolutionary novel take three other forms: the anti-ideology novel, the novel of terror, and (least common) the tour of the social revolution. Each of these subgenres grafts existing versions of the revolutionary novel to selected conventions of the post-apocalyptic repertoire.

Set in an evacuated antisocial world, apocalyptic fiction discloses the conditions of "bare life"[21] and describes the struggles of subjects abandoned by the state. The protagonists' dire situations give proof of their status as the damned. The most enlightened characters typically reflect on the historical process that led to their dilemmas, and the narrator conveys an aura of judgment, whether or not the substance of that judgment is revealed. Unlike fully apocalyptic visions, however, revolutionary novels rarely regard history as a closed process. They tend, instead, to look back at a closed chapter within an ongoing story—for example, the Soviet experiment, Third World solidarity movements of the 1960s, postcolonial state formation. Positioned, as it were, on a hillock overlooking the ruins of a past revolution but not yet high enough to foretell the end of time, their narrators review revolutionary failures and mourn the loss of those removed from history by delusions of the rapture, even as they collect the materials needed for a post-catastrophe existence.

This apocalyptic interpretation of the revolutionary novel modifies several genre conventions of the historical romance. To start with, it renounces the modest smallness of the sidekick hero in order to penetrate the consciousness of revolutionary leaders directly; fictions built around the point of view of Che Guevara, Toussaint L'Ouverture, Madame Mao, Haile Selassie, Stalin, and Lenin have appeared in the past decade. "Armed prophets" themselves become the mouthpieces for an apocalyptic rhetoric that is often contradicted by their inner lives. Adopting the perspective of a revolutionary figurehead imaginatively brings the revolutionary leader down to the same level as exiled writers and intellectuals. The latter tend to be depicted in this fiction more humanely than any principally political figure.

A second innovation in the new revolutionary novel involves the treatment of communication. Blocked or incomplete transmissions of revolutionary ideas are ubiquitous and commonly result in misdirected letters, missed rendezvous, failed performances, smudged sketches, interrupted performances, and other figures of miscommunication. Twentieth-century revolutionary fiction often pivots on scenes of speech making that conclude with a political conversion.[22] In twenty-first-century fiction, however, ideological expression more commonly flows in closed, repetitive circuits, producing either horrific effects or none at all. Conversion plots disappear, and the motives for commitment become opaque. From the post-apocalyptic vantage point, a deep chasm lies between revolutionary ideals and the chaotic experience of rebellion.

This anti-ideological tendency leads to a focus on bodily rather than intellectual commonalities. The post-apocalyptic narrative of survival becomes the main story in the depiction of political turbulence, and political changes of heart are figured by physical symptoms or visceral empathy. Especially in those narratives focused on the use of violence, torture, and terror, physical sensation becomes the irrefutable emblem of political virtue, and narratives are often carefully organized to highlight the bodily suffering of the most sympathetic characters. They are sympathetic as a result of their survival, almost regardless of political, intellectual, or ideological position. Simply living through revolution becomes sufficient for heroism, and the idealistic reformer shrinks into the merely physical person.

Finally, the apocalyptic narrative supplements the numbness of the survivor with interludes of wonder at the sublimity of historical processes; it expresses stunned shock at the actuality of change. Leaping up for a moment to ponder devastation, the twenty-first-century novel of revolution displaces the form's conventional confidence in progress with amazement at the fact of radical ruptures, even when it reveals the ill effects and brevity of that change. When joined with shifts in characterization and figuration, this tonal difference pulls the twenty-first-century novel of revolution toward a new genre, as summarized in the table.

Innovations in Twenty-First-Century Revolutionary Fiction

	TWENTIETH-CENTURY NORMS	TWENTY-FIRST-CENTURY TRENDS
HERO	Invented character close to historical leader	Leaders, central actors— including historical figures
SETTING	Civil unrest, public crisis	Aftermath, viewing revolutionary upheaval in retrospect or perpetual present
CONFLICT	Private dilemmas that correlate to climax in public events	Physical survival, reconciling bodily endurance with intellectual failure
POINT OF VIEW	Restricted knowledge, limited historical foresight	Cynical, ironic, retrospective
RESOLUTION	Sudden with lingering aftershock	Sublime shifts of focus—not necessarily in concluding passages

These emerging genre elements are visible in fiction about the Green Revolution in Iran; guerrilla warfare in Cuba; nationalist uprisings in the Dominican Republic, the Philippines, and Bangladesh; Maoism in China; and even the Jacobin movements in France and its colonies. Taken together, these many post-apocalyptic adaptations of the historical romance reveal the ways that a swath of dedicated contemporary authors have begun to rethink the dynamics of political and cultural revolution.

THE ANTI-IDEOLOGY NOVEL

Recent novels by William T. Vollmann, Ian Buruma, Miguel Syjuco, Anahita Firouz, Ken Kalfus, Julia Alvarez, Ana Menéndez, and Henry Bromell, and Susan Choi (not to mention contemporary English authors with a sizable readership in the United States, such as Hilary Mantel, Hari Kunzru, and James Meek) invert the conversion novel's narrative of commitment to revolutionary ideology. Tracking political disillusionment, they take ideology as the sign of vulnerability to social processes because, in this new fiction, all ideologies are equally suspect. Socialist, nationalist, radical anarchist, and theocratic agendas are all probed for their weakest points, and many novels pointedly equate systems of thinking that are on the face of things incompatible in order to undercut ideology in general.

In his elaborately constructed and diligently researched National Book Award winner *Europe Central* (2005), for example, William Vollmann alternates between the perspectives of Nazi and Soviet ideologues, highlighting the toll paid by committed military and artistic adherents on both sides of the Eastern Front in World War II. Similarly, Ian Buruma's *China Lover* (2008) examines the appeal of a Japanese actress for male protagonists with three different ideological orientations: a devoted nationalist during the Japanese occupation of Manchuria, a gay American Japanophile during the American occupation, and a Japanese-born leftist drawn into the Palestinian struggle. Relying on both his own experience as a longtime foreign correspondent in Asia and original research, Buruma uses the image of the actress to illuminate the surprisingly similar visions of an ideal Japan that underlie each ideology. Miguel Syjuco's *Ilustrado* (2009) adopts a similar strategy for his exploration of the political landscape of the Philippines; his protagonist (also named Miguel Syjuco) leaves Manhattan to return to his hometown of Manila in the course of his work on a biography of his recently deceased literary hero, Crispin Salvador. The body of the novel is made up of a collage of excerpts from the fictional Salvador's varied career as well as passages from Miguel's diary, scholarly notes, and the biography in progress. These plural voices refract any single event (for example, a corruption scandal in Manila), interpreting it simultaneously from viewpoints ranging from revolutionary nationalism to postmodern cynicism. Whether authors choose to compare two ideologies active in a single moment (like Vollmann, as well as Anahita Firouz in *In the Walled Gardens* [2002], James Meek in *The People's Act of Love* [2005], and Ken Kalfus in *The Commissariat of Enlightenment* [2002]), narrate their transformation over time (like Buruma, as well as Julia Alvarez in *In the Name of Salomé* [2000], Ana Menéndez in *Loving Che* [2004], Henry Bromell in *Little America* [2001], Susan Choi in *American Woman* [2004], and Hari Kunzru in *My Revolutions* [2007]), or multiply them nearly indefinitely (like Syjuco), though, the underlying goal remains essentially the same. They all make ideological commitment a narrative problem rather than an outcome.

In part, this approach reflects the classical liberal view of the status quo as lacking any ideology. Modern liberalism frequently imagines itself as a content-free process that protects the form of political debate without filling in that form with any particular content.[23] From this perspective, any system that involves commitment to a substantive interpretation of social life appears necessarily stagnant and prone to error. For this reason, Cold War liberalism in the United States routinely traced institutional problems in the Soviet Union back to ideological positions, charging that social ills necessarily resulted from poor information and/or rigidly dogmatic interpretations of data. During the dismantling of Soviet Communism, the same argument played out in reverse, as various ideological positions were supposedly invalidated by their presumed effects. From both directions, liberalism saw causal links between revolutionary ideology and post-revolutionary institutions.

This is the logic that Theda Skocpol, the leading American political theorist of revolution in the late twentieth century, rejects in her field-shaping book *States and Social Revolution*. While granting that ideology can and does have a unifying effect during periods of revolutionary organizing, Skocpol specifically rejects the notion that ideology determines the character of later institutions or the methods used during revolutionary struggle: "Any line of reasoning that treats revolutionary ideologies as blueprints for revolutionaries' activities and for revolutionary outcomes cannot sustain scrutiny in the light of historical evidence"[24] In her masterful comparative study of the French, Russian, and Chinese revolutions, Skocpol demonstrates that massive social transformation occurs only when particular domestic and geopolitical conditions arise. This emphasis on social conditions rather than ideological truth or error offers a reading of both the failure and the causes of revolutions that complicates liberal truisms. While Fukuyama's worldview can imagine no revolution where there is no ideology, Skocpol's structural explanation provides a framework for understanding how revolutionary movements may arise in contexts where multiple ideologies are expressed—or even none at all.

Interestingly, despite the anti-ideology sentiments of so many authors, Skocpol's turn to structural and social motivations for revolutionary activity has few echoes in contemporary fiction. Of the novels that directly tackle the nature of ideology, perhaps only Choi's *American Woman* moves significantly in this direction. Choi's retelling of the kidnapping of Patty Hearst and Hearst's subsequent radicalization as a member of the Symbionese Liberation Army is concerned first with exposing flaws in the revolutionary protocol for handling of captivity; following commonplace psychological explanations for the captive's identification with her captors, Choi demonstrates how extreme conditions of isolation and dependence make the Hearst character's conversion to revolutionary ideology possible, even inevitable. "Tied up alone in a closet," she looks forward to the brief moments of physical contact when "someone would adjust her blindfold, maybe yank a few times on her rope"; their proximity exerts pressure on her captors, too, as they begin to experience a "positive yen to effect a conversion" (266). This familiar narrative assumes that de-conversion will follow a change in circumstances, especially a restoration of networks of support and intimacy closer to those of the captive's earlier life.

The pop psychology of the Stockholm syndrome—relied on by revolutionaries and counter-revolutionaries alike—is precisely the narrative that Choi undercuts, however, with structural analysis. *American Woman* is told mainly from the point of view of Jenny Shimada, a Japanese American comrade in a Weatherman-like group whose experience living underground makes her an ideal handler for the SLA cell in hiding. Shimada (also based on a historical person) bonds with the Hearst figure, only to discover in the novel's dramatic climax that, rather than rescuing the captive, she has been set up as a sacrificial victim so that the Hearst figure can prove her loyalty to the cell. Her own growing ambivalence about revolutionary zeal is then traced back to her family's multilayered experience with American racism (a history concretized by internment during World War II), very much as the Hearst character's perhaps surprising level of commitment is explained by the experiences of exclusion and isolation that characterized her haute-bourgeois upbringing. In the trial following their capture, both women revert to survival strategies associated with their families of origin, and both have to "rub the flint tirelessly, until new lights of kinship spring up" (356). In this anthropological manner, Choi's novel locates both commitment and its opposite in a broader social landscape. Rather than regarding ideological commitment as either a psychological aberration or an intellectual error, Choi suggests that various relationships to revolutionary ideologies may themselves be social effects rather than causes. No doubt this culturalist explanation for ideological commitment has its limits, suggesting as it does a kind of inarguable correctness to versions of the self derived from the experience of segregation;[25] nonetheless, especially in relation to more satirical depictions of female partisans (for example, Philip Roth's *American Pastoral* [1997] and Joan Didion's *Book of Common Prayer* [1977]),[26] Choi's novel is remarkable for the even-handedness it displays in attributing social causes to both revolutionary and counter-revolutionary sentiments, rather than allowing (à la Roth) only the anti-revolutionary to have an authentic relationship to his or her roots.

Choi's novel is also, as noted, exceptional; perhaps only Buruma's more journalistic approach to the collapse of the prewar Japanese economy compares. Far more frequently, twenty-first-century revolutionary fiction renders the protagonist's world inexplicable once ideological coherence begins to dissipate. Nearly all the novels concerned with ideological commitment close with their protagonists stranded and adrift—facing a major loss that results directly from their tangled commitments. Syjuco's eponymous hero finally tracks down his subject's love-child in a remote village, only to discover that she has suddenly departed, leaving him stranded, aborted, evacuated: "Our protagonist opened the first box. It was empty. He opened the second. Empty. The third. Empty" (299). Similarly, Menéndez's heroine (another researcher hunting for traces of her long-lost Cuban mother, a painter devoted to Che) also learns of her subject's suicide. Yet another archivist, Alvarez's multiply exiled Spanish professor, finally learns that her mother, a revolutionary nationalist poet, was so weakened by childbirth that she died shortly thereafter. Even Firouz's novel of underground leftists in the final hours of pre-revolutionary Iran follows this pattern—closing with its two protagonists, would-be lovers, reflecting on the events that have prevented their successful union. Once ideology fails, these novels conclude, little is left except a disillusioned, barren freedom. "This was the end," Firouz's radical hero concludes, "and when it came it felt like no glory had ever graced it. No honor could ever persist. . . . Freedom begins now. I'll free myself. I'll leave everything behind" (328–329).

Reza then briefly elects to commit himself fully to a cause that, within pages, is described as doomed by its own "rapacious, shortsighted, ill-experienced" advocates (332). At best in works in the anti-ideology subgenre, a single literary or artistic text might survive as a monument to this historical vacuum.

This seemingly inescapable drive toward the apocalyptic abyss consistently provides a moment of closure for anti-ideology fiction, but it does not solve the problem of motivating the long middle of these narratives. In order for anti-ideology novels to undercut commitment, they have to identify, without enlivening, the ideas and political language whose barrenness they presume. They must develop plots that can sustain the conventional dialectical unfolding of history without ceding too quickly to an apocalyptic scenario that shuts down that process. They also need to convey the disappointment of former ideologues without boring their readers to tears with tedious passages demonstrating the vacuity of that self-same prose. Different tactics for tackling the problem of motivation create the greatest variation in this subset of the novel of revolution. Only Vollmann invests fully in the agonizing process of tracking the minute realignments of party lines—tracing, for instance, Dmitry Shostakovich's complex wrestling with Bolshevik imperatives over the last thirty years of his life. One or two authors follow Choi in providing descriptions of the mechanisms for generating ideological statements, focusing on the revolutionary cell's difficulty in accessing tape recorders, paper, and radio time, for example, as well as the psychology of the long sessions of self-criticism required to probe the cell members' commitment to the official line. Knowledge of these procedures then allows readers to decode the compromises and coercion underlying official pronouncements. To some extent, this interest in the mechanisms of ideological expression over narrative content derives from political thrillers, so we see similar devices in play in more generic interpretations of the anti-ideology novel, such as *Little America*. Brommell's CIA thriller describes the tactics that mid-twentieth-century operatives use to exert control over a fictional oil-rich Hashemite kingdom in the Middle East. These subversive ploys are, as is conventional for the genre, largely at odds with the democratic ideals espoused by American political leaders. However, Bromell twists that convention by suggesting that the ideology being undermined is not so much the liberal geopolitical rationale (freedom by any means necessary) as the spy's justification of his profession. The second layer of *Little America* follows, once again, a child (here, a son) digging into the archive of his parent's life. The procedures of the father-spy's work turn out to undercut even his own WASPy, patrician notion of political realism. Something of the same strategy informs Hilary Mantel's brilliant novel of the early phases of the English Reformation, *Wolf Hall* (2009). Her descriptions of the day-to-day tasks undertaken by the commoner Thomas Cromwell in his quest to become Henry VIII's most trusted adviser supplant any dry exploration of the theological controversies of the sixteenth century. This layer of narrative detail reinforces her interpretation of the Reformation as an essentially middle- or merchant-class rebellion against aristocratic privilege.

In addition to examining the procedures for generating ideology, rather than the ideology itself, many twenty-first-century novels focus on the emotional subtext of ideological speech. Parent–child quest narratives are especially prone to this approach. Some take this strategy to such extremes that ideological commitment disappears entirely into emotional concerns. Menéndez, for example, suggests that the erotic involvement with Che Guevara described by her narrator's mother in a lyrical but suitably vague manuscript was more likely the product of an obsessive, deprived imagination than an encounter in the physical world. No political thinking or observation animates this artist figure; she simply rhapsodizes about the earthy smell that her revolutionary lover emanates. Her personal devotion to the stinky revolutionary soon transforms into outright worship as she lives in penury, painting and repainting his iconic image.

Even when the revolutionary sympathizer's motives are not entirely emotional, but also contain a form of intellectual fulfillment—as, say, in Alvarez's novelization of the life of the Dominican poet Salomé Urena de Henríquez and Carolina De Robertis's depiction of the Tupamaro movement in Uruguay in *The Invisible Mountain* (2009)—the emotional content of the mother–child relationship still takes up more space in the foreground than does any account of the statements made in a political tenor. "We children had no idea what the fighting was about," Alvarez's Salomé asserts at the beginning of the first chapter. "One side was red and the other side was blue—color being the only way we could tell one side from the other" (13). Beginning as she will continue, in other words, Alvarez establishes her heroine's revolutionary credentials while expressing her narrator's near-total disregard for nuances of party or ideology. Although De Robertis is considerably more interested in distinguishing Peronist populism from Cuban Marxist-Leninism and Uruguayan nationalism than Alvarez is in differentiating the red and blue sides, both novelists share the strategy of linking a daughter's revolutionary or proto-revolutionary sensibility first to unusually deep empathy for the mother and second to lesbian desire. This entanglement of rebellious political and erotic lives is echoed by Choi (also lesbianism), Syjuco, Buruma, Firouz, and Kalfus—all of whom associate rebels with extra-marital longing. Descriptions of the emotional and physical aspects of desire displace accounts of the political dilemmas presumed to flower on the same tree. In some contexts, this emphasis on intimacy may be read as a concerted response to the excisions of certain populations (women, sexual minorities, children) from the heroic nation-building narratives of a previous generation; however, the popularity of this approach in works treating subjects that do not have a strong tradition of nationalist writing available in English (for example, Iranian fiction) suggests that it may relate just as much to the presumed prurience of American readers.

The last strategy that twenty-first-century authors use when attempting to depict the work of ideology in an anti-ideology narrative is elliptical shorthand. This can be a risky approach, since it relies somewhat on a reader's familiarity with obscure or topical subjects, but it does allow some entry into the intellectual world of the committed protagonist. Buruma's *China Lover* uses this strategy, providing ample detail, for example, about the recurring presence of anti-Semitism along the spectrum of Japanese ideologies that he examines and overusing phrases such as "our glorious national history" and "wonderful revolutionary leader" in his effort to portray the effects of ideology on reported speech. A more robust version of ideological shorthand appears in De Robertis's *Invisible Mountain*. Although spending more time with family letters than political documents, the novel contains several fine passages that survey popular discussions of public issues. "Everything's changed" one elliptical sequence begins: "It's temporary./ It's disastrous./ This is practically a dictatorship./ Oh, come on./ *You* come on. Look at the police./ True./ See?" (246). Compressed into an anonymous chorus, these non-narrative passages recall the form and diction of some of the pamphlets and spray-painted slogans described in the surrounding text, thus reinforcing rather than undercutting the urgency of that prose.

Perhaps the most effective use of the shorthand strategy, however, appears in *My Revolutions*, Kunzru's compelling narrative of the lesser-known British counterparts of the German Bader-Meinhof gang and the Italian Red Brigades. Like Choi, Kunzru emphasizes the demands of self-criticism and the social and emotional toll taken by isolation within a self-defining group organized around erotically charged, ascetic leaders. However, Kunzru quite elegantly counterbalances the potential for a purely psychological explanation not by emphasizing the themes of racial and familial community that

Choi underscores (even though these themes have figured prominently in some of his other work), but by allowing his hero to take a principled stand in the denouement. He finally betrays the revolutionary band to which he committed himself because he refuses to take a life. Rather than being led deeper into ideological compromises and twists and turns of political necessity, the hero remains faithful to the antiwar sentiments so painfully hammered out in the novel's earlier passages. Even while noting their devolution into an "acronymic jumble of letters" and their dispersal across a sprawling "international network with nodes in Frankfurt, Milan, Beirut, Bilbao," the hero continues to employ these principles ("armed love," "escape the binary madness of East and West") in order to extract himself from the most ironic consequences of the failed revolution (230). For Kunzru and a few of the other authors in this subgenre, the establishment of this kind of abbreviated, accelerated, but not entirely illegitimate ideological code motivates both the final exhausted turn away from ideology and the careful attention to its development illustrated in preceding passages.

While it is tempting to imagine that these different approaches to the problem of representing ideology correlate with particular political stances taken by the authors, this turns out not to be the case. The political spectrum represented by works in this group stretches from anarchist and libertarian left-wing social democracy (Vollmann, Kunzru, Alvarez, Meek, and De Robertis), through more centrist liberalism (Brommell, Kalfus, Mantel, and Firouz) and multicultural criticism of left-wing social democracy (Choi and Buruma), to largely apolitical or anti-political postmodernism (Syjuco and Menéndez). Literary strategies simply do not line up with political convictions; formal choices have no inherent political meaning in this genre. If, in other words, Fukuyama's thesis about the end of ideology seems to have been embraced by a number of authors whose fiction explores the nature of political commitment, his corollary about the inevitable triumph of liberal democratic principles does not follow. The anti-ideology novel is consistent in unraveling the coherence of committed worldviews of previous generations but importantly diverse in its range of sympathies in the present and variable in the literary strategies it employs.

TERROR IN THE NOVEL OF REVOLUTION

If the abandonment of the perhaps overly great coherence provided by ideology often leaves the novel of revolution in a condition of anxiety, that mood is heightened to an almost unbearable degree in fiction that explores the role of terror. While revolutionary narratives that grant some pride of place to ideological reasoning can frame violence as heroic self-sacrifice, a defense of universal human rights, or simply an expedient means to an end, post-ideology fiction rarely has this recourse. As Michael Hardt and Antonio Negri put it, in the twenty-first century, "distinctions between legitimate and illegitimate violence, between wars of liberation and wars of oppression, tend to blur."[27] Without ideology, neither states nor rebels find secure grounds for rationalizing the use of force in any widely persuasive sense. Lacking legitimation, any exercise of force can appear terroristic. Stripped of an ideological message, the violent non-state actor who may otherwise have been designated a revolutionary, rebel, or freedom fighter devolves into the terrorist, while states find it increasingly difficult in principle to distinguish themselves from these actors on any grounds other than size, longevity, and resources.

In the revolutionary novel, a contemporary concept of terroristic violence sometimes attaches to a single ideology or figure (for example, China's Mao, Ethiopia's Mengistu, or Iran's Khomeini), and the leader's irrational personal thirst for power motivates all violence. However, psycho-political entry into the inner lives of revolutionary icons is not a requirement for this subgenre. Just as often, the political passions of the mob or the state launch the terror narrative. The unifying element of this subgenre, in short, is not the political meaning attributed to revolutionary action but the reliance on the pulpy, passive body, figures rendered as if it were immediately, uncontroversially legible. This motif colors Kathryn Davis's *Versailles* (2003), Anchee Min's *Becoming Madame Mao* (2000), Maaza Mengiste's *Beneath the Lion's Gaze* (2009), Laleh Khadivi's *Age of Orphans* (2009), Dalia Sofer's *Septembers of Shiraz* (2007), Tahmina Anam's *Golden Age* (2007), and Rachel Kushner's *Telex from Cuba* (2008).

Each of these novels involves at least one memorably mangled body. *A Golden Age*, Anam's account of the struggle to wrest an independent Bangladesh from the grip of the Pakistani army, for example, returns repeatedly to descriptions of the bloody fingers of Sabeer, a largely apolitical newlywed whose fingernails were extracted by counterrevolutionary torturers. The plot of Mengiste's novel, which describes the overthrow of Emperor Haile Selassie of Ethiopia, turns on the meaning of another torture tactic—the wrapping of the victim's body in plastic to prevent blood spatter; this crucial detail finally reveals the identity of the anonymous young woman brought to the protagonist's hospital in the opening pages. Khadivi builds her lyric novel about Iranian Kurds under the shah around a similar figure of the massacred mother.

Memories of this loss motivate her son as he becomes a state-sanctioned torturer himself—raping women with his rifle once he is conscripted into the
shah's army. The titular age of orphans quickly becomes for Khadivi an age of
terroristic vengeance for deprivation.

The burned body of a wealthy father signals essentially the same theory of
the avenging torturer in Sofer's narrative of Jews in revolutionary Iran. Only
the father's calculated admission of responsibility for the poverty that his torturer endured during the shah's regime and his questionable promise of financial restitution secures his release. Similarly, Min begins *Becoming Madame
Mao*, her novelization of the biography of Mao's third, widely hated wife,
with a graphic description of the pus-infused foot-binding cloths that Jiang
Ching reportedly tore off as a child. Min attributes the future Madame Mao's
relentless pursuit of power to her need to compensate for the agonizing pain
caused by foot-binding. In a related effort to link a specifically female experience of the body to revolutionary terror, Davis's *Versailles* describes the rise
of the French Revolution exclusively through the sensory world of Marie Antoinette—focusing in its final pages not on the mob's reactions to her famous
beheading but on the queen's own experience of her physicality. In a final act
of rebellion, as Davis would have it, Marie Antoinette "removed the bloody
rag [from] between [her] legs, rolled it up, and stuffed it in a chink in the
wall" before her once heavily adorned hair is shorn for execution (201–202).
Imperial figures from the French court to the palaces of Haile Selassie (who
"walked through his marble halls and to his royal throne, removed himself
from the mustiness of mud walls and the undignified stench of his own body"
[Mengiste 75]) exist in relation to a contaminating viscerality rather than the
spectacle, publicity, and/or symbolic presence of the divine in this fiction.
The revolutionary leaders themselves provide some of the most powerful and
obsessively reproduced images of the terrorized body; their terroristic violence
derives, we infer, from a resentful preoccupation with their own physicality.

In all these recent novels of revolution, though, including those unconcerned with political leaders, images of the bloody, oozing, viscous body on
the verge of death recur. The acts of torture that produce this damaged flesh
are regularly traced back to physical suffering on the part of the torturer (usually hunger), and this translation of hunger into violence triggers continuing
cycles of bloody retribution.[28] Mengiste, for example, populates her Addis
Ababa with hordes of corpses and turns her one-time revolutionary student
hero into a collector and burier of the dead. One damaged or bloody body
acts on another, we are shown, and in this fiction these acts are essentially

apolitical. No matter what ideology they claim to endorse, the torturers serve the goddess of their own rage and pain. "You should never have gone abroad, should never have worn that priceless white pearl necklace and that pair of black high-heeled shoes," Min's Madame Mao fumes before arranging the public humiliation and brutal interrogation of her rival, Wang Guang-mei; "you should never have stolen my role. . . . Take your turn across my stage of hell" (285). Any public political explanation for torture merely serves as a screen for intensely personal visceral responses in the novel of revolutionary terror.

In this fiction, however, it is important to notice that the primary image of the damaged body is not the corpse. Although corpses certainly appear—from the numerous bodies in *Beneath the Lion's Gaze* to the heads stuck on pikes by angry Jacobins in *Versailles* and the prisoner rapidly executed by a cynical guerrilla in a demonstration killing in Kushner's *Telex from Cuba*—the most powerful images are those of the still throbbing, pulpy flesh. The terror narrative requires that the body retain some memory of agony and that whoever observes the torture empathizes to some degree with the sensation of abuse. Rather than being understood in a strategic or tactical sense, the exercise of force has the putatively moral status of an injury; political or ideological elements are reduced to "local motives," when the "main purpose and outcome of war" are understood to be fleshly.[29] As an infliction of collective injury, terror takes a step outside time into a place where borders are undifferentiated and unendurable sensations swamp all cognitive functioning—when "she could no longer tell which body parts had leaked which stains on the cement floor," as De Robertis's heroine puts it in the torture sequence in *The Invisible Mountain* (303). Reduced to raw sensation, the world of the terrorized body lacks contour, history, and volition. In scale, it is both enormous and primary (encompassing the entire physical universe) and minuscule (shrinking to the millimeters of contact between the skin and any external objects). The universe of this terrorized body is also fundamentally singular and irreducible. Public rhetoric of the sort produced by Madame Mao in her operatic efforts to extract propaganda value from physical suffering is always imagined as falsified in this fiction. The closing passages of Khadivi's novel, which find her aged soldier alone in the mountains seeking access to the legends and rituals of the Kurds whom he was forced to subjugate, are typical. On occasion, erotic or gastronomic pleasure can overcome the torture victim's isolation, but the restoration of a capacity for these sensations is in no way guaranteed. Hovering so close to death, the terrorized body usually does not survive the detailed episodes of crisis that feature so prominently in this fiction.

This insistent emphasis on sensation occurs in the context of an assault on ideological reasoning that authorizes violence. Recent revolutionary fiction depicts the revolutionary impulse and movement as faltering once it is faced with the brute physicality of bloody suffering; moving portrayals of the less dramatic condition of chronic food shortages, back-breaking and humiliating labor, or endemic poverty and exclusion from institutions of power (all treated as legitimate motives in revolutionary fiction of earlier decades)[30] give way to accounts of the physical losses exacted by the revolutionary struggle itself. Despite this anti-ideological climate, though, the literary effect of the description of the terrorized body retains a political charge. Few, if any, novels of revolution are entirely impartial in their accounts of terror. Even depictions of protracted civil wars (as in the Russian experience) tend to stack the corpses up higher in one corner than in the others, and novelists are, of course, under no obligation to adhere to the historical record when enumerating atrocities. The authors of fiction devoted to describing revolutionary terror focus their imaginative powers wherever they like, attaching responsibility for the damaged body to whom- or whatever they perceive as the most horrifying villain.

For Anam and Khadivi, for example, portrayals of terror serve nationalist agendas—a victorious nationalism for the former and an unfulfilled one for the latter. Min's and Davis's complementary explorations of widely reviled female leaders suggest that they are testing the limits of a universalizing feminist empathy. Sofer, Mengiste, and Kushner examine revolutionary terror from the point of view of educated, relatively wealthy exiles and, to varying degrees, use memories of terror to position themselves as critics of revolution, even if they are also critics of the counter-revolutionaries (as in Kushner's description of the American families of United Fruit Company executives evacuated from Cuba). In short, the bloody body is not nearly as politically transparent or morally legible as its status as a replacement for ideological confusion might suggest. It conveys a range of political attitudes, some of which recall the confused official logic surrounding the American so-called war on terror: the opposition between *their* (irrational, excessive, illegitimate, and fanatical) terror and *our* (just, proportionate, nobly sacrificial, and non-dogmatic) war, for example. The terror subgenre of the revolutionary novel provides a host of historical analogues for reflecting on the meanings that terror and terrorism have acquired in the new millennium, even while it challenges readers to recognize, often from an apocalyptically heightened sense of judgment, the horrific toll exacted by revolutionary experiences in earlier decades.

WRITING THE SOCIAL REVOLUTION

Because the terror novel returns so obsessively to sensory experience, it exceeds even the anti-ideology novel in its renunciation of historical knowledge. At its farthest extreme, the terror novel sinks into a pure immediacy from which it imagines no remove. This habit makes any vision of the cessation of revolutionary upheaval very difficult to achieve—as well as any account of social reorganization—since the passage of time, let alone collective human activity, has been rendered nonsensical. There is simply no world or process on the other side of terror in this view: specific incidents that trigger terror may subside, but the condition never disappears. There is no life after terror—only a perpetual present. The anti-ideology novel also undercuts a vision of life after the revolution, because it so strongly links post-revolutionary failures to the errors of leaders and/or fellow travelers. All that remains after the revolution is its reversal and betrayal, in this version. Both of the most common variations on the revolutionary novel share a foundation, in other words, in their erasure of the social revolution—the process that, according to Skocpol, reveals how "basic changes in social structure and in political structure occur together in a mutually reinforcing fashion. And these changes occur together in intense sociopolitical conflicts in which class struggle plays a role."[31] For Skocpol and many others on the left, post-revolutionary social transformation necessarily relates to and reinforces political struggle; the social—especially class-based—revolution is the necessary completion of a process initiated by the seizure of political power.

Although Skocpol's account of the causes of social revolution has attracted scrutiny in recent decades,[32] her periodization of revolutions into two steps is not uncommon. Slavoj Žižek's recent reconsideration of Lenin's political theory also centers on this theme. "The fundamental lesson of revolutionary materialism," he writes, "is that revolution must strike twice."[33] We can easily lose sight of the second, or social, revolution, however, because its slower processes usually lack the glamour and exhilaration of political upheaval. As Neil Lazarus has argued in his study of West African literature of the 1970s, literary forms for exploring dramatic military and political events often come more readily to hand than do those that can describe the difficult, long-term process of rebuilding social life on new foundations.[34] Furthermore, the quotidian aspects of the social revolution are explicitly cultural—sometimes threatening precisely those niches of entrenched power that artists and intellectuals have carved out for themselves. "For a social revolution to be successful," Manning

Marable argues, "the classes or social groups who are being governed from above must crack the hegemony of ideas, values and belief held by their own people and others who perpetuate and rationalize the status quo."[35] Writing the social revolution, in other words, involves not only describing the transformation of social structures but also engaging with the writer's own position in the cultural processes that have contained and constrained revolution. By contrast, the novels of ideology and terror make the literary a space of refuge from systemic thinking and physical pain; any hegemonic functions of the literary recede behind their compensatory pleasures. Perhaps the necessity of grappling with this difficult problem helps explain why novels of social revolution are the least common twenty-first-century variant of the revolutionary novel.

The most direct approach to the novel of social revolution appears in Christina García's *Monkey Hunting* (2003). Her sketches of post-revolutionary Havana focus on the ethics and medical practices of the Chinese community in Cuba. The hero, Chen Pan, signs on as an indentured laborer in Cuba during the dictatorship of Fulgencio Batista, escapes from a brutal sugar plantation, and establishes a new identity as an antiques dealer. The novel deepens its sympathetic portrait of Chen's post-exilic longings by making his situation analogous to the questions of racial and sexual discrimination explored by his Afro-Asian son and lesbian niece. Several of García's vignettes stress the emergence of unanticipated cultural encounters after the revolution. New couples emerge, and their interracial and transnational unions rattle the powers that be and extend revolutionary solidarity to cultural conflicts. This description of social change as a process that survives and supersedes political revolution recalls themes of the anti-ideology novel, and García's emphasis on the comforts provided by sex and food retains important motifs from terror fiction and the migrant novel. In both contexts, cuisine sustains cultural memory as well as the body. As in so many other recent revolutionary novels, depictions of political conflicts surrounding food distribution and other unmet material needs are supplanted by cultural questions. As an indentured servant, for example, Chen endures the insult of unsalted rice gruel, but his deprivation is described as aesthetic, not economic or even physical. What he needs, it turns out, is not a higher caloric intake but *croque monsieurs*, "tiny pickles and beer," "steamed mussels in wine broth," and "rum punch"—in short, assimilation into Cuban food culture (142). These tasty treats and many others in similar passages suggest that cultural needs overpower political or economic suffering in *Monkey Hunting*.

When culture is detached from economics, the scandal of the plantation system rests on its reliance on residual racism, not the organization of labor. In *Monkey Hunting*, anti-black prejudice unites Chinese and Spanish Cubans, but it is symbolically overcome by transcontinental monkey stories, much as a medley of transnational folk medicines soothe Lucrecia, Chen Pan's "Congolese" wife. As in Gerald Vizenor's *Griever* (1986), which interweaves Native American and Chinese trickster stories, *Monkey Hunting* finds cultural hybridization more transformative than political struggle. In this respect, García's vision aligns with revisionist accounts of revolution.

More historically sweeping and, from the point of view of mainstream American liberalism, politically unconventional approaches to the topic of social revolution appear in Madison Smartt Bell's trilogy on the Haitian revolution—*All Souls' Rising* (1995), *Master of the Crossroads* (2004), and *The Stone That the Builder Refused* (2006)—and Peter Carey's *Parrot and Olivier in America* (2009). Both authors set themselves the difficult task of describing the social context and effects of eighteenth-century political revolutions. Without giving in to the temptation to psychologize the revolutionary leader and without ignoring cultural conflicts, both take the project of social transformation as their central drama. Bell and Carey convey their judgments of the known failures of the Haitian and American revolutions, respectively while exploring the tangled motives, ideologies, opportunities, and conflicts that shaped each rebellion.

Bell's deeply researched trilogy describes the rising and cresting action of the first successful black revolution in the Western Hemisphere from multiple points of view. His carefully balanced cast of characters immerses the reader in the mental worlds of male and female white planters, maroons and practitioners of Vodun, military leaders and soldiers, French liberals and smallholder Jacobins, and members of Toussaint L'Ouverture's forces, as well as the many facets of the mixed-race urban milieu. Antoine Hébert, a newly arrived French doctor who is searching for his sister (who disappeared, along with her child), provides the first point of entry into the colonial milieu. His reasoned responses to the naked violence used to maintain order on the plantations, as well as his resistance to racial hierarchy, establishes his credentials as a vehicle of sympathy for contemporary readers. With scientific foresight, he rejects the fictions of radical racial difference used to bolster the slave economy and exposes the duplicity of the logic of the planter class. He attacks, for example, the belief that "*la bienfaisance* had arranged the constitution of the Negro so that he (like the mule again) could best be retained in the path of virtue by beating and whipping" (*All Souls' Rising* 136). By the end of the first volume of the trilogy, Hébert has been partially integrated into Haitian society, having fathered a child with a mulatto courtesan and taken charge of his sister's plantation. His is a new kind of plantation, though—housing Toussaint's troops and offering medical care to its nonetheless still enslaved laborers. Hébert's integration is thus also a kind of captivity,[36] developing out of his largely involuntary service as a medic in Toussaint's army. This captivity motif makes the doctor a portal not only between present to past, but also between racially marked antagonists in revolutionary Haiti. Like the trilogy and the revolution itself, he is occupied and possessed by several forces.

The logic of possession is vital to Bell's writing. A practitioner of Vodun rites,[37] Bell has described the writing of historical fiction as a process of being mounted by the dead, much as a Vodun worshipper becomes the horse for Loa. Considered from this angle, his polyphonic narrative integrates the Enlightenment desire for balance in complex systems with the intricate patterns of a *vévé* (the elaborate, highly symmetrical drawings created during a Vodun ceremony). Bell's trilogy builds up the rising action of the revolution by allowing the Loa with different temperaments to claim center stage. His narrative alternates between the pacific Ghede and the martial Petro rites, moving from town or plantation to military encampments, and in each location a range of figures appear—from Madame Arnaud (who invokes the French-speaking Loa Mistress Charlotte) to the doctor's lover, Nanon (an erotic Erzulie). Central to this Vodun metahistory,[38] though, is the most devout practitioner depicted in the work, the one-time maroon-turned-soldier-turned-maroon, Riau.

From Riau's perspective, we discover the roots and goals of the revolution for a major swath of Toussaint's followers. Born in Africa, like the vast majority of slaves on the brutal Haitian plantations, Riau seeks a return. He describes the Vodun figure of the crossroads as the point where access to Africa/La Guinée opens:

> The whitemen believe that everything is a story. In their world that may
> be so. I will never live there. What men may do is flat like a road and goes
> along the skin of the world but because it does not begin in one place or
> end in another it is not a road at all. At the crossroads is where we must
> always meet but the other road does not lie on the earth. It comes out
> of the sky down the *poteau mitan* and through the earth *en bas de l'eau*,
> where Guinée is the sunken island beneath the waters, where the *loa* wait

to meet us. That is the cross and what it means and it is everywhere. (*All Souls' Rising* 27)

For Riau, the revolution—like ritual ecstasy—offers this plunge beneath the waters, a return not to the geographical space of Africa but to its metaphysical significance, its status as a world beyond the visible earth. Although, as Bell's narrative is careful to remind us, Toussaint was a professed Christian and banned Vodun worship from his encampments, Riau's understanding of the revolution as a crossroads space organized around the *poteau mitan* (center pole) of the symbolic leader informs the trilogy. Bell's depiction of the campaigns, rhetoric, and logic of revolution pivot around this sense that the entire world—including both political and cultural registers—is altered by the revolution.

For this reason, Bell's Haitian trilogy does not read like a narrative of a failed revolution, even though it is punctuated and framed by passages following Toussaint's imprisonment in France. Because Bell is so centrally concerned with the social logic of slavery, colonial racial hierarchy, and religious practice, the fallen leader's fate does not determine the outcome of the revolution. Bell also actively resists analogies between contemporary Haiti's tragedies and the revolution. His narrative instead describes the emergence of new social forms (publicly acknowledged interracial coupling, the social advancement of mulatto officers, multiracial communities of care, new forms of social isolation, the unlearning and relearning of racially charged language, and so on) made possible by the revolution. He presents a culturally specific, Vodun-influenced account of the political events that lay the groundwork for social change.

The task of assessing a social revolution in progress is also central to Carey's selective retelling of Alexis de Tocqueville's travels in the new American republic. Beginning in rural England and France during the late eighteenth and early nineteenth centuries, *Parrot and Olivier* initially appears to be contrasting the effects of revolutionary thought on a radical printer's son and a politically conflicted French aristocrat. The English Parrot, although sympathetic to the underground radical movement, loses more by it when his activist father is arrested and he is forced to flee his homeland for France; the French Olivier, although only dabbling in rebellion to annoy his reactionary family, benefits from revolution in his country more fully. For one thing, he remains the sheltered master who takes Parrot, as his would-be servant, with him on a tour of the new United States. He continues to exercise aristocratic privilege even when the bonds of servitude dissolve on the pair's arrival in Philadelphia. In the American setting, Parrot and Olivier's finances make them dependent on each other (for wages and co-signing of notes), as does their complicated shipboard rivalry for the affections of Mathilde, a liberated painter. In the American passages, the novel's focus shifts, in other words, from the dissolution of feudal bonds to the formation of a new system of market-driven class relations. Carey's novel suggests that the American social revolution continues to struggle with a feudal legacy of inequality.

Aesthetically, for example, Parrot and Olivier are complementary rather than equal. Parrot's narration is characterized by earthy, tender passages. He reflects, for instance, that Mathilde and her mother are to him "both so dear, so familial, so fond of me and I of them, and if they had been at the wine an hour or two before I got there, that was how we lived. I liked it, our sour red mouth" (92). Olivier's narration, by contrast, has an icier, more analytic tone, benefiting from the moments when it is disrupted by amazing discoveries—for example, the fizz of soda water, the energy of corn-husking machines, and the wonders of carbon paper. In the second half of the novel, the two plots diverge for some time, and the two heroes fall into parallel sorts of ruin—as they risk domestication in America. Only when they encounter each other again in the penultimate scene does the full impact of the incomplete middle-class social revolution in the United States become evident. When a bedraggled Olivier arrives at his former servant's home on the Hudson after choosing not to marry an American heiress, he obliviously appropriates Parrot and Mathilde's best bedroom, even though he is very much a "former master" by this point (370). Parrot has largely transformed himself and unlearned the habits of a professional manservant. Olivier, however, has not remade himself as fully. Like the wealthy Americans with whom he has been socializing, he romanticizes an aristocratic life that he cannot renounce, imagining that it can persist without an underclass. Frustrated that he can live as neither a full-fledged democrat nor an aristocrat, Olivier drunkenly berates Parrot in a brilliant screed derived from *Democracy in America*. Olivier predicts that as an American, Parrot will

> follow fur traders and woodsmen as [his] presidents, and they will be as barbarians at the head of armies, ignorant of geography and science, the leaders of a mob daily educated by a perfidious press which will make them so confident and ignorant that the only books on their shelves will be instruction manuals, the only theater gaudy spectacles and the

paintings made to please that vulgar class of bankers, men of no moral character, half-bourgeois and half-criminal, who will affect the tastes of an aristocracy but will compete with each other like wrestlers at a fair, wishing only to pay the highest price for the most fashionable artist. (380)

This vision of cultural degradation is quickly and ironically rejected in the closing dedication. "There is no tyranny in America, nor ever could be," Parrot responds. "Your horrid visions concerning fur traders are groundless. The great ignoramus will not be elected. The illiterate will never rule" (381). Carey leaves his two protagonists locked in an ongoing dispute about post-revolutionary culture. Their interdependence negates both Parrot's vision of a total democratic revolution and Olivier's revisionist longing for a self-perpetuating aristocracy. Carey sets two versions of the revolutionary novel against each other, overturning in the process triumphalist narratives of the United States as the enemy of tyranny as well as anti-American narratives of the "half-bourgeois and half-criminal" leadership of the new nation.

Although Carey is Australian by birth and has lived in New York for many years, his unwriting of American exceptionalism probably should not be entirely chalked up to an expatriate's skepticism about the default ideologies of the host country. Carey does, after all, delight in the trickster possibilities allowed by the philistine environment of the New World. His painters, for example, engage in an elaborate system of forgeries, funded in part by their successful efforts at insurance fraud. This system allows them to produce high-quality Audubon-style art books that are marketed back to the aristocrats of Europe. There is art in Carey's America, even if it is best appreciated elsewhere. Also, his retelling of Tocqueville's travels pointedly avoids reproducing the historical French aristocrat's damning portrait of slavery in the southern states. Rather than taking cheap shots at banality and materialism, he relates the strange ideals of the Americans (as Parrot and Olivier understand them) to European revolutions that the Americans in the novel seem only dimly to comprehend. The rapid swerve outward to Australia that takes place midway through the novel serves much the same function—situating pro- and anti-revolutionary attitudes in a broader geopolitical vision. Taking that long view, Parrot finally tones down Olivier's apocalyptic judgments: "[A] man could not be angry with a child of the awful guillotine," he reflects; "[Olivier] sighed and walked up to the house alone, poor sausage" (380). On this kinder note, the dispute between Carey's two heroes over the nature of social revolution gives way to problems of historical memory and a nearly maternal empathy.

Social Revolution in Post-Apocalyptic Fiction

If the writings of García, Bell, and Carey are any indication, fictional tours of social revolution have achieved less generic consistency than have the anti-ideology and terror variants on the novel of revolution. Their tonal range veers from comedy and lyric to metahistorical romance, and their scope extends from brief impressionistic vignettes to multi-volume epics. Perhaps for this reason, a number of authors who choose to address the social revolution have moved away from historical fiction altogether and taken a major detour through the apocalyptic novel. A durable and flexible genre, apocalyptic narrative attracted a flurry of critical attention in the late 1980s and early 1990s as part of the end-of-history debate,[39] and another burst of narratives in this form has, perhaps predictably, appeared since 2000. The theological interests evident in some of the new apocalyptic fiction show the influence of the passage of the millennium mark itself, as well as the attacks on the World Trade Center and the Pentagon on September 11, 2001, but the most prominent concerns of the narratives are the long-lived themes of environmental, technological, and/or epidemiological catastrophe. The open question of what kind of social life, if any, might survive a devastating material collapse links this genre to the overtly political themes of the historical novel in general and the revolutionary novel in particular. Precisely in their interest in the day-to-day mechanics of survival[40] and the radiant relics they find scattered around their devastated landscapes, apocalyptic narratives provide crucial figures for social revolutions yet to come.

Although relatively uninterested in specific policies or crises,[41] twenty-first-century post-apocalyptic narratives such as Cormac McCarthy's *The Road* (2006), Kevin Brockmeier's *Brief History of the Dead* (2006), Jim Crace's American narrative *The Pesthouse* (2007), Marcel Theroux's *Far North* (2009), Margaret Atwood's *Year of the Flood* (2009), and Chris Adrian's *Children's Hospital* (2006) share the revolutionary novel's concern for collective life. These works concentrate on describing the protagonists' passage through a damaged land and their quest for other survivors with whom to make common cause. They seek the grounds of a new social relation and often cling, rather desperately, to messianic visions of the child—whether from the point of view of the father (*The Road*), the mother (*Far North*), or a new collective sexual subject (*The Year of the Flood*). Inhabiting, like Brockmeier's protagonists, a transitional city of the dead, the subjects of the post-apocalyptic novel convey an intense need for new modes of survival and the reproduction of the social unit. These are oddly hopeful works; they typically devote less of their narrative energy to horror than to the slow crawl out of the wreckage and toward signs of other survivors.

That said, a complex disappointment in most versions of reform features prominently in the apocalyptic novel. Atwood, for example, offers a scathing satire of the cultish aspects of veganism as well as the agribusiness opposed by these purists, and Theroux's anti-modern Quaker settlers in Siberia appear just as woefully unprepared for the brutality released by social breakdown as do Adrian's doctors and Brockmeier's theologians. Crace takes particularly pointed potshots at religious fundamentalists in his depiction of the so-called Finger Baptists, an anti-metallurgy sect that pushes nostalgia for agrarian feudalism to a dangerous extreme. Nonetheless, this familiar disassembling of ideological systems should not overshadow the fact that these apocalyptic novels continue to hold out a vision of a regenerated social order as their ideal. In comparison with the relentless skepticism of the anti-ideology novel, in particular, these futuristic scenarios allow a greater portion of revelatory salvation to survive the chaotic disarray imagined as endemic at the end of the world.

These novels are also not especially interested in assigning blame for the apocalypse or detailing its causes. Although Brockmeier implicates Coca-Cola in the dissemination of an anthrax-like plague, the mechanics of that corporate malfeasance are never specified. He concentrates instead on the foolishness of a former public-relations officer's exhausting efforts to cover up evidence of culpability that has survived in the afterlife. Brockmeier's motif is erasure, not destruction, and *The Brief History of the Dead* fittingly concludes with the final disappearance of the dead people recalled by the last human survivor of a pandemic. At that moment, even the cause of all this disappearance itself disappears. This interest in the aftereffects of an event with an indeterminate cause arguably defines the genre as a whole. The German critic Klaus Scherpe, for one, has asserted that in postmodern narratives, there really is no need to describe the causes of apocalypse, since genetic manipulation, nuclear threat, and environmental degradation are among the routine dangers of the social world as we know it. "The producibility of the catastrophe *is* the catastrophe," Scherpe proclaims; no single catastrophic event appears singularly dramatic.[42] The total social situation and all positions on it bear responsibility for catastrophic collapse.

If, for this reason, ideology as a problem largely disappears from the postapocalyptic vision of social revolution, so, too, does terror—or, at least, the site of terror shifts from politically motivated, factional torture to the risks taken in a desperate quest for food, clothing, and shelter. Although extreme violence (especially rape and enslavement) is a staple of this fiction, it results not from the intellectual errors or miscalculations of any single group but from the common condition of scarcity. The treatment of cannibalism by McCarthy in *The Road*, for example, is notable more for its level of detail than its uniqueness. The same motif appears, although less centrally, in Atwood's *Year of the Flood* and Theroux's *Far North*, as well as in Paul Auster's earlier contribution to the genre, *In the Country of Last Things* (1987). When resources are limited, these authors suggest, people cluster around certain valuable commodities—including, where possible, the vulnerable human body. Terror then derives not so much from specific events or ideas as from proximity to the other person's or group's perpetual hunger, while by extension safety arises mainly in nomadic foraging.

This last motif explains why of these several neotribal visions, Atwood's is the rosiest. However silly the rituals of the vegan sect she imagines initially appear to her two protagonists, their beatification of Saint Euell Gibbons (among others) does prove vital. Atwood's survivors of the Waterless Flood ultimately endure because they intentionally preserve a kind of traditional knowledge that outlasts the delusions of plague-ridden, hyper-commercial Gomorrah. The members of the God's Gardeners cult become the monks of a new Dark Age, providing continued access to ecological knowledge on the verge of disappearing. In this respect, their activities resemble the archival habits of Theroux's protagonist, Makepeace Hatfield; she squirrels away thousands of volumes of books that she is unable to read (as well as a pianola that she cannot play), while her destructive nemesis parasitically pillages old scientific sites. Similarly, in a society that has lost the capacity to produce metals, Crace's heroine makes a talisman of single penny, saving this evidence of a lost world. In all these visions, new sustainable groups—the seeds of the social revolution—form around collections of auratic texts, while menacing antagonists cluster around the human commodity. In the tradition of apocalyptic narratives stretching back at least as far as the biblical book of Daniel, the glowing word (sometimes, as in a crucial passage in Theroux's *Far North*, reduced to fire itself) provides the contact point between the worlds that precede and follow catastrophe. The perpetual wandering of new tribes carrying the word offers the apocalyptist's best hope for a post-revolutionary renewal.

Granted, the uniformly small size of these visions of primitive communism lends an anarchic, even libertarian, flavor to twenty-first-century accounts of the social revolution. No states or state functionaries ever seem to survive environmental or epidemiological crisis, and communication networks also disappear when the technologies that enable them collapse. (Brockmeier's last woman alive, for example, "had never known any software designers, so there were no software designers. She had known plenty of petty customer service types, and street people, and dirty screaming kids," and so these low-tech isolates are the most common survivors in the city of the dead [183].) Political revolution becomes impossible in novels that imagine a catastrophe without causality, because there is no state power to seize. Even the family patriarch is a morally compromised figure in most of these works, and sexual violence is endemic. Only as long as the new tribes organize themselves around principles other than ownership of the woman, it is suggested, might a more viable form of the state emerge. The rather surprising preponderance of female survivors and narrators of the apocalypse suggests that a social revolution built on a foundation of gender egalitarianism starts with the small group. (Strikingly, racial egalitarianism hardly figures in this body of writing, and several works continue the pattern that Jacqueline Foertsch describes as the "servant-savior-savant" treatment of nonwhite characters in science fiction of the 1950s.)[43] These are, in short, visions of social revolution stripped of the public and political forum and all the attendant issues of the large group. Urban concentrations of population, wealth, and knowledge—along with specialization of labor and development of the commodity form—are typically envisioned as antithetical to sustainable social organization. The nomadic, flexible, regendered social group that apocalyptic fiction places at the foundation of the new order requires a new spatial and social form through which to express itself.

Emerging from the ruins of twentieth-century revolutionary fiction (and movements), then, we find a self-consciously restricted social sphere that is detached from the traces of political action, yet still containing within itself important symbols of continuity with dissenting and literate traditions. Perhaps these apocalyptic visions, together with the complex ironies of Bell's and Carey's unraveling of New World democratic revolutions, are the closest that twenty-first-century writers can currently come to sustained visions of social renewal, given that so many contemporary initiatives are organized around an aggressive neoliberal assault on the state. Chapter 3 argues that direct depictions of the landscape of neoliberalism are far more advanced in twenty-first-century fiction devoted to the international than to the domestic setting. In this chapter, the relevant corollary might be that while political revolution is as still possible to imagine in historical fiction, the social rebuilding associated with successful egalitarian alternatives to neoliberalism remains, for the foreseeable future, a speculative endeavor in U.S. fiction. Urgent as the social revolution appears to many authors, its depiction requires taking a step out of the framework of the nation as we know it and into worlds elsewhere—or, if I may put it this way, elsewhen. To envision the social revolution in twenty-first-century U.S. fiction requires a move past the end of history into another time frame altogether.

5 TOWARD THE WORLD NOVEL

Genre Shifts in Twenty-First-Century Expatriate Fiction

> The dream of the great American novel is past. We need to write the global novel.
> Maxine Hong Kingston, "The Novel's Next Step"

> I am working myself up to writing a kind of epic global novel. I suppose a lot of people are always working themselves up to writing that kind of novel.
> Kazuo Ishiguro, "In Conversation with Kazuo Ishiguro"

S INCE AT LEAST the late 1980s, one of the great ambitions of a certain type of contemporary writer has been the invention of the "world" novel. Maxine Hong Kingston, Kazuo Ishiguro, and others have imagined a new "epic" that spans many locations, documents the simultaneous and multidirectional movements of the world's populations, and registers without being swamped by the new communication technologies. They hope that such works will address the major issues of our era, including peace, ecological crisis, and nuclear threats. Modeled in part on the meatiest nineteenth-century Russian social novels, the new global fiction they envision will be long and macrocosmic, and it will incorporate the many kinds of English spoken in the urban crossroads of the new world order. The world novel, in other words, moves geopolitical fiction from the local and personal scale of the "Peace Corps novel" to a vaster global canvas.

Kingston conceives of the world novel as replacing that Holy Grail of an earlier generation—the so-called great American novel.[1] Yet several of the features thought to characterize the world novel also seem to derive from the earlier form: multi-stranded narration, broad geographical reach, cosmopolitan ethics, multilingual sensitivity, and a renewed commitment to realism.[2] With the possible exception of multilingualism, all these characteristics could describe John Dos Passos's *U.S.A.* trilogy (1930–1936), for example, as well as they characterize recent novels celebrated for their worldliness, such as Junot Díaz's *Brief Wondrous Life of Oscar Wao* (2007), Chimamanda Ngozi Adichie's *Half of a Yellow Sun* (2006), and Shirley Geok-lin Lim's *Joss and*

Gold (2001). The world novel may not replace the ambitious national novel so much as grow out of it and extend its vision.

Recognizing this continuity in form, a number of critics have identified national narratives that may inspire the nascent project of the global novel. Benedict Anderson proposes José Rizal's classic of the Filipino anti-imperial movement, *El Filibusterismo* (1891), as a model, while Malcolm Bradbury offers Angus Wilson's East–West fantasy, *As If By Magic* (1973), and Guy Reynolds suggests *Worlds of Color* (1961), the final volume of W. E. B. DuBois's trilogy of African American family life. Timothy Brennan's candidate for a proto-global fiction is Julio Cortázar's *Hopscotch* (1963), and Salman Rushdie's somewhat underrated novel of Bombay musicians turned international celebrities, *The Ground Beneath Her Feet* (2000), has been mentioned more than once in this context as well. Kingston herself names Mario Vargas Llosa's apocalyptic vision of a Brazilian community of outsiders in *The War of the End of the World* (1981) as an inspiration.[3]

Sometimes the influence of this state-of-the-nation fiction on the geopolitical novel is thought to be a liability, as in Joseph Slaughter's critical assessment of the influence of the Goethian bildungsroman on human-rights talk and the postcolonial novel,[4] but this not always the case. In *Culture in the Age of Three Worlds*, Michael Denning imaginatively pairs his own suspicion of the "marketing category" of the world novel with an investigation into mid-twentieth-century American proletarian literature. Denning suggests that the best global fiction (Gabriel García Márquez and José Saramago) grows out of the dialogue between nationalism and internationalism developed by an earlier generation of leftist writers; he contrasts this critical internationalism with the blander international style favored by multinational media conglomerates in the present, urging its revival.[5] Although the specific ideologies of the left-wing writers whom Denning discusses rarely seem to be explicitly affirmed in U.S. fiction of past ten or twenty years, his periodization suggests a method for explaining the transition from national narrative to world novel. Extrapolating from Denning, we can hypothesize that the world novel arrives when the genres of national writing reach out to incorporate politically charged elements of the global scene. Straining against the limits of national models, the new global fiction invents methods and resuscitates certain aspects of an older literary internationalism in its effort to wrestle with the conditions of the present. The world novel emerges when the generic syntax of the national novel cross-breeds with older genres. These syntactic innovations allow the world novel to grapple with contemporary semantic material.[6]

Without contesting this pattern for the emergence of new genres, not all observers agree that the threshold for the world novel has been reached. In his survey of contemporary fiction, Bruce Robbins asserts that "generic rules . . . severely limit the instruction [that the American novel] can deliver about the world and America's place in it." Among the constraining principles that Robbins identifies is the rule that "history abroad will never be less than an atrocity" that motivates celebratory immigration narratives, along with the corollary that these atrocities will be represented by way of "mercifully short" narrative detours.[7] To the extent that recent American fiction travels abroad, according to Robbins, it remains captive to the expatriate's narrative of romantic or erotic self-discovery. Even though this story may occasionally shade off into ethical questions posed by do-gooders or an occasional investigation of commodity logic, by and large new fiction, in Robbins's view, tells us little about the world because it insists on laying blame for international problems either too forcefully or too lightly at the door of Americans. Robbins concludes that no fully "worldly" fiction has yet appeared in the most recent U.S. literature because twentieth-century formulas for describing the adventures of American travelers still have too strong a hold.

While Robbins's account of the absurdist strain in contemporary expatriate narrative is as compelling as his treatment of expatriation as the root narrative for the world novel, his assertion that the norms of the genre remain fixed in twenty-first-century fiction is less persuasive. Many other genres of contemporary fiction have proved quite flexible—from the proto-digital migrant narrative to the new thrillers, neoliberal allegories, and revolutionary fictions—and the same is true of the expatriate novel. Authors of expatriate fiction have heeded calls for the renewal of the political novel just as closely as have those in other genres.

The well-documented and heavily publicized career of Dave Eggers, for example, illustrates the turn in expatriate narratives. Eggers's career began with his exceptionally self-conscious memoir of personal and familial loss, *A Heartbreaking Work of Staggering Genius* (2000), but his second effort was a "do-gooder" novel of the sort Robbins describes. *You Shall Know Our Velocity* (2002) chronicles the adventures of ill-informed young Americans on a whirlwind one-week journey around the world, seeking to distribute a large sum of inherited money to those in need. Eggers's subsequent writing has taken an even less personal turn by documenting the worlds and voices of persons distant from his suburban upbringing. Winner of the Prix Médicis étranger, his nonfiction novel *What Is the What* (2006) recounts the life story of Valentino

Achak Deng, a Lost Boy of Sudan, and his retelling of oral history in *Zeitoun* (2009) similarly focuses on immigrant experiences—this time in the aftermath of Hurricane Katrina. If Eggers is, as some have described him, a "one-man zeitgeist" representative of major developments in American letters, then both his specific experiments with limiting first-person point of view and his shift toward international and activist content deserve our attention.[8] Eggers's career may suggest, too, why the world novel emerges from the expatriate context: the world novel's political and institutional sensibility requires a recovery from narcissistic consumerism, so the expatriate novel's account of the well-heeled traveler's self-discovery provides a natural starting point.

After all, since the 1920s, the American literature of expatriation has strongly associated international travel with erotic and aesthetic liberation. Alienated from American culture and drawn toward a European and/or primitive alternative, the expatriate hero aspires to a bohemian placelessness,[9] even though crucial lines of material support anchor him in a home country. Expatriate writing develops a vision designed to correct for the home country's failures and, consequently, addresses a home audience. The expatriate's voluntary travels anticipate an eventual return, thus distinguishing them from forced exile. The multiply exiled and imprisoned Nazim "Hikmet," as Carolyn Forché puts the matter in her scathing portrait of a twenty-year-old would-be radical expatriate in Turkey, "did not choose to be Hikmet."[10] The expatriate, however, elects displacement in order to accomplish a self-assigned task of self-transformation.

Whether in the guise of the Gilded Age tourism of Mark Twain and Henry James, the more openly alienated artists of Ernest Hemingway's and Gertrude Stein's Lost Generation, the post–World War II voluntary exile of James Baldwin and Paul Bowles, or Vietnam War–era hip travel, then, the expatriate hero leaves home to "explore other freedoms," all the while "safely retaining links to his homeland."[11] Many variations distinguish different approaches to the quest for personal freedom; generational, social, and stylistic differences matter. Claude McKay's black transnational sensibility, for example, is not identical to Hemingway's primitivism, even though both participate in a masculinist project reconsidered by women of the Left Bank and elsewhere.[12] Not all expatriates are alienated from the United States in the same manner or for the same reasons, nor are their ties to their home country equally strong. Nonetheless, as a group, expatriate writers share a focus on self-cultivation in the context of foreign travel. They explore an essentially ethical (rather than political) project of cultural critique by means of an often rapturous individualism.[13] *The Sun Also Rises* (1926) remains the touchstone text for the expatriate narrative for a reason: it treads the line between immersion in the foreign spectacle and reversion to heavy American cultural baggage (class snobbery, ethnic and racial chauvinism, sexual hang-ups) particularly well, and the project of personal renewal on display in Hemingway's novel is clearly compromised, contained, and incomplete. It chastises its homebound readers for their parochialism at the same time that its hero must repair to ever more dangerous, exotic, and fantastic locales in order to continue discovering himself. Hemingway's expatriate arrives in Spain already damaged by his American origins and his renovation promises to be a precarious long-term undertaking, especially when conceived in this essentially oppositional, individualist sense.

After all, if the expatriate were to engage fully with others beyond the confines of his self-defined community of aesthetes, he would become a migrant. As discussed in chapter 1, recent migration fiction has been and remains largely preoccupied with its protagonists' efforts to release themselves from a repetitious traumatic history in order to connect more effectively with others in the technologically mediated environment of the present. Expatriates, by contrast, typically remain engaged with the host country as visitors—sometimes very knowledgeable ones—but transients nonetheless. They consume the host's offerings and contribute only their own erotic urges and conversation before departing. Unlike the international volunteers in *For Whom the Bell Tolls* (1940), expatriates fear lasting changes to the host country; they hope for a Spain that continues its rituals, fiestas, bull fighting, and eternal sunniness just as if they had never visited. Before reuniting with his troublesome love interest, Hemingway's classic expatriate hero closes the solo portions of his narrative floating on a raft that "rocked with the motion of the water" and peering out at "the narrow gap that led into the open sea" (242).

In this respect, too, expatriates differentiate themselves from the do-gooders discussed in chapter 2. So dedicated to making an impact on the host country that they are frustrated at their failure to accomplish more than they do, the Peace Corps volunteers plunge into a condition resembling the expatriates' self-regard only as a last resort, by default. While the expatriate focuses intentionally on self-cultivation, the Peace Corps volunteer experiences the self as a limit, a hole into which one falls, and the volunteer's return home often figures as a failure of that self, rather than its healing or triumph—as we sometimes find in the expatriate novel. For Hemingway's Jake Barnes, the status of his personal illusions about having had a "good time" matter most, not the

Expatriate Fiction Versus the World Novel

	EXPATRIATE FICTION	WORLD NOVEL
HERO	Voluntarily mobile, person of means, strong aesthetic and erotic drive, solitary	Migratory, divided, often multilingual
OTHERS	Lovers, bearers of culture, puritanical reminders of home, fundamentally separate from the hero	Dilemmas and attributes similar to the hero's
SETTING	Alien, exotic culture with aesthetic charm	Multiple sites; global transition points, networks; world cities
CONFLICT	Personal freedom vs. norms of home; how to achieve an authentic self	How to depict the world, how to act on global trends
RESOLUTION	Formation of small community of the likeminded or couple	New collective action, achievement of epic vision

fate of the barmen, maids, and concierges with whom he interacts, just as for Bowles, the reunification of all sides of the travelers' romantic triangle brings *The Sheltering Sky* (1949) to a close, regardless of the losses experienced by the locals they encounter.

Of course, as Forché's poem "Expatriate" suggests, by the 1970s and 1980s, many of the conventions of this interwar narrative of expatriation summarized in the table were so familiar that they made easy targets of satire. A novel such as Thomas Pynchon's *Gravity's Rainbow* (1973) may be the ultimate expression of this tendency; Slothrop's manic and pornographic ramblings through the postwar Zone, as well as his efforts to locate a viable Counterforce to the transnational array of institutions aligned against him, sends up the most narcissistic aspects of expatriate writing quite beautifully. Similarly critical versions of the expatriate narrative have continued to blossom in the twenty-first century, and this may be the strain of international fiction most deserving of Robbins's rebuke. Satires directed at the inward focus of the young American abroad rarely do much to disrupt that self-regard. They underscore the contradictions of this form without altering them.

If, however, we consider under the heading of expatriate fiction not only narratives about young, unattached Americans on European sojourns (works that do sometimes differ more from their predecessors than we may initially assume) but also novels written by and about expatriates from elsewhere relocating to the United States, a new set of patterns emerges. While still clearly in dialogue with the modernist classics, these novels also appeal to a different set of generic conventions.[14] They modify the romantic unreality of the international scene, often by comparing the lenses employed by expatriates from different backgrounds. Works in this vein are often triangulated narratives staging a cultural collision that throws the institutional and political situation of the United States into sharp relief. A third group of writings—those I call the work of the new nomads—establishes yet another set of variations on the expatriate theme. In the works of this group, the expatriate novel's definitive center—the wounded self that is seeking aesthetic compensation abroad— gives way to relatively more depersonalized figures for global exchanges. A particular sort of worldly contemplation characterizes these writings.

Even if, when considered singly, none of these variants of the expatriate novel entirely fulfills critical or authorial desires for an informative, innovative, purely extra-national world novel, in the aggregate the nearly thirty works described in this chapter do signal a significant mutation of the expatriate narrative. This group of writings reveals the shifting syntax of the genre. In the expatriate novel, as in other versions of international fiction, U.S. literature tests geopolitical visions appropriate to the twenty-first century.

THE CONTEMPORARY AMERICAN ABROAD

Fiction that describes the adventures of Americans abroad reproduces the traits of modernist expatriate writing most faithfully. Many novels in this vein specifically mention members of Hemingway's generation. They recognize a debt to their literary predecessors as well as a need to revise the habits of the modernists. In some novels, such as Gary Shteyngart's *Russian Debutante's Handbook* (2003), this revisionist impulse triggers a thorough satire of genre conventions. The first third of Shteyngart's first novel sends up the erotic and professional ambitions of discontented immigrants, but the remainder converts Vladimir Girshkin, its Russian American hero, from "a man who couldn't measure up to the natives" to "Vladimir the Expatriate, a title that signified luxury, choice, decadence, frou-frou colonialism" (179). Shteyngart's consumerist hero is unable to master either the American world he has fled or the central European environment he has entered. He might imagine himself a conqueror luring American innocents into his elaborate Ponzi scheme, but he is quickly and repeatedly thrown off-kilter by his own investment in the same expatriate quest for erotic and aesthetic fulfillment on which he preys. "Fifty percent functional American and fifty percent cultured Eastern European in need of a hair cut and a bath," Vlad lacks the secure identity and moral authority necessary for advising a home audience (409).

Beyond these ironies of characterization, Shteyngart's novel also points out the limits of other generic rules governing modernist expatriation. As the title indicates, one of Shteyngart's targets is the guidebook outlining the etiquette of cross-cultural encounters. In *The Sun Also Rises*, transgressors like Robert Cohn who violate the expatriate's norms are punished violently, but Shteyngart's novel rejects that convention. Girshkin ("part P. T. Barnum, part V. I. Lenin" [3]) turns expatriate precisely from a position of being, like Cohn, only partially assimilated; his Russian Jewish background excites interest, not scorn. Furthermore, in addition to repeatedly dropping the name of Hemingway, "the patron saint of the expatriate scene," Shteyngart rewrites one of the signature fishing passages from *Sun* (301). While Jake Barnes achieves rapture in a Spanish trout stream, Girshkin several times describes the lascivious consumption of cooked fish before deepening the parody with the introduction of a midget-size poet named Fish, who "looked like an unwashed twelve-year-old" despite having "the voice of Milton Berle" (303). Shteyngart's Fish promises a uniquely postmodern vision achieved by means of Manhattan's latest designer drug, "horse powder"; after ingesting it together, Fish and Girshkin plunge into the "bottomless joy of anesthesia"—only to emerge, a mere fifteen minutes later, into an everyday world of buttons and party planning (306). Shteyngart, in other words, overplays Hemingway's hyperbolic moments of expatriate revelation, sending them through the mill of his own deflationary slapstick humor.

Similar moments of parodic allusion to expatriate classics abound in recent depictions of the American abroad. The dissatisfied youngsters who populate Arthur Phillips's *Prague* (2002), Tom Rachman's *The Imperfectionists* (2010), and Rosa Shand's *Gravity of Sunlight* (2000) also recall Hemingway's would-be sensualists. Richard Russo's *Bridge of Sighs* (2007), which travels from upstate New York to Venice and back, refers at several key moments to Henry James's Italian stories. Cynthia Ozick's *Foreign Bodies* (2010) explicitly updates the situation of James's *The Ambassadors* (1903), as arguably do portions of Chang-Rae Lee's war novel *The Surrendered* (2010). Peter Cameron's *Andorra* (1997) and *The City of Your Final Destination* (2002) employ Jamesian narrators who know more than the rather oblivious protagonists about the moral corruption of the worlds that the expatriates enter. Self-consciousness about the derivativeness of the expatriate project of aesthetic renewal and erotic liberation through travel provides a starting point for these new novels.

The path of these satires often leads from a blushing acknowledgment of the contemporary expatriate's belatedness to a direr sense of entrapment in a dangerous alien culture. Phillips's protagonist becomes so enmeshed in shady dealings in Budapest that only in the final pages does he finally muster the energy to propel himself outward toward the titular fairy-tale city of Prague. All of Russo's characters are inexorably drawn back to the economically depressed town from which they initially fled. And both of Cameron's novels end with a Hoffmanesque eeriness in which repatriation or imprisonment abroad seem to be the only options. The hero of *Andorra*, for example, attempts to flee this miniature police state in a boat and finds himself walking down "the wet, rocky shoal, at the base of the embankment," going "quite far—perhaps a quarter of a mile—" before encountering a place where he can access the path above; even at that elevated position, he finds only "a burnt spot where a fire had been" (263). Rather than providing release through a second-order aestheticization of the experience of travel, then, as earlier expatriate writers have done, twenty-first-century fictional treatments of Americans abroad point out the inaccessibility and burned-over status of creative projects, choking off the motives as well as the means for further mobility.

The spatial figures recurring in these works reveal a similar investment in reduction and enclosure. As in the new migrant novel, many locations are shadowed by sister cities. Phillips's Budapest is haunted by Prague, Shteyngart's Prague is permeated by Moscow and Manhattan, while Russo's New York and Venice are always presented in relation to his invented upstate community. In *The City of Your Final Destination*, Cameron embraces this principle most fully—filling rural Uruguay with shades of European capitals and even populating his traveler's point of relative origin (Kansas) with the traces of an older imperial world order. His possibly Egyptian—no, Iranian or maybe Canadian—hero, Omar, longs while traveling for midwestern cuisine, that "Indian cooking filtered through British imperialism and modified for Americans" (38). In this frequently employed figure of paratactic regression, the intensity of perception that a Hemingway hero devotes to local particularities gives way to the presentation of a potentially homogeneous world space. For the twenty-first-century expatriate, travel becomes an experience of the inescapability of one's origin. The authors of this expatriate fiction largely give up the modernist's project of mapping the new, choosing to move instead among relatively undifferentiated urban spaces strongly reminiscent of a home that, it turns out, has not been left so far behind after all.

The inescapability of urban consumerism, in particular, suggests that the country–city opposition is being reimagined in the twenty-first-century novel. Whether or not the extra-fictional urban form itself has undergone a fundamental alteration, as Saskia Sassen has argued, in fiction of the new millennium, the city provides the shock of the familiar more often than the shock of the new.[15] The city is ubiquitous for contemporary expatriates, and their quest for cultural particularity less central. They travel with "this small, good world," as Russo puts it in *The Bridge of Sighs*, with constant access to American security behind them (642). And, like the financial analyst in Peter Mountford's gripping *A Young Man's Guide to Late Capitalism* (2011), they enjoy easy access to pisco sours, cell-phone reception, and professional peers even in war-torn Bolivia.

In this first subset, then, twenty-first-century expatriate fiction deviates somewhat from its generic predecessors while remaining largely inside the parameters sketched in the 1960s by travel writer Paul Theroux. Observing cultural conflict in East and Central Africa, Theroux charged that Tarzan is an expatriate and vice versa. The first casualty of a Tarzan-ish approach to expatriation, Theroux argues, is curiosity about one's new environment. "When the expatriate feels he knows the country in which he is working, he loses interest," and personal ambitions supersede care for others, Theroux writes.[16] When he composed this piece, Theroux had recently been expelled from Malawi for political activity, and he is understandably relentless in his condemnation of other expatriates' acquiescence to the conditions that support their mobility. Their quietude, Theroux concludes, leads white expatriates finally to compromise with repressive state authority and economically self-serving racism. No matter what politics the expatriate might espouse, Theroux would have us measure narratives of this type by the unspoken relationships that they allow to go unchallenged.

Although contemporary expatriate fiction does often attend to racial logic, Theroux's attack highlights the silence that this group of novels maintains about international politics. Even when some forms of state power are depicted (as in the police chases featured in Cameron's *Andorra* and Shteyngart's *Russian Debutante's Handbook*), curiosity about the motives, strategies, and circumstances of alternative modes of state power is noticeably absent. At most, these novels observe the bureaucracies through which power is implemented abroad, but political events are usually imagined as cultural effects, rather than being related in any significant way to knowable institutions or histories. When Idi Amin seizes power in *The Gravity of Sunlight*, for example, this is a shocking disturbance, largely unanticipated by Shand's white heroine. Novels about Americans in quest of aesthetic experiences abroad are, as Robbins has rightly suggested, largely disinclined to investigate the political conditions that may have laid some groundwork for a supposed cultural homogeneity.

The Contemporary Expatriate in America

By contrast, fiction about expatriates from elsewhere in the world encountering conditions in the United States often addresses institutional authority. In part, this topic follows from interest in the situation of foreign nationals in America since September 11. Joseph O'Neill's *Netherland* (2008), Teddy Wayne's *Kapitoil* (2010), and Claire Messud's *Emperor's Children* (2006) take up this subject most directly, while Colum McCann's *Let the Great World Spin* (2009) and Susan Choi's *Person of Interest* (2009) adopt a more indirect approach. All these novels interrogate the limits of the American collectivity, a question that is openly political from the outset. Also, all of them show some comfort with sociological description, exploring specific professional idioms and generating plot twists and linguistic innovations out of arguably American variants of professional norms. The abandoned national homes of the expatriate protagonists tend not to color their everyday movements, as they do in fiction of exile or immigration; sometimes (as in Choi's novel), even the name of the country of origin is suppressed. Instead, direct and thorough engagement with the new narrative present takes center stage. From the parks and avenues of Queens neighborhoods in *Netherland* and the Bronx underpasses in *Let the Great World Spin* to the midwestern college town in *A Person of Interest*, the private Los Angeles high schools in Nell Freudenberger's *Dissident* (2006) and the dissection of the Manhattan public-relations business in Rana Dasgupta's *Solo* (2008), the specific milieus that frame foreign expatriates' American experiences are precisely mapped. They describe both their home countries, to which they periodically return, and their new environs in equally tangible terms. Neither is consigned to a shadowy and mythic past. They situate the United States on a variegated international map rather than universalizing its time-space or depopulating the present by means of repeated swerves through memories of atrocity.

Another major difference between narratives of Americans abroad and those of foreigners in America is that, rather than doubling up the novel's topos, the expatriate-in-America subgenre doubles up the protagonists. All these novels involve paired heroes, one of whom observes the other's adventures. Typically, the narrating expatriate has a higher level of mobility or cultural capital than the second, more embedded figure, but this relative privilege usually dissipates as the novel proceeds. This chiasmatic structure inverts the modernist prototype for this sort of narration, *The Great Gatsby* (1925). In the reported action of Fitzgerald's novel, Nick Carraway initially appears to be a relative outsider, admiring Jay Gatsby's apparent success; however, over the course of the narrative, he takes a position closer to the seat of power than Gatsby's elaborate charade of insiderism allows. In contemporary expatriate fiction, the same ironic logic pertains; these are still novels, to varying degrees, that describe the downfall of a nearby friend. As a group, however, they express their distinctive geopolitical sensibility by relating that downfall from within, as it were, and exporting an ultimately more heroic rise to an other who remains more opaque to narration. In these novels, in other words, it is not Fitzgerald's "rich" who are different from and more romantic than the novel's "you and me," but the expatriate "poor." These novels typically make a downwardly mobile middle-class narrator the ironic observer of a poor person's relative rise.

These rich and poor double protagonists are usually brothers. McCann's narrative tracks one Irish sibling who follows his monkish brother from Dublin to the Bronx in the months before the latter's death; Abraham Verghese's *Cutting for Stone* (2009) makes the brothers twins who differ in their responses to their Anglo-Indian parents' expatriation first in Ethiopia and later in the United States. Messud's *Emperor's Children* varies the pattern a bit by placing an uncle–nephew relationship at the center, but it also treats the theme of expatriation more obliquely, locating Australian and British expatriates in the context of intra-state mobility. Freudenberger's novel initially appears to be devoted to a single protagonist, the titular Chinese dissident, but the plot eventually turns on the discovery that the supposed dissident, who has taken a position as artist-in-residence in an upper-middle-class Los Angeles high school, is playing a part scripted by his more adventurous comrade-in-arms, a conceptual artist. Several other novels treat the fraternity metaphor more figuratively—comparing the expatriate experiences of fellow sportsmen (O'Neill's cricketers in *Netherland*), professional colleagues (Choi's mathematicians in *A Person of Interest* and Wayne's financial analysts in *Kapitoil*), or involuntary housemates (Jonathan Raban's homeowner and contractor in *Waxwings* [2003]). However the male protagonists are paired, though, they are always paired. This pattern rarely appears in tales of Americans abroad, which represent the American as being alone or immersed in a larger group of age mates (*Prague*) or professionals (*The Imperfectionists*) operating as a single hive-mind. The dyadic structure of the foreign expatriate story simply does not characterize narratives of extra-national space, even though both variants stay with the modernist convention of depicting the traveler primarily as a masculine self-questioner (or the figure that Nina Baym calls the "beset" man longing for a space of freedom beyond the confines of a feminized convention).[17]

Not surprisingly, then, fraternal rivalry organizes the stories of these beleaguered sojourners; one brother routinely undercuts the authority of the other, usually from below, as it were. McCann's more conventional narrator comes to appreciate his ascetic sibling's devotion to prostitutes. Raban's professorial European exile admires the entrepreneurial energy and linguistic creativity of the contractor who renovates his home. Verghese's American-educated doctor is saved by his less formally trained twin's last-minute donation of a kidney, and O'Neill's Anglo-Dutch financier learns to situate his own personal dilemmas relative to the more intense struggle for survival faced by his Trinidadian cricket teammate. Although the protagonists of Gish Jen's *World and Town* (2010) are tough women rather than pair-bonded men, the pattern holds. Jen's highly assimilated and educated Chinese American narrator learns a great deal from a less fortunate Vietnamese girl whom she sees as a version of herself.

In the final third of *Netherland*, O'Neill's Anglo-Dutch narrator offers a particularly memorable instance of the way the less advantaged expatriate illuminates the world for his better-off observer. During an awkward Christmas holiday in southern India, Hans watches locals walking in the forest and reflects: "I keep on seeing these men. I do not think of Chuck [the Trinidadian] as one of them, even though, with his very dark skin, he could have been one of them. I think of Chuck as the Chuck I saw. But whenever I see these men I always end up seeing Chuck" (230). By coming to know Chuck as a fellow expatriate in New York, Hans learns to read alternative routes, histories, and faces; his map of the world expands to include these wavering perceptions of the mobility of others. It is not solely his own movements on which he need (or can) rely to image a geopolitical scene. After all, although Chuck had repeatedly drawn Hans's attention to the original Dutch presence in New York, the real "nether" regions of the novel turn out not to be the faded history of Europeans in the New World but Chuck's bare brown cricket fields.

In the final passages of the novel, Hans magnifies images of this new Ground Zero, with the help of Google Maps, before swerving out to the planetary level, where "a human's movement is a barely intelligible thing" and "the USA as such is nowhere to be seen" (252). His detour into his less fortunate fellow expatriate's "netherland" provides a necessary gathering of momentum that allows him to propel himself out into the putatively post-national, cosmopolitan space. As their titles indicate, similar metaphors of triangulated flight are crucial to *Let the Great World Spin* and *Waxwings* as well. Similar effects are achieved in *Solo*, *A Person of Interest*, *Kapitoil*, and *Cutting for Stone*, as the narrators zoom out to a broader geopolitical vision using the tools provided by specific professions (public relations, mathematics, risk analysis, and medicine, respectively). Together, the foreign expatriate novels use a socially advantaged European narrator to collect reflections of the livelier dramas surrounding protagonists from the developing world before absorbing both into a new synthesis at the level of the technologically mediated global image.

In these narratives of cultural conflict, however, the voice of the "nether" migrant is consistently hard to hear. Sometimes the nether twin is simply stalled institutionally through visa problems (as in the novels by Freudenberger, Verghese, Raban, and Wayne), but just as often the narrator cannot reach him because he is dead (as in the works narratives of O'Neill, McCann, Messud, and, differently, Choi). This tendency prevents the expatriate novel from expressing any overly romantic fondness for the heroic other. However, it could also be read as an effort to contain potentially disturbing political effects of genuine international and cross-class solidarity. That is, even while being cognizant of the incompleteness of single-voiced narratives of expatriation, these novels extinguish some of their own glimmers of a new proto-global subject by casting that figure into the past—killing him off in order to sustain the safer figure of the jaded middle-class skeptic as the only viable actor in the present.

This latter, less charitable reading is reinforced by these novels' consistent use of irresolute endings. From the final family Ferris wheel ride in *Netherland* to the imagist discovery of birds in flight in *Waxwings* and the protagonist's recognition of his father's voice on the long-distance line in *Cutting for Stone*, these novels tend to use family reconciliations to produce figurative rather than active closure. These reunions differ from those in the closing scenes of national allegories, where a household reassembles after terrible trials. In the expatriate-in-America novel, the tired protagonists return to their various spheres of professional competence and renew romantic or kinship relations that have remained largely intact. These conclusions suggest that public conflicts can, in the end, be only recognized, not acted on, and that bourgeois family life is finally the only feasible playing field. In a reversal of Sergei Eisenstein's charge to the artist, they "distract audiences" from "a current conflict" rather than exacerbating it.[18] These novels tend to close with an appeal to domestic realism, rather than with any more forceful challenge to the syntax of this grounding genre of modernist expatriation. Despite their use of politically charged twin protagonists and their stronger commitment to mapping the present, in other words, works in this second cluster of expatriate writings also reveal some (but not all) of the generic limits to a world vision evident in the narrative of the American abroad.

The New Nomads

Some of the most formally innovative expatriate fiction is devoted to the perpetual expatriate or stateless nomad; often these works are narrated from the point of view of disaffected diplomats. Like the Peace Corps novel, they hearken back to Graham Greene's *Quiet American* (1955). Greene's detached, deracinated observer of American naïveté has a kinship with the administrator-spy at the heart of *The Great Fire* (2003), Shirley Hazzard's complicated novel of English and Australian citizens adrift in post-1945 Asia, for example. We first meet her narrator, Alfred Leith, as he sits on a departing train, studying a book-jacket photograph of his father, a man "renowned for private detachment" (4). That inherited reserve helps Leith interpret his observations of the equally incomprehensible American and Japanese occupants of his multinational milieu. A similarly impersonal administrative eye can be detected in Micheline Aharonian Marcom's ambitious trilogy *Three Apples Fell from Heaven* (2001), *The Daydreaming Boy* (2004), and *Draining the Sea* (2008). Marcom writes from a lush, hypnotic sensibility that links the survivors of extreme violence in Turkey, Beirut, and Guatemala. In the same spirit, both Lee's *Surrendered* and Karen Tei Yamashita's *I Hotel* (2010) use nested narratives to explore the shattered consciousnesses of people whose lives have been altered by war in East Asia. Lee's and Yamashita's characters reflect on their own moments of surrender to military, erotic, and/or theological forces, and the novels themselves link these sections to one another through a logic unconstrained by place, family, or plotted causality. Resisting the Faulknerian drive toward a deep and intensely local historical causality, Lee depicts institutional locations—empty storefronts, low-rent apartments, cars, and hotels— made meaningful only by the geopolitical narrative linking their inhabitants.

Yamashita repeatedly probes the ideological as well as the interpersonal and institutional networks necessary to understand the story of a single block in San Francisco's Chinatown during the 1960s and 1970s. In a brief discussion of David Mitchell's narrative experiments in *Cloud Atlas* (2004), Rita Barnard describes the point of view employed in these decentered narratives as a "multiple, mobile optic, both internal and external to its successive narrators."[19] Barnard compares this perspective to a surveillance satellite tracking a multipolar global crisis and suggests that it updates the print-culture national simultaneity so famously described by Anderson.[20]

Another, less technological figure for the mobile sensibility of the new nomad appears in Jane Alison's *Natives and Exotics* (2005). With a more Woolfian lightness of tone, Allison describes the upbringing of the stepdaughter of an American diplomat posted in Central America during the 1980s. Framed by passages devoted to the travels of Charles Darwin and Alexander von Humboldt, this character develops a geo-botanical consciousness that takes native and exotic plant species as a counterpoint for human migrations underwritten by the imperial relations that link Scotland, the Azores, and Australia. In Alison's novel, the diplomat's daughter has no more possibility of repatriating to a home that she never knew than does an orange produced by grafting. Alison imagines new human and plant species that are native nowhere and therefore unsettle systems of classification that purge exotics or refuse their import. In her vision, as Humboldt reflects, "matters of creation were becoming clearer; extraordinary connections were afoot" (7).

Neither Alison's Woolfian interest in internal monologue nor her turn to botanical metaphors is unique in contemporary fiction. Both Michael Cunningham most clearly and (as discussed in chapter 1) Salvatore Scibona more indirectly have helped to revive appreciation for some of Woolf's narrative tactics in *The Hours* (1998) and *The End* (2008), respectively. And botany arguably comes second only to a preoccupation with entering the mental world of the financier as an indicator of contemporaneity in twenty-first-century American literature. Drawing perhaps on the dazzling precedent set by Russell Banks in early chapters of *Continental Drift* (1985), a number of recent novels turn capital and ecology into images of each other, making either a naturalized market or a marketized nature the basis for contemporary cultural flows. Vivek Berberian's *Das Kapital* (2007) brings these figures together most pointedly, through a tripartite plot concerned with Cypriot agriculture and short selling in the international paper market, but we might also recall Ruth Ozeki's denaturalization of female physical development in *My Year of Meats*

(1999) and Andrea Barrett's explorations of the global distribution of expertise in natural history in *Servants of the Map* (2003), as well as Leslie Marmon Silko's exploration of biopiracy in *Gardens of the Dunes* (1999).

This triangular field (nature-culture-capital) reorganizes the concerns of eco-fiction, as well as the geopolitical novel proper. To appreciate the full impact of the new nomadic sensibility on the genre, however, it may be helpful to consider in some detail a final and more literal adaptation of the expatriate novel: Aleksandar Hemon's *Nowhere Man* (2004). Although Hemon has also made distinguished contributions to the immigrant novel, as discussed in chapter 1, *Nowhere Man* shifts his concerns away from the delayed traumas of culture shock and toward a depiction of the arguably placeless sensibility of the expatriate-cum-nomad. Hemon's carefully composed narrative builds up the world of its title character, Jozef Pronek, by triangulating among Chicago, Sarajevo, and Kiev, before coming to rest in a version of Shanghai that absorbs qualities of all the former locations. Hemon's spaces in this novel are inter-urban rather than international because he repudiates the premises of national narratives. Pronek repeatedly identifies himself as a Sarajevan, rather than a Bosnian—using the latter designator only when it offers a mild improvement over even cruder labels. "I am complicated," he responds when a potential employer asks whether he is a Serb or a Muslim; his stomach heaving, he finally adds, "You can say I am the Bosnian" (146). The provisional nature of this acceptance of national identity is also important to an earlier passage when Pronek encounters, of all people, President George H. W. Bush and is left "bedazzled by the uncanniness" of the American's alien expressions of national pride (106). A taste for nationalism is not itself a national characteristic, however. Hemon's hero experiences the distasteful falseness of a range of ethnic and national generalities; these moments analogize American boosterism to Serbian nostalgia for *pravoslav* solidarity and strategically performed Russian anthems.

In short, even before his migration to Chicago and immersion in the pan-ethnic stew of English-language learners (a crucial scene in the world novel, according to Kingston), Pronek is already ambivalent about narratives of national belonging. His expatriation precedes his geographical mobility by several steps; it is voluntary and subjective rather than rooted in the forced exile of the wartime refugee. At the same time, rather than simply literalizing his alienation from a home culture or immersing him in a new aesthetic environment that cures him of a rootless modern anomie, Pronek's physical displacement reinforces his anti- or a-nationalism. In Hemon's novel, a dissociated nomadism begins at home and extends to all levels of identity. Pronek reinvents himself several times before migration—first as John Lennon in a high-school Beatles tribute band and later as Blind Jozef Pronek, during a blues phase. This process continues in Chicago when he canvases for Greenpeace, introducing himself as his childhood friend "Mirza from Bosnia," "Sergei Katastrofenko from Ukraine," "Jukka Smirdiprdiuskas from Estonia," "John from Liverpool" (once again), "Nobody," "Phillip from Luxembourg," "Joseph from Snitzlland," and even the generic "Someone Else" (179–180). The ersatz versions of musical celebrity that he initially adopted in order to disrupt the official music culture of home and school becomes a general principle. Pronek is a nowhere man from the outset, expatriated early and often—not through crisis but simply as a means of self-assertion.

Despite his recurring interest in an apparently global popular music, Hemon's nowhere man does not drift toward the relativistic narcissism of the American expatriate abroad—recognizing only variants of a dully familiar urban commercialism everywhere he travels. Instead, *Nowhere Man* fuses Pronek's complicated detachment from other people's misperceptions of nationality to a special adaptation of the fraternal motif observed in the expatriates-in-America subgenre. Pronek's metaphysical brother is a childhood acquaintance from Sarajevo whom he encounters by chance at a language school in Chicago. Observing one of the more advanced classes, this unnamed narrator hears Pronek "reading in a very low voice, as if confessing," a newspaper passage that describes the intimacy experienced by the conjoined twins Ronnie and Donnie. "Donnie is me, and I am Donnie," Pronek mumbles (23). Bringing the narrator's doubling of Pronek into the open, this passage anchors his performances of multiple selves in a logic of two-ness. This introduction to Pronek anticipates the doubling that finally resolves his story.

As *Nowhere Man* winds down, Pronek moves toward a more comfortable, romantically coupled state and replaces his retroactively embarrassing Beatles songs with a rendition of *sevdalinka*, a "Bosnian blues" that is "so sad that it makes you free" (210). Even after conjoining his American and European selves through song, a painful abyss surrounding Pronek's "real me" still persists, and the narrative does leave him dizzy with "violent adrenaline," claiming his own place by screaming "Here! Here!" This frenzy is soon contained, when the volatile night world of the narrator is made tolerable by the presence of an equal other. Pronek's narrating double manages this crisis scene by speaking to himself in the first person—first in Bosnian and then in English:

"Calm down, I'm telling him, everything will fall into place" (221). This voice provides not a twinning of rich and poor or white and brown brothers, then, but a therapeutic synthesis that can contain a multitude of past and future selves. The importance of this device is underscored by the peculiar final section.

In "Nowhere Man," the seventh part of *Nowhere Man*, the unnamed narrator of the opening section—a voice close to the disembodied presence that comforts Pronek during his crisis but also borrowing details very similar to those found in his story—again takes the helm. On a honeymoon in Shanghai, this narrator intently reads a biography of a Ukrainian spy known as Evgenij Pick, Joseph Pronek, Dr. Montaigne, and Evenij Mihailovich Kojevnikoff, among other pseudonyms. In a swirl of metafictional references culminating in a self-deprecating description of Pick's associate "Alex Hemmon, a former member of the Purple Gang in Detroit, a hit man who has to kill somebody every time he gets drunk (which he does habitually), and who moonlights as a professional trombonist" (233), Hemon renews his earlier emphasis on Pronek's multiple identities, resolving them again in the figure of the physically conjoined twin. In the novel's final image, the unnamed narrator absorbs all these variations into himself, even going so far as to imagine that he has swallowed the mouse that featured in Pronek's wild crisis scene earlier in the novel: "It is right inside me now, clawing at the walls of my chest, trying to get out" (242). As in the novel's third section, when a Ukrainian American roommate closely observes Pronek and falls in love with him, the narrator and his subject become intimately identified at several levels. Rather than preserving the distance between brothers so vital to narrative ironies in the expatriate-in-America novel, *Nowhere Man* collapses distance in favor of an unusually close fraternal bond maintained in full knowledge of the dispersed, multi-stranded, post-national universe that its subjects inhabit. This traveling fraternity keeps various world locations and inter-urban networks alive, even as it undercuts its own or other people's nationalist nostalgia.

In the end, then, when considered in light of its many related companion texts, Hemon's *Nowhere Man* fully illustrates the generic mutations undergone by the twenty-first century expatriate novel and suggests its movement toward a form we might plausibly call the world novel. The geopolitical map of this emergent genre differs markedly from the jigsaw-puzzle pieces of modernist contributions to the expatriate genre. The twenty-first-century expatriate novel sends multinational doubles traveling through an overlapping simultaneity of diverse spaces and selves. In place of the modernist expatriate's sometimes ecstatic sense of release from the confines of his home culture, it expresses an exhaustion with nostalgia and refuses sentimentality about origins. Finally, the central discovery of the contemporary expatriate narrative less often involves the narrator's heroic achievement of an aestheticized self than an intensified perception of an other with whom he retains some close identification. The twenty-first-century expatriate novel describes a world of conflict, antagonism, and affection—a world in which space is politically marked, even if an existing political ideology is rarely affirmed.

In short, dozens of expatriate novels published in the past decade imagine specific non-American locations as well as paths toward them without resort to an earlier generation's clichés about atrocity and Third World wretchedness. This fiction inhabits its own distinctive world. Its expatriates may occasionally allude to the immigrant's conventionally more celebratory narrative or the do-gooder's uplift ambitions, but by and large the twenty-first-century expatriate novel resists the early- and mid-twentieth-century American story of the heroic rise. The protagonist of this genre typically turns out to be not a self-made man but someone more like Herbert Marcuse's one-dimensional man[21]—a subject who occupies an institutional non-space in which romantic love or family life partially, but never entirely, compensates for a profound sense of vulnerability. This protagonist yearns for a fraternity that he does not fully know how to enjoy because he remains so intensely aware of the enormous disparities in power, wealth, access to care, language, and life chances that characterize the international scene. The resulting narratives of partially disrupted friendships and chance connections may not be political novels in the most familiar sense; they rarely describe ideological struggle or conversion outright. Yet these works do demonstrate an emerging recognition of the formative effects of global inequities on travel and the mobile subject. In these mutations of the expatriate narrative, then, the geopolitical consciousness of the world novel begins to show its face. This new form has a coherent spatial, social, narrative, and ethico-political orientation that differs significantly from its twentieth-century predecessors. Together with the changes to the migration narrative, Peace Corps thriller, national allegory, and revolutionary novel, these observable generic mutations suggest that U.S. fiction is truly grappling with the pragmatics of global mobility and inequality and is learning to speak in a new voice, one that opens the door to a different kind of engagement with the world beyond the borders of the United States.

NOTES

INTRODUCTION

1. Mary McCarthy, "The Lasting Power of the Political Novel," *New York Times Book Review*, January 1, 1984.

2. David Shields, *Reality Hunger: A Manifesto* (New York: Knopf, 2010), 50.

3. Bill Marx, "Dr. Strangereader: Or How I Learned to Stop Worrying About Suburban Novels and Love International Fiction," *Ploughshares* 26, nos. 2–3 (2000): 204.

4. Edmund White, quoted in Ian Jack, "A Very Uncertain Country," *Guardian*, March 10, 2007.

5. Bruce Robbins, "The Worlding of the American Novel," in *The Cambridge History of the American Novel*, ed. Leonard Cassuto (New York: Cambridge University Press, 2011), 1096–1106. See also Robert Boyers, *Atrocity and Amnesia: The Political Novel Since 1945* (New York: Oxford University Press, 1985).

6. Tim Parks, "The Dull New Global Novel," *New York Review of Books*, February 9, 2010.

7. John Whalen-Bridge, *Political Fiction and the American Self* (Urbana: University of Illinois Press, 1998), 18.

8. Morris Edmund Speare makes conversion central to the genre in *The Political Novel: Its Development in England and America* (New York: Oxford University Press, 1924).

9. William Sharpe, review of *Politics and the Novel*, by Irving Howe, *Political Science Quarterly* 108, no. 1 (1993): 206–207.

10. For a feminist critique of Howe, see Sharon M. Harris, "Introduction: Literary Politics and the Political Novel," in *Redefining the Political Novel: American Women Writers, 1797–1901*, ed. Sharon M. Harris (Chattanooga: University of Tennessee Press, 1995), vii–xxiii.

11. Stuart A. Scheingold, *The Political Novel: Reimagining the Twentieth Century* (New York: Continuum, 2008), 8–12.

12. See, for example, Marianne DeKoven's overview "The Politics of Modernist Form," *New Literary History* 23, no. 3 (1992): 675–690.

13. Popular and high-brow narratives focused on presidents often justify the concentration of power in the executive branch, on which see Sean McCann's insightful study, *A Pinnacle of Feeling: American Literature and Presidential Government* (Princeton, N.J.: Princeton University Press, 2008).

14. Susan Suleiman, *Authoritarian Fictions: The Ideological Novel as a Literary Genre* (New York: Columbia University Press, 1983).

15. On literary liberalism, see David Cowart, *History and the American Novel* (Carbondale: Southern Illinois University Press, 1989); and Anthony Hutchinson, *Writing the Republic: Liberalism and Morality in Political Fiction* (New York: Columbia University Press, 2007).

16. Fredric Jameson, "The Cultural Logic of Late Capitalism," in *Postmodernism, or the Cultural Logic of Late Capitalism* (Durham, N.C.: Duke University Press, 1991), 1–50; Walter Benn Michaels, *Shape of the Signifier: 1967 to the End of History* (Princeton, N.J.: Princeton University Press, 2004).

17. Mark McGurl summarizes his argument in "The Program Era," *Critical Inquiry* 32, no. 1 (2005): 102–129.

18. Ibid., 125.

19. Christopher Newfield, *Unmaking the Public University: The Forty-Year Assault on the Middle Class* (Cambridge, Mass.: Harvard University Press, 2008).

20. Gordon Hutner, *What America Read: Taste, Class, and the Novel, 1920–1960* (Chapel Hill: University of North Carolina Press, 2009).

21. On anti-social logic, see Michael Clune, *American Literature and the Free Market, 1945–2000* (Cambridge: Cambridge University Press, 2010).

22. Newfield, *Unmaking the Public University*; Mark Bousquet, *How the University Works: Higher Education and the Low-Wage Nation* (New York: New York University Press, 2008).

23. Chad Harbach, "MFA vs. NYC," November 6, 2010, *Slate*, http://www.slate.com/articles/arts/culturebox/2010/11/mfa_vs_nyc.html (accessed January 23, 2013).

24. Nathan Oates, "Political Stories: The Individual in Contemporary Fiction," *Missouri Review* 30, no. 3 (2007): 156–171.

25. Laura Miller, "Are MFA Programs Ruining American Fiction?" May 17, 2011, *Salon*, http://www.salon.com/2011/05/18/mfa_programs/ (accessed February 26, 2013).

26. Bloggers stressed the necessity of internationalism in "20 More Under 40," June 16, 2011, The Millions, http://www.themillions.com/2010/06/20-more -under-40.html (accessed January 23, 2013).

27. Phillip Wegner, A Life Between Two Deaths, 1989–2001: U.S. Culture in the Long 1990s (Durham, N.C.: Duke University Press, 2009); Adam Thurschwell concurs in "Writing and Terror: Don DeLillo on the Task of Literature After 9/11," Law and Literature 19, no. 2 (2007): 277–302.

28. Franco Moretti develops the concept of distant reading in Graphs, Maps, Trees: Abstract Models for a Literary History (New York: Verso, 2005).

29. Tzvetan Todorov, "The Origin of Genres," New Literary History 8 (1976– 1977): 159–170.

30. Mikhail Bakhtin, The Dialogic Imagination: Four Essays, ed. Michael Holquist, trans. Caryl Emerson and Michael Holquist (Austin: University of Texas Press, 1982); György Lukács, The Theory of the Novel: A Historico-Philosophical Essay on the Forms of Great Epic Literature, trans. Anna Bostock (Cambridge, Mass.: MIT Press, 1974).

31. According to Fredric Jameson, "the aesthetic act is itself ideological" (The Political Unconscious: Narrative as a Socially Symbolic Act [Ithaca, N.Y.: Cornell University Press, 1981], 62).

32. Rick Altman, "A Semantic/Syntactic Approach to Film Genre," Cinema Journal 23, no. 3 (1984): 6–18.

33. Jacques Derrida, "The Law of Genre," trans. Avital Ronnell, Critical Inquiry 7, no. 1 (1980): 55–81.

34. On Blanchot's multigenre fiction, see Leslie Hill, "Introduction," in Maurice Blanchot: The Demand of Writing, ed. Carolyn Bailey Gill (New York: Routledge, 1996), 2.

35. See, for example, Barry Langford's treatment of genre shifts in Film Genre: Hollywood and Beyond (Edinburgh: Edinburgh University Press, 2005); and Jamie Sexton, "US 'Indie-Horror.': Critical Reception, Genre Construction, and Suspect Hybridity," Cinema Journal 51, no. 2 (2012): 67–86.

36. See, for example, Elaine Scarry's caricature of political criticism in On Beauty and Being Just (Princeton, N.J.: Princeton University Press, 2001).

37. Amanda Anderson, "Character and Ideology: The Case of Cold War Liberalism," New Literary History 42, no. 2 (2011): 209–229.

38. Fredric Jameson, "Persistencies of the Dialectic: Three Sites," Science and Society 62, no. 3 (1998): 362–363.

39. Ezra Pound, The ABC of Reading (1934; New York: New Directions, 1960).

40. Max Horkheimer and Theodor W. Adorno, *The Dialectic of Enlighten-ment*, trans. Edmund Jephcott (1944; Stanford, Calif.: Stanford University Press, 2002), 214.

41. Theodor W. Adorno, Else Frenkel-Brunswik, Daniel J. Levinson, and R. Nevitt Sanford, *The Authoritarian Personality* (1950; New York: Norton, 1993)

42. John Gerring, "Ideology: A Definitional Analysis," *Political Research Quar-terly* 50, no. 4 (1997): 957–994.

43. The "F scale" is developed in Adorno et al., *Authoritarian Personality*.

44. Ronald Inglehart, Miguel Basáñez, Jaime Díez-Medrano, Loek Halman, and Ruud Luijkx, eds., *Human Beliefs and Values: A Cross-Cultural Sourcebook Based on the 1999–2002 Values Surveys* (Mexico City: Siglo XXI, 2004).

45. Timothy W. Luke, "An Apparatus of Answers: Ecologism as Ideology in the 21st Century," *New Political Science* 31, no. 4 (2009): 487–498; Radhika Desai, "From National Bourgeoisie to Rogues, Failures and Bullies: 21st Century Impe-rialism and the Unraveling of the Third World," *Third World Quarterly* 25, no. 1 (2004): 169–185.

46. Michael Hardt and Antonio Negri, *Empire* (Cambridge, Mass.: Harvard University Press, 2001).

47. Richard Ohmann, "English and the Cold War," in *Politics of Knowl-edge: The Commercialization of the University, the Professions, and Print Culture* (Middletown, Conn.: Wesleyan University Press, 2004), 1–41. Michael Szalay takes this thesis a step further, arguing that American novelists of the 1950s and 1960s served as strategists for the Democratic Party, in *Hip Figures: A Literary History of the Democratic Party* (Stanford, Calif.: Stanford University Press, 2012).

48. Manfred B. Steger and Jennifer M. Gidley, "Guest Editors' Introduction," *New Political Science* 31, no. 4 (2009): 423–430.

49. Michael Freeden defines "decontestation" in *Liberal Languages: Ideo-logical Imaginations in Twentieth-Century Progressive Thought* (Princeton, N.J.: Princeton University Press, 2005), 230.

1. FROM ROUTES TO ROUTERS

1. Ali Behdad, *A Forgetful Nation: On Immigration and Cultural Identity in the United States* (Durham, N.C.: Duke University Press, 2005), 175.

2. Other trauma theories of migration include Katarzyna Marciniak, *Alien-hood: Citizenship, Exile, and the Logic of Difference* (Minneapolis: University of Minnesota Press, 2006); Gilbert H. Muller, *New Strangers in Paradise: The Im-migrant Experience and Contemporary American Fiction* (Lexington: University

Press of Kentucky, 1999); Sarah Phillips Casteel, *Second Arrivals: Landscape and Belonging in Contemporary Writing of the Americas* (Charlottesville: University of Virginia Press, 2007); and David Cowart, *Trailing Clouds: Immigrant Fiction in Contemporary America* (Ithaca, N.Y.: Cornell University Press, 2006).

3. These are Thomas J. Ferraro's examples in *Ethnic Passages: Literary Immigrants in Twentieth-Century America* (Chicago: University of Chicago Press, 1993).

4. William Q. Boelhower emphasizes cross-border movement in "The Immigrant Novel as Genre," *MELUS* 8, no. 1 (1981): 3–13.

5. On assimilation, see Muller, *New Strangers in Paradise*; on neo-slave narratives, see Judie Newman, *Fictions of America: Narratives of Global Empire* (New York: Routledge, 2007).

6. James Clifford, *Routes: Travel and Translation in the Late 20th Century* (Cambridge, Mass.: Harvard University Press, 1997).

7. Cowart calls these figures the "standard mythemes" of the migrant novel in *Trailing Clouds*, 7–8.

8. Mikhail Bakhtin, "Forms of Time and of the Chronotope in the Novel: Notes Toward a Historical Poetics," in *The Dialogic Imagination: Four Essays*, ed. Michael Holquist, trans. Caryl Emerson and Michael Holquist (Austin: University of Texas Press, 1981), 109.

9. Hamid Naficy, *An Accented Cinema: Exilic and Diasporic Filmmaking* (Princeton, N.J.: Princeton University Press, 2001).

10. Pheng Cheah, *Spectral Nationality: Passages of Freedom from Kant to Postcolonial Literatures of Liberation* (New York: Columbia University Press, 2003); Aihwa Ong, *Flexible Citizenship: The Cultural Logics of Transnationality* (Durham, N.C.: Duke University Press, 1999); Timothy Brennan, *At Home in the World: Cosmopolitanism Now* (Cambridge, Mass.: Harvard University Press, 1997); Amitava Kumar, *Passport Photos* (Berkeley: University of California Press, 2000); Rosemary Marangoly George, *The Politics of Home: Postcolonial Relocations and Twentieth-Century Fiction* (New York: Cambridge University Press, 1996), chap. 6.

11. David Morley, *Home Territories: Media, Mobility, and Identity* (New York: Routledge, 2000).

12. Paul Gilroy, *Postcolonial Melancholia* (New York: Columbia University Press, 2005), 146, xv.

13. Paul Buhle makes this argument in "Introduction: The 1960s Meet the 1980s," in *Popular Culture in America*, ed. Paul Buhle (Minneapolis: University of Minnesota Press, 1987), ix–xxvii.

14. David Foster Wallace, "E Unibus Pluram: Television and US Fiction," *Review of Contemporary Fiction* 13, no. 2 (1993): 151–193.

15. Naficy, *Accented Cinema*, chap. 2.

16. Manuel Castells, *The Rise of the Network Society*, vol. 1 of *The Information Age: Economy, Society, and Culture* (New York: Blackwell, 1996); Arjun Appadurai, *Modernity at Large: Cultural Dimensions of Globalization* (Minneapolis: University of Minnesota Press, 1996).

17. Castells, *Rise of the Network Society*, 502.

18. Morley analyzes the cultural geography of cyberspace in *Home Territories*, chap. 8. On access issues, see Henry Jenkins, *Convergence Culture: Where Old and New Media Collide* (New York: New York University Press, 2006); on copyright and the historical archive, see Jessica Litman, *Digital Copyright: Protecting Intellectual Property on the Internet* (New York: Prometheus, 2001).

19. Aharon Kellerman, *Personal Mobilities* (New York: Routledge, 2006), 132.

20. Generational conflict has been a major theme of the Digital Natives project organized by the Berkman Center for Internet & Society at Harvard University. See "Youth and Media, http://youthandmedia.org/projects/digital-natives/ (accessed February 26, 2013). On fragmentation and solipsism, see, among others, Rey Chow, "Listening Otherwise, Music Miniaturized," in *The Cultural Studies Reader*, ed. Simon During (New York: Routledge, 1996), 462–478.

21. Sven Birkerts excoriates declining literacy in *The Gutenberg Elegies: The Fate of Reading in an Electronic Age*, 2nd ed. (New York: Macmillan 2006), while Cathy N. Davidson argues that distributed attention can democratize the classroom in *Now You See It: How Technology and Brain Science Will Transform Schools and Business for the 21st Century* (New York: Penguin, 2012).

22. "If you're looking for language that will help you approach our nigh-unbearable historical experiences you can reach for narratives of the impossible: sci-fi, horror, fantasy, which might not really want to talk about people of color at all but that take what we've experienced (without knowing it) very seriously indeed" (Edwidge Danticat, "Interview with Junot Díaz," *BOMB*, December 4, 2007).

23. Nick Nesbitt studies Francophone revolutionary nationalism in *Voicing Memory: History and Subjectivity in French Caribbean Literature* (Charlottesville: University of Virginia Press, 2003).

24. Antonio Benítez-Rojo describes the Caribbean basin as a furnace of differences in *The Repeating Island: The Caribbean and the Postmodern Perspective*, trans. James Maraniss (Durham, N.C.: Duke University Press, 1992). On exile romanticism, see Martin Munro, "Introduction: Inhabiting Haiti," in *Exile and Post-1946 Haitian Literature: Alexis, Depestre, Ollivier, Laferrière, Danticat* (Liverpool: Liverpool University Press, 2007), 1–37.

25. So argues Carine M. Mardorossian, *Reclaiming Difference: Caribbean Women Rewrite Postcolonialism* (Charlottesville: University of Virginia Press, 2005).

26. Ileana Rodríguez, *House/Garden/Nation: Space, Gender, and Ethnicity in Postcolonial Latin American Literatures by Women*, trans. Robert Carr and Ileana Rodríguez (Durham, N.C.: Duke University Press, 1994).

27. Munro, "Introduction: Inhabiting Haiti," 16.

28. Renee Shea, "The Dangerous Job of Edwidge Danticat," *Callaloo* 19, no. 2 (1996): 382–389.

29. Carine M. Mardorossian, "From Literature of Exile to Migrant Literature," *Modern Language Studies* 32, no. 2 (2002): 15–33; Rocio Davis, "Oral Narrative as Short Story Cycle: Forging Community in Edwidge Danticat's *Krik? Krak!*" *MELUS* 26, no. 2 (2001): 65–81; Heather Hewett, "At the Crossroads: Disability and Trauma in *The Farming of Bones*," *MELUS* 31, no. 3 (2006): 123–145.

30. Mardorossian, "From Literature of Exile."

31. Valerie Kaussen, *Migrant Revolutions: Haitian Literature, Globalization, and U.S. Imperialism* (New York: Rowman & Littlefield, 2007).

32. Constant has been living in exile in the United States since 1994. In 2008, he was convicted of mortgage fraud, as reported in Kirk Semple, "Ex-Militia Chief from Haiti Sentenced to up to 37 Years for Fraud," *New York Times*, October 29, 2008.

33. See Danticat's question to Díaz about the delirious style in Danticat, "Interview with Junot Díaz."

34. The word *chabine* is Caribbean slang for a biracial person with fair skin, light eyes, and black hair. See Nesbitt, *Voicing Memory*, 12.

35. Fred L. Gardaphé, *Italian Signs, American Streets: The Evolution of Italian American* Narrative (Durham, N.C,: Duke University Press, 1996); Anthony Julian Tamburri, *A Semiotic of Ethnicity: In (Re)cognition of the Italian/American Writer* (Albany: State University of New York Press, 1998); Mary Jo Bona, *Claiming a Tradition: Italian American Women Writers* (Carbondale: Southern Illinois University Press, 1999); Robert Viscusi, *Buried Caesars, and Other Secrets of Italian American Writing* (Albany: State University of New York Press, 2006); Thomas J. Ferraro, *Feeling Italian: The Art of Ethnicity in America* (New York: New York University Press, 2005).

36. Ioanna Laliotou, *Transatlantic Crossings: Acts of Migration and Cultures of Transnationalism Between Greece and America* (Chicago: University of Chicago Press, 2004).

37. Fernand Braudel, *The Mediterranean and the Mediterranean World in the Age of Philip II*, 2 vols. (Berkeley: University of California Press, 1996).

38. Kenneth Womack and Amy Mallory-Kani, "'Why Don't You Just Leave It Up to Nature?': An Adaptationist Reading of the Novels of Jeffrey Eugenides," *Mosaic* 40, no. 3 (2007): 157–173.

39. Several of Fard's contemporaries described him as "Asiatic" or "Oriental." See Doris Witt, *Black Hunger: Food and the Politics of U.S. Identity* (New York: Oxford University Press, 1999), 117.

40. Scibona has described his debt to *Mrs. Dalloway*, in "A Conversation with Salvatore Scibona About *The End*," April 2008, http://www.theendnovel.com/theendnovel/Pre-pub._Interv._The_End_Novel_Salvatore_Scibona.html (accessed February 26, 2013).

41. In *Ethnic Passages*, Ferraro argues that education is crucial to Anya Yezierska's self-writing.

42. On trauma and migration, see Michael Rothberg, *Traumatic Realism: The Demands of Holocaust Representation* (Minneapolis: University of Minnesota Press, 2000); Magdalena Zabrowska, *How We Found America Reading Gender Through East European Immigrant Narratives* (Chapel Hill: University of North Carolina Press, 1995); and Marciniak, *Alienhood*.

43. Many dissident or exile writings treat Soviet Communism as a kind of trauma, as does, for example, Josef Skvorecky, *The Engineer of Human Souls: An Entertainment on the Old Themes of Life, Women, Fate, Dreams, the Working Class, Secret Agents, Love, and Death*, trans. Paul Wilson (New York: Knopf, 1977).

44. Guido Snel, "The Footsteps of Gavilo Princip: The 1914 Sarajevo Assault in Fiction, History, and Three Monuments," in *History of the Literary Cultures of East-Central Europe*, vol. 1, *Junctures and Disjunctures in the 19th and 20th Centuries*, ed. Marcel Cornis-Pope and John Neubauer (Amsterdam: Benjamins, 2004), 211.

45. Curtis A. Keim, *Mistaking Africa: Curiosities and Inventions of the American Mind* (Boulder, Colo.: Westview Press, 1999).

46. Dinaw Mengestu uses this phrase in a brief essay on Barack Obama's election to the presidency, "The Past Remains with Us," *Granta* 122: "Betrayal," summer 2011.

47. Mengestu praises Baldwin's "restrained, eloquent fury" in his response to questions posed by Reader's Almanac, http://blog.loa.org/2011/06/dinaw-mengestu-on-american-writers-who.html; Cole groups Baldwin with Coetzee and Naipaul as masters of a first-person "middle space between reportage, essay, and invention," in "A Conversation with Teju Cole," January 26, 2011, Tin House, http://www.tin

house.com/blog/6650/a-conversation-with-teju-cole.html; similarly, Abani asserts that reading Baldwin's *Another Country* (1962) at age ten was a profound moment in his ethical education, in "Chris Abani on the Stories of Africa," June 2007, TED, http://www.ted.com/talks/chris_abani_on_the_stories_of_africa.html (all accessed February 26, 2013).

48. A reference to the assassination in May 1997 of the Congolese leader Laurent Kabila identifies the setting of Mengestu's *Beautiful Things That Heaven Bears*, 42.

49. For a more on melancholia and identity politics, see Judith Butler, *The Psychic Life of Power: Theories in Subjection* (Stanford, Calif.: Stanford University Press, 1997); Wendy Brown, *States of Injury: Power and Freedom in Late Modernity* (Princeton, N.J.: Princeton University Press, 1995); and David L. Eng, "Melancholia in the Late Twentieth Century," *Signs* 25, no. 4 (2000): 1275–1281.

50. Espen Aarseth, *Cybertext: Perspectives on Ergodic Literature* (Baltimore: Johns Hopkins University Press, 1997).

51. Binyavanga Wainaina, "How to Write About Africa," *Granta* 92: "The View from Africa," winter 2005.

52. "We are being described as the 'next India,'" Helon Habila wrote in "Is This the Year of the Nigerian Writer?" *Times* (London), August 8, 2007. He concludes that "the Indians have one thing we don't have, a healthy publishing industry at home."

53. Mohsin Hamid, "Now That I've Finally Been Admitted to Britain, It Seems That Everyone Else Suddenly Wants to Leave," *Guardian*, August 6, 2008.

54. Evelyn Nien-Ming Ch'ien sees this practice as a move toward a transnational literary language, in *Weird English* (Cambridge, Mass.: Harvard University Press, 2004).

2. THE ANXIOUS AMERICAN

1. George Packer, "Third World, Second Hand," *Mother Jones*, June 1989, 42–43.

2. Edmund White's description is summarized in Ian Jack, introduction to "Best of Young American Novelists 2," *Granta* 97, spring 2007, 7–11.

3. Quoted in Harris Wofford, "The Future of the Peace Corps," *Annals of the American Academy of Political and Social Science* 365 (1966): 134.

4. Sargent Shriver, "Two Years of the Peace Corps," *Foreign Affairs*, July 1963, 699.

5. Cultural intervention of the sort imagined by Shriver should be differentiated from the "cultural diplomacy" practiced by the British Council, the Alliance

Française, and other state-sponsored organizations. See Helena K. Finn, "The Case for Cultural Diplomacy: Engaging Foreign Audiences," *Foreign Affairs* 82, no. 6 (2003): 15–20.

6. Wofford, "Future of the Peace Corps," 145.

7. Histories of the Peace Corps include Stanley Meisler, *When the World Calls: The Inside History of the Peace Corps and Its First Fifty Years* (Boston: Beacon Press, 2011); Laurie L. Charles, *Intimate Colonialism: Head, Heart, and Body in West African Development Work* (Walnut Creek, Calif.: Left Coast Press, 2007); Elizabeth Cobbs Hoffman, *All You Need Is Love: The Peace Corps and the Spirit of the 1960s* (Cambridge, Mass.: Harvard University Press, 1998); Michael E. Latham, *Modernization as Ideology: American Social Science and "Nation Building" in the Kennedy Era* (Chapel Hill: University of North Carolina Press, 2000); and Fritz Fischer, *Making Them Like Us: Peace Corps Volunteers in the 1960s* (Washington, D.C.: Smithsonian Institution Press, 1998).

8. Julius Amin, "The Peace Corps and the Struggle for African American Equality," *Journal of Black Studies* 29, no. 6 (1999): 809–826.

9. Jonathan Zimmerman reports on interviews conducted with more than 100 African-American volunteers in "Beyond Double Consciousness: Black Peace Corps Volunteers in Africa, 1961–1971," *Journal of American History* 82, no. 3 (1995): 999–1028.

10. Shriver, "Two Years of the Peace Corps," 707.

11. This definition of liberalism restates the main themes of James Kloppenberg, *The Virtues of Liberalism* (New York: Oxford University Press, 1998).

12. Kathleen D. McCarthy, *The American Creed: Philanthropy and the Rise of Civil Society, 1700–1865* (Chicago: University of Chicago Press, 2003).

13. Horror writer John Coyne has edited at least four collections of Peace Corps writing, and his online bibliography lists "thousands of books by 971 RPCV and 52 by Peace Corps staff" (Peace Corps Writers, http://peacecorpswriters.org/pages/depts/aboutus/aboutus.html [accessed February 26, 2013]). Similar statistics appear in Hoffman, *All You Need Is Love*.

14. The Maria Thomas Award is publicized, along with a range of writing by RPCVs, on the Web site of Peace Corps Writers (http://peacecorpswriters.org).

15. With more than thirty-two novels and nearly as many volumes of nonfiction to his credit, Theroux is certainly the most prolific and one of the best-known professional writers to emerge from the Peace Corps (he served in Malawi before being expelled for participation in a failed coup). Many of Theroux's novels are thrillers—including A *Dead Hand: A Crime in Calcutta* (Boston: Houghton Mifflin, 2010)—and several earlier works are set in part or in whole in Africa:

Fong and the Indians (Boston: Houghton Mifflin, 1968), *Girls at Play* (Boston: Houghton Mifflin, 1969), *Jungle Lovers* (Boston: Houghton Mifflin, 1971), *The Black House* (Boston: Houghton Mifflin, 1974), and *My Secret History* (New York: Putnam, 1989). However, because Theroux's twenty-first-century fiction mainly concerns South American and South Asian settings only indirectly related to his Peace Corps service, it is omitted from this chapter.

16. Tzvetan Todorov, "The Typology of Detective Fiction," in *The Poetics of Prose* (New York: Blackwell, 1978), 70–78.

17. Robert Lance Snyder, "Eric Ambler's Revisionist Thrillers: *Epitaph for a Spy, A Coffin for Dimitrios*, and *The Intercom Conspiracy*," *Papers on Language and Literature* 45, no. 3 (2009): 227–260.

18. Sean McCann, *Gumshoe America: Hard-Boiled Crime Fiction and the Rise and Fall of New Deal Liberalism* (Durham, N.C.: Duke University Press, 2000).

19. Michael Denning, *Cover Stories: Narrative and Ideology in the British Spy Thriller* (London: Routledge, 1987). John Buchan's most famous thriller is *The Thirty-Nine Steps* (London: Blackwood, 1915).

20. Brian Diemert, *Graham Greene's Thrillers and the 1930s* (Montreal: McGill–Queens University Press, 1996).

21. On stasis in the Cold War thriller, see Anthony Waine, "Anna Seghers's *Transit*: A Late Modern Thriller—Without Thrills," *Neophilologus* 89 (2005): 403–418.

22. John Coates, "Experimenting with Genre: Green [sic] and *The Confidential Agent*," *Renascence* 55, no. 1 (2002): 63.

23. These themes have been crucial to policy-focused critiques of the Peace Corps. See Irving Bernstein, *Promises Kept: John F. Kennedy's New Frontier* (New York: Oxford University Press, 1991); Michael Maren, *The Road to Hell: The Ravaging Effects of Foreign Aid and International Charity* (New York: Free Press, 1997); and Nelson W. Polsby, *Political Innovation in America: The Politics of Policy Initiation* (New Haven, Conn.: Yale University Press, 1984).

24. The DSM-IV-TR states that "individuals with Dissociative fugue may have a Mood disorder, Posttraumatic Stress Disorder or a Substance-Related Disorder" (American Psychiatric Association, *Diagnostic and Statistical Manual of Mental Disorders*, 4th ed., rev. [Washington, D.C.: American Psychiatric Association, 2000], 524).

25. Jan Goldstein, "The Wandering Jew and the Problem of Psychiatric Anti-Semitism in Fin-de-Siècle France," *Journal of Contemporary History* 20 (1985): 521–52. See also Ian Hacking's beautifully written *Mad Travelers: Reflections on the Reality of Transient Mental Illness* (Charlottesville: University of Virginia Press, 1998).

26. Freud's debate with Josef Breuer, the co-author of *Studies on Hysteria*, on this subject is discussed in Eli Zaretsky, *Secrets of the Soul: A Social and Cultural History of Psychoanalysis* (New York: Vintage, 2004), 29.

27. Carl Elliott, *Better Than Well: American Medicine Meets the American Dream* (New York: Norton, 2003), 178.

28. Mihaly Csikszentmihalyi, *Flow: The Psychology of Optimal Experience* (New York: Harper & Row, 1991).

29. Robert W. Rudnicki attributes the disorientation of Walker Percy's southern protagonists to the lack of a functioning regional identity, in *Percyscapes: The Fugue State in Twentieth-Century Southern Fiction* (Baton Rouge: Louisiana State University Press, 1999).

30. In the first fifty years of the Peace Corps, at least 279 volunteers died during their service from illness, injury, and suicide as well as assault and murder. See Fallen Peace Corps Volunteers: Memorial Project, fpcv.org (accessed February 26, 2013). Several congressional hearings on the safety of volunteers have been held—most recently in 2011.

31. The polemical association of Peace Corps officials with missionaries is complex, especially given the tension between volunteers and missionaries in some postings. See Zimmerman, "Beyond Double Consciousness."

32. For statistics on violence in the Peace Corps, see Russell Carollo and Mei-Ling Hopgood's seven-part special report "Mission of Sacrifice: Peace Corps Volunteers Face Injury, Death in Foreign Lands," *Dayton Daily News*, October 26, 2003.

33. Bob Shacochis, review of *American Taboo: A Murder in the Peace Corps*, by Philip Weiss, July 20, 2004, *Salon*, http://www.salon.com/2004/07/20/weiss/ (accessed February 26, 2013).

34. Laura Miller, review of *Whiteman*, by Tony D'Souza, May 16, 2006, *Salon*, http://www.salon.com/2006/05/16/dsouza/ (accessed February 26, 2013).

35. P. F. Kluge, review of *American Taboo: A Murder in the Peace Corps*, by Philip Weiss, April 7, 2004, Peace Corps Writers, http://www.peacecorpswriters .org/pages/2004/0407/407rvamtaboo.html (accessed February 20, 2013).

36. Ikhide R. Ikheloa, "Whiteman: The Heart of Our Darkness," April 27, 2006, Nigerians in America, http://www.nigeriansinamerica.com/articles/997/1/White‏man-The-Heart-of-Our-Darkness/Page1.html (accessed January 23, 2013).

37. On Peace Corps Writers, Coleman's *Volunteer* is grouped with other novels that critically examine the Peace Corps sensibility: Tama Janowitz, *A Cannibal in Manhattan* (New York: Crown, 1987); Anita Shreve, *The Last Time They Met:*

A Novel (Boston: Little, Brown, 2001); and Shirley Goek-Lin Lim, Joss and Gold (New York: Feminist Press at the City University of New York, 2001).

38. O'Neill—who became security director for the Peace Corps, the Red Cross, and Save the Children—was captured and eventually escaped, according to John Coyne, "The Peace Corps Volunteer as a Fictional Character," August 21, 2009, Peace Corps Worldwide, http://peacecorpsworldwide.org/pc-writers/2009/08/21/character/ (accessed February 26, 2013).

39. For example, George Alexander Lethbridge Banbury, Sierra Leone, or the White Man's Grave (London: Sonnenschein, 1889); and F. Harrison Rankin, The White Man's Grave: A Visit to Sierra Leone in 1834 (London: Bentley, 1836). For a contemporary reassessment of European fears of health risks in West Africa, see Philip Curtin, Death by Migration: Europe's Encounter with the Tropical World in the Nineteenth Century (New York: Cambridge University Press, 1989).

40. The limitations of professional expertise are also central to Richard Dooling's later thrillers Critical Care (New York: Morrow, 1992), Brain Storm (New York: Random House, 1998), and Bet Your Life: A Novel (New York: Harper-Collins, 2003).

41. Graham Greene's African novels, The Heart of the Matter (New York: Viking, 1948) and Journey Without Maps (Garden City, N.Y.: Doubleday, Doran, 1936), are explicitly mentioned as one of the sources that Westfall consults before traveling to Sierra Leone in Dooling's White Man's Grave, 42.

42. Dooling's Brain Storm (a satire of hate crime prosecution) and his nonfiction dissections of anti-swearing rules and the hostile workplace clause have won him fans among neoconservative reviewers.

43. This is the evaluation of travel writer Tom Bissell, "Unflowered Aloes: Why Literary Success Is a Product of Chance, Not Destiny," Boston Review, April–May 2000.

44. Paul Virilio introduces these terms in an interview with Sylvère Lotringer and Michael Taormina, "After Architecture: A Conversation," Grey Room 3 (2001): 32–53.

45. Mark Jacobs, "A Serious Conversation," Counterpunch, June 19, 2003.

46. David Holloway, "The War on Terror Espionage Thriller, and the Imperialism of Human Rights," Comparative Literature Studies 46, no. 1 (2009): 20–44.

47. Tom Bissell asserts that "the Peace Corps, if nothing else, has midwifed some first-rate American literature with an internationalist bent" ("Destination: Central Asia," June 22, 2006, "The Literary Guide to the World," Salon, http://www.salon.com/2006/06/22/central_asia/ [accessed January 23, 2013]).

48. Jack Kerouac, *On the Road* (New York: Penguin, 1951), 280. See also Robert Holton's brilliant "Kerouac Among the Fellahin: *On the Road* to the Postmodern," *Modern Fiction Studies* 41, no. 2 (1995): 265–283.

49. "Talking with . . . Tony D'Souza" [interview with John Coyne], June 3, 2006, Peace Corps Writers, http://www.peacecorpswriters.org/pages/2006/0603/603talk dsouza.html (accessed February 26, 2013).

50. In his interview with Coyne, D'Souza describes his disenchantment with the Peace Corps as the result of its unwillingness to protect volunteers during outbreaks of violence, as well as other American officials' inability to even name political figures in the Ivory Coast.

51. For example, in an aside on *Whiteman*, Christine Smallwood asks, "Did another story of a white man's existential crisis in Africa need to be told?" ("Lost Belongings" [review of *The Konkans*, by Tony D'Souza], February–March 2008, Bookforum, http://bookforum.com/inprint/014_05/2077 (accessed February 26, 2013).

52. For more context on Côte d'Ivoire, see Siddhartha Mitter's comprehensive essay "Ebony and Ivoirité: War and Peace in Ivory Coast," *Transition* 12, no. 4 (2003): 30–55. On post–September 11 mutations to the thriller more generally, see Holloway, "War on Terror Espionage Thriller."

53. The exception would be a brief mention of essays on racial fantasies that the Peace Corps applicants were supposedly asked to write in Norman Rush's *Mortals* (2003).

54. Erik Erikson, "Autobiographic Notes on the Identity Crisis," *Dedalus* 99, no. 4 (1970): 733.

55. This is one of the few Peace Corps novels that has inspired a body of scholarly commentary. See Dave Kuhne, *African Settings in Contemporary American Novels* (Westport, Conn.: Greenwood Press, 1999); John Cullen Gruesser, *White on Black: Contemporary Literature About Africa* (Urbana: University of Illinois Press, 1992); and Dennis Hickey and Kenneth C. Wylie, *An Enchanting Darkness: The American Vision of Africa in the Twentieth Century* (East Lansing: Michigan State University Press, 1993).

56. Although art historians sometimes dismiss the complex carvings of the Makonde as tourist art, in Thomas's *Antonia Saw the Oryx First*, Makonde sculpture and matrilineal social structures are associated with the Tanzanian independence movement. See Leon V. Hirsch, "The Authenticity of Makonde Art," *African Arts* 26, no. 1 (1993): 10, 12, 14, 100.

57. In this respect, these novels employ the pragmatic administrative thinking that John Marx attributes to the full range of contemporary authors in *Geopolitics*

and the Anglophone Novel, 1890–2011 (New York: Cambridge University Press, 2012).

58. Gabrielle Danchick, review of *Fieldwork*, by Mischa Berlinski, *New York Post*, February 18, 2007. Danchick places Berlinski's novel in the context of backpacker narratives by Alex Garland, *The Beach* (New York: Riverhead, 1997); Katy Gardner, *Losing Gemma* (New York: Riverhead, 2002); Scott Landers, *Coswell's Guide to Tambralinga: A Novel* (New York: Farrar, Straus and Giroux, 2004); and George Mastras, *Fidali's Way: A Novel* (New York: Scribner, 2009). Kevin Hannam and Irena Ateljevic treat backpacker fiction as a distinct genre, identifiable by its distinction between travel and tourism, in "Introduction: Conceptualising and Profiling Backpacker Tourism," in *Backpacker Tourism: Concepts and Profiles*, ed. Kevin Hannam and Irena Ateljevic (Tonawanda, N.Y.: Channel View Press, 2008), 1–6. Julie Wilson describes her own canon of backpacker authors in "Backpacker Icons: Influential Literary 'Nomads' in the Formation of Backpacker Identities," in *The Global Nomad: Backpacker Travel in Theory and Practice*, ed. Greg Richards and Julie Wilson (Tonawanda, N.Y.: Channel View Press, 2004), 123–148.

59. Orner was a Worldteach volunteer in Namibia in 1991 and 1992. Worldteach is an independent nongovernmental organization similar to the Peace Corps.

60. Richard Wiley has also published a more conventional Peace Corps novel, *Festival for Three Thousand Maidens* (New York: Dutton, 1991), based on his experiences teaching English in Korea from 1967 to 1969, as well as the PEN/Faulkner Award–winning World War II novel *Soldiers in Hiding: A Novel* (Boston: Atlantic Monthly Press, 1987).

61. Sadako Ogata, former United Nations High Commissioner for Refugees, asserts the centrality of refugee questions to geopolitics in *The Turbulent Decade: Confronting the Refugee Crises of the 1990s* (New York: Norton, 2005).

62. Dambisa Moyo argues that "millions in Africa are poorer today because of aid" (*Dead Aid: Why Aid Is Not Working and How There Is a Better Way for Africa* [New York: Farrar, Straus and Giroux, 2009], xix).

63. Slavoj Žižek, "The Violence of Liberal Democracy," *Assemblage*, April 1993, 92.

64. Norman Rush, *Whites: Stories* (New York: Knopf, 1986), and *Mating* (New York: Knopf, 1991).

65. Rush's writing has been widely reviewed in major American periodicals. Not everyone loves his garrulous style. See, for example, John Updike's panning of *Mortals* in "Botswana Blues," *New Yorker*, June 2, 2003.

66. Rush has said that he based the insurgency on Patrice Lumumba's uprising in the Belgian Congo (present-day Democratic Republic of the Congo) in

1960, as well as Alice Lakwena's Holy Spirit movement in Uganda, in "Talking with . . . Norm Rush" [interview with Ron Singer], January 3, 2001, Peace Corps Writers, http://www.peacecorpswriters.org/pages/2001/0103/103talkrush.html (accessed February 26, 2013).

67. Ibid.; Norm Rush, "Spying and Lying" [review of *The Tailor of Panama*, by John Le Carré], *New York Times Book Review*, October 20, 1996.

68. Many Peace Corps memoirs mention locals' suspicion that volunteers are really CIA agents; Rush has literalized this idea in the person of his main character.

69. Sheldon G. Weeks, "A Disappointing Novel" [review of *Mating*, by Norman Rush], *Africa Today* 40, no. 1 (1993): 79–80.

70. The phrase "alien politics" appears in James Wood's otherwise positive "Thinking" [review of *Mortals*, by Norman Rush], *New Republic*, June 23, 2003; in "Botswana Blues," Updike chides Rush for not writing about American subjects. Surprisingly, many reviewers praise *Mating* for being a good novel, even though it is set in Africa.

3. NEOLIBERAL ALLEGORIES

1. Fredric Jameson, "Third-World Literature in the Era of Multinational Capitalism," *Social Text* 15 (1986): 65–88.

2. Fredric Jameson, "The Cultural Logic of Late Capitalism," in *Postmodernism, or the Cultural Logic of Late Capitalism* (Durham, N.C.: Duke University Press, 1992), 1–50.

3. Aijaz Ahmad, "Jameson's Rhetoric of Otherness and the 'National Allegory,'" *Social Text* 17 (1987): 3–25.

4. Nicholas Brown explains reactions to Jameson's essay as effects of academic micropolitics and Cold War macropolitics in *Utopian Generations: The Political Horizon of Twentieth-Century Literature* (Princeton, N.J.: Princeton University Press, 2005), 9–10.

5. Imre Szeman, "Who's Afraid of National Allegory? Jameson, Literary Criticism, Globalization," *South Atlantic Quarterly* 100, no. 3 (2001): 803–827; Vitaly Chernetsky, *Mapping Postcommunist Cultures: Russia and Ukraine in the Context of* (Montreal: McGill–Queens University Press, 2007); Glenn Willmott, *Unreal Country: Modernity in the Canadian Novel in English* (Montreal: McGill–Queens University Press, 2002); Amy Zalman, "Gender and the Palestinian Narrative of Return in Two Novels by Ghassan Kanafani," in *Literature and Nation in the Middle East*, ed. Yasir Suleiman and Ibrahim Muhawki (Edinburgh: Edinburgh University Press, 2006), 48–78; Leerom Medovi, *Rebels: Youth and the Cold War*

Origins of Identity (Durham, N.C.: Duke University Press, 2005); Evan Mwangi, *Africa Writes Back to Self: Metafiction, Gender, Sexuality* (Albany: State University of New York Press, 2009); Christopher L. Hill, *National History and the World of Nations: Capital, State and the Rhetoric of History in Japan, France, and the United States* (Durham, N.C.: Duke University Press, 2008). Neil Lazarus asserts that Jameson's essay on Third World literature raises "massively consequential questions" and goes a long way toward answering them in *The Postcolonial Unconscious* (New York: Cambridge University Press, 2011), 107.

6. Srinivas Aravamudan, "In the Wake of the Novel: The Oriental Tale as National Allegory," *Novel* 33, no. 1 (1999): 5–31; Oliver Lovesey, "Chained Letters: African Prison Diaries and 'National Allegory,'" *Research in African Literatures* 26, no. 4 (1995): 31–45; Thomas Palakeel, "Third World Short Story as National Allegory?" *Journal of Modern Literature* 20, no. 1 (1996): 97–102.

7. Joseph Slaughter, "Master Plans: Designing (National) Allegories of Urban Space and Metropolitan Subjects for Postcolonial Kenya," *Research in African Literatures* 35, no. 1 (2004): 49.

8. The National Endowment for the Arts documented the declining percentage of readers in the United States in "To Read or Not to Read: A Question of National Consequence" (Washington, D.C.: National Endowment for the Arts, 2007), http://www.nea.gov/research/ToRead_ExecSum.pdf. Statistics compiled by the American publishing industry indicate that at most 3 percent of annual publications in English are translations. See Esther Allen, "Translation, Globalization and English," in *To Be Translated or Not to Be: PEN/IRL Report on the International Situation of Literary Translation*, ed. Esther Allen (Barcelona: Institut Ramon Llull, 2007), 24, http://llull.cat/IMAGES_2/Trad%20ENG.pdf (both accessed March 4, 2013).

9. Tzvetan Todorov, "The Origin of Genres," *New Literary History* 8 (1976–1977): 159–170.

10. Francine Prose, review of *Sacred Games*, by Vikram Chandra, *People*, January 15, 2007, 41.

11. Paul Gray, review of *Death of Vishnu*, by Manil Suri, *Time*, February 21, 2001; Helen Haywood, review of *Death of Vishnu*, by Manil Suri, *New Statesman*, January 22, 2001.

12. Review of *In Other Rooms, Other Wonders*, by Daniyal Mueenuddin, *People*, February 16, 2009; Karin Aguilar-San Juan, review of *Dream Jungle*, by Jessica Hagedorn, *Women's Review of Books*, March 2004, 5.

13. Caroline Hallsworth, review of *Half of a Yellow Sun*, by Chimamanda Adichie, *Library Journal*, September 1, 2006; Jim Dwyer, review of *PU-239 and Other Russian Fantasies*, by Ken Kalfus, *Library Journal*, August 1, 1999.

14. Stephen Morrow, review of *Lost City Radio*, by Daniel Alarcón, *Library Journal*, December 1, 2006.

15. David Harvey, "Neoliberalism as Creative Destruction," *Annals of the American Academy of Political and Social Science* 610, no. 1 (2007): 21–44.

16. The ambivalent role played by consumerist idealism in the context of neoliberalism is a major theme of Inderpal Grewal, *Transnational America: Feminisms, Diasporas, Neoliberalisms* (Durham, N.C.: Duke University Press, 2005).

17. Aiwa Ong, *Flexible Citizenship: The Cultural Logics of Transnationality* (Durham, N.C.: Duke University Press, 1999); David Harvey, *Spaces of Global Capitalism: Towards a Theory of Uneven Geographical Development* (New York: Verso, 2006).

18. Jean Comaroff and John L. Comaroff, "Millennial Capitalism: First Thoughts on a Second Coming," *Public Culture* 12, no. 2 (2000): 305–335.

19. On occultism, see Gauri Viswanathan, "The Ordinary Business of Occultism," *Critical Inquiry* 27, no. 1 (2000): 1–20.

20. I am recapping main themes of Franco Moretti, "Conjectures on World Literature," *New Left Review* 1 (2000): 54–68.

21. Fernando Coronil, *The Magical State: Nature, Money, and Modernity in Venezuela* (Chicago: University of Chicago Press, 1997).

22. Recent Rust Belt narratives include Richard Russo, *Empire Falls* (New York: Knopf, 2001); and Philipp Meyer, *American Rust* (New York: Spiegel & Grau, 2009). For experimental versions, see George Saunders, *Civilwarland in Bad Decline: Stories and a Novella* (New York: Random House, 1996); Ben Marcus, *The Age of Wire and String* (Normal, Ill.: Dalkey Archive Press, 1995); and many of the novels of Joyce Carol Oates.

23. For a sampling of writing on expatriation, see Amitava Kumar, ed., *Away: The Indian Writer as Expatriate* (New York: Routledge, 2004).

24. Amitava Kumar, "Louder Than Bombs: What's So Hot About Indian Writing?" *Transition* 79 (1999), 80–101.

25. Menakshi Mukherjee, "The Anxiety of Indianness: Our Novels in English," *Economic and Political Weekly*, November 27, 1993, 2607–2611. See also Margaret Sabin on Pankaj Mishra's *Romantics*, in *Dissenters and Mavericks: Writings About India in English, 1765–2000* (New York: Oxford University Press, 2002).

26. Manjushree Thapa discusses the division between Nepali liberals and progressives in "Reaching One's Own People, Reaching the World," *Manoa* 13, no. 3 (2001): 37–53. Kumar directs attention to the working-class diaspora in "Louder Than Bombs."

27. On this, see Gaurav Desai's beautifully argued essay "Old World Orders: Amitav Ghosh and the Writing of Nostalgia," *Representations* 85 (2004): 125–148; and Yumna Siddiqi, "Police and Postcolonial Rationality in Amitav Ghosh's *The Circle of Reason*," *Cultural Critique* 50 (2002): 175–211.

28. Dirk Wiemann, *Genres of Modernity: Contemporary Indian Novels in English* (Amsterdam: Rodopi, 2008), 73.

29. Paul Sharrad complains that Mishra's *Romantics* contains too much "calculated address to a foreign audience" (review of *The Romantics*, by Pankaj Mishra, *World Literature Today* 74, no. 3 [2000]: 584).

30. Brian T. Edwards discusses the continuing appeal of Orientalism in *Morocco Bound: Disorienting America's Mahgreb, from Casablanca to the Marrakech Express* (Durham, N.C.: Duke University Press, 2005).

31. Srinivas Aravamudan, *Tropicopolitans: Colonialism and Agency, 1688–1804* (Durham, N.C.: Duke University Press, 1999).

32. For a careful reading of the modern Indian novel's dialogue with European realism, see Ulka Anjaria, *Realism in the Twentieth-Century Indian Novel: Colonial Difference and Literary Form* (Cambridge: Cambridge University Press, 2012).

33. This is the romantic "centrality of the suffering and active ego" that sees "the world as something outside which is apparently incapable of penetrating to those recesses from which all awareness starts" (Frederick Garber, "Self, Society, Value, and the Romantic Hero," *Comparative Literature* 19, no. 4 [1967]: 321).

34. Ghosh and Mishraj invoke Wordsworthian melancholy, rather than the Blakean prophetic mode that advances a nineteenth-century critique of Orientalism, according to Saree Makdisi, *Romantic Imperialism: Universal Empire and the Culture of Modernity* (New York: Cambridge University Press, 1998).

35. This trope of the interrupted idyll through American Romanticism is traced in Leo Marx's classic study *The Machine in the Garden: Technology and the Pastoral Ideal in America* (New York: Oxford University Press, 1964).

36. Thomas Pfau argues that emotion anticipates cognition for the Romantics, especially social cognition, in *Romantic Moods: Paranoia, Trauma and Melancholy, 1790–1840* (Baltimore: Johns Hopkins University Press, 2005), 27–28.

37. Morton D. Paley argues that "the imminence of an apocalypse that will be succeeded by a millennium" is "a major topos" for the Romantics (*Apocalypse and Millennium in English Romantic Poetry* [New York: Oxford University Press, 1999], 1).

38. Edie Meidav also describes a traveler arriving in Sri Lanka and encountering utopian communities gone awry in *The Far Field: A Novel of Ceylon* (Boston:

Houghton Mifflin, 2001), and Michael Ondaatje's widely read *Anil's Ghost* (New York: Knopf, 2000) uses essentially the same formula in the more contemporary forensic detection genre.

39. These passages teeter between W. J. T. Mitchell's second and third senses of ekphrastic description: hope and fear: "Ekphrastic hope and fear express our anxieties about merging with others," and verbal reproduction of the visual scene keeps this ambivalence alive (*Picture Theory: Essays on Verbal and Visual Representation* [Chicago: University of Chicago Press, 1994], 163).

40. Ann Bermingham describes Romantic approaches to framing and composition in *Landscape and Ideology: The English Rustic Tradition, 1740–1860* (Berkeley: University of California Press, 1989), chap. 2.

41. Exogamous marriage is a key component in Doris Sommer's description of national romance in *Foundational Fictions: The National Romances of Latin America* (Berkeley: University of California Press, 1993), 18–19.

42. Developing terms borrowed from Karl Mannheim, Nicholas M. Williams describes this kind of crisis as chiliastic, concerned with an Eternal Now that collapses past–future and subject–object distinctions, in *Ideology and Utopia in the Poetry of William Blake* (Cambridge: Cambridge University Press, 1998), 144.

43. Shahnaz Habib, "The Book Bench: Exchange with Daniyal Mueenuddin," *New Yorker*, March 3, 2009.

44. For a discussion of this theme in American Romanticism, see David Blight's history *Race and Reunion: The Civil War in American Memory* (Cambridge, Mass.: Harvard University Press, 2001).

45. "The theme of the comic is the integration of society," writes Northrop Frye in *Anatomy of Criticism: Four Essays*, ed. Robert D. Denham (1957; Toronto: University of Toronto Press, 2006), 40.

46. Sommer, *Foundational Fictions*; Lee Edelman, *No Future: Queer Theory and the Death Drive* (Durham, N.C.: Duke University Press, 2004). See also Rosemary Marangoly George, *The Politics of Home: Postcolonial Relocations and Twentieth-Century Fiction* (New York: Cambridge University Press, 1996).

47. So argues Sharon Marcus, *Apartment Stories: City and Home in Nineteenth-Century Paris and London* (Berkeley: University of California Press, 1999).

48. Krishan Kumar and Ekatarina Makarova outline a similar dynamic in the United States in "The Portable Home: The Domestication of Public Space," *Sociological Theory* 26, no. 4 (2008): 324–343.

49. Catherine Kroll, "Rwanda's Speaking Subjects: The Inescapable Affiliations of Boubacar Boris Diop's *Murambi*," *Third World Quarterly* 28, no. 3 (2007): 655–663.

50. Simon Gikandi, *Reading the African Novel* (London: Heinemann, 1987); Ernest Emenyonu, *The Rise of the Igbo Novel* (New York: Oxford University Press, 1978); Derek Wright, ed., *Contemporary African Fiction* (Bayreuth: Bayreuth African Studies, 1997).

51. Said A. M. Khamis notes parallel developments in non-Anglophone writing in "Signs of New Features in the Swahili Novel," *Research in African Literatures* 36, no. 1 (2005): 91–108.

52. Wole Ogundele, "Devices of Evasion: The Mythic Versus the Historical Imagination in the Postcolonial African Novel," *Research in African Literatures* 33, no. 3 (2002): 132.

53. Adélékè Adéèkó, "Power Shift: America in the Nigerian Imagination," *Global South* 2, no. 2 (2008): 22.

54. Binyavanga Wainaina, "How to Write About Africa," *Granta* 92: "The View from Africa," winter 2005.

55. The *Granta* editor's head note to Wainaina's piece indicates that it is the most frequent "hit" on the entire *Granta* site.

56. In her masterful synthetic account of the Nigerian literary scene, Wendy Griswold argues that unlike the faith in rationality expressed in crime fiction, political novels reflect intellectuals' collective loss of faith in the Nigerian Dream following the collapse of the oil boom, in *Bearing Witness: Readers, Writers, and the Novel in Nigeria* (Princeton, N.J.: Princeton University Press, 2000), 262.

57. The Isak Dinesen fad of the 1980s has been the subject of scathing commentary. See, for example, Ngugi wa Thiong'o, "Literature and Society," in *Writers in Politics: Essays* (London: Heinemann, 1981), 1–33.

58. Madeleine Hron, "*Ora na-azu nwa*: The Figure of the Child in Third-Generation Nigerian Novels," *Research in African Literatures* 39, no. 2 (2008): 27–48.

59. For more on the colonial miseducation of the child as well as the ambivalent appeal of modernity, see Willmott, *Unreal Country*, 23–26.

60. On adolescent rebellion in American national allegories, see Medovoi, *Rebels*.

61. By comparison, recent novels written by white Americans describing Africa tend to deemphasize the patriarch. See, for example, Russell Banks, *The Darling* (2004); and Dave Eggers, *What Is the What: The Autobiography of Valentino Achak Deng: A Novel* (2006). Even Barbara Kingsolver's *Poisonwood Bible: A Novel* (New York: HarperFlamingo 1998), which describes the adventures of a missionary family following the devout father to the Congo, stresses the autonomy of the daughters.

62. As is Aminatta Forna's much more magical *Ancestor Stones* (New York: Atlantic Monthly Press, 2006), a novel that links the voices of a mother, co-wives, and grandmothers through their relation to a patriarch.

63. Achille Mbembe, *On the Postcolony* (Berkeley: University of California Press, 2001), chap. 3.

64. Adéèkó makes the last point in "Power Shift."

65. This is Mike Davis's term for a partially urbanized countryside filled with industrial farms in *Planet of Slums* (New York: Verso, 2006), 9.

66. Related narratives of psychological turmoil in the Afro-British context appear in two of Helen Oyeyemi's novels: *The Icarus Girl* (2005) and *White Is for Witching* (New York: Nan A. Talese/Doubleday, 2009).

67. Mbembe discusses rhetorical excess and the postcolonial state in *On the Postcolony*, 105.

68. On correspondence between American policy objectives and academic funding for Slavic studies, see David Engerman, *Know Your Enemy: The Rise and Fall of America's Soviet Experts* (New York: Oxford University Press, 2009).

69. Edith W. Clowes makes this point about Solzhenitsyn and argues that Zamiatin is updated in the "meta-utopias" of Grigory Zinoviev, Abram Terts, and Venedict Erofeev in *Russian Experimental Fiction: Resisting Ideology After Utopia* (Princeton, N.J.: Princeton University Press, 1993).

70. Jeremy Morris, "From *Chudak* to *Mudak*? Village Prose and the Absurdist Ethics of Evgenii Popov," *Modern Language Review* 99, no. 3 (2004): 696–710; Angela Brintlinger, "The Hero in the Madhouse: The Post-Soviet Novel Confronts the Soviet Past," *Slavic Review* 63, no. 1 (2004): 43–65; Kathleen Parthé, "The Righteous Brothers (and Sisters) of Contemporary Russian Literature," *World Literature Today* 67, no. 1 (1993): 91–99.

71. Ironic uses of socialist realism are described in Marina Balina, Nancy Condee, and Evgeny Dobrenko, eds., *Endquote: Sots-Art Literature and Soviet Grand Style* (Evanston, Ill.: Northwestern University Press, 2000); N. N. Schneidman describes the socialist realist aims of authors of "patriotic fiction" in *Russian Literature, 1995–2002: On the Threshold of the New Millennium* (Toronto: University of Toronto Press, 2004); Mark Lipovetsky argues that socialist realism provides plot structures for gangster stories in "New Russians as a Cultural Myth," *Russian Review* 62, no. 1 (2003): 54–79; Kathleen Parthé considers sentimental village novels implicitly critical of socialist realism and the collective farm in *Russian Village Prose: The Radiant Past* (Princeton, N.J.: Princeton University Press, 1992).

72. Like Chernetsky in *Mapping Postcommunist Cultures*, Mark Lipovetsky describes a flourishing of postmodernism in contemporary Russian literature in *Rus-*

sian Postmodernist Fiction: Dialogue with Chaos (Armonk, N.Y.: Sharpe, 2000); "postrealism" is the term used in N. L. Leiderman and M. N. Lipovetskii, *Sovremannaia russkaia literatura* (Moscow: Editorial URSS, 2001), reviewed by N. N. Schneidman, *Slavic Review* 62, no. 1 (2003): 223–224. Alexander Etkind develops the concept of magical historicism in "Stories of the Undead in the Land of the Unburied: Magical Historicism in Contemporary Russian Fiction," *Slavic Review* 68, no. 3 (2009), 631–658.

73. Lipovetsky, "New Russians as a Cultural Myth"; Valentina G. Brougher, "The Occult in Russian Literature of the 1990s," *Russian Review* 56, no. 1 (1997): 110–124. Etkind gives several examples of fascinations with sectarian practices in "Stories of the Undead." On feminist and queer writing, see Chernetsky, *Mapping Postcommunist Cultures.*

74. Rosalind Marsh, *Images of Dictatorship: Portraits of Stalin in Literature* (London: Routledge, 1989).

75. Charles A. Knight argues that national preoccupations define satire, dividing them into outward-looking "satiric nationalism" and inward-looking "satiric exile," in *The Literature of Satire* (Cambridge: Cambridge University Press, 2004).

76. Steven Weisenberger argues that cannibalistic violence signals the anti-ideological politics of contemporary satire in *Fables of Subversion: Satire and the American Novel, 1930–1980* (Athens: University of Georgia Press, 1995), 140.

77. Drastic shifts and contrasts in scale are key to many accounts of time–space compression in the global economy, but this literary use of scalar contrast clearly owes a great deal to Rabelais as well. See Mikhail Bakhtin, *Rabelais and His World*, trans. Helene Iswolsky (Bloomington: Indiana University Press, 1984).

78. Frye argues that utopia is a subgenre of satire, in addition to often serving as a target of satire, and that the two forms belong together, in *Anatomy of Criticism*, 223–240.

79. This distinction between utopian plans and the utopian impulse is made in Fredric Jameson, *Archaeologies of the Future: The Desire Called Utopia and Other Science Fictions* (Durham, N.C.: Duke University Press 2005).

80. Jill E. Twark catalogues similar effects in housing narratives set in the German Democratic Republic, in *Humor, Satire and Identity: East German Literature in the 1990s* (Berlin: de Gruyter, 2007).

81. In 2009, Fujimori was convicted of corruption and human rights abuses committed during Peru's war against leftist guerrillas. See Joshua Partlow and Lucien Chauvin, "Peru's Fujimori Gets 25 Years," *Washington Post*, April 8, 2009.

82. Similar concerns animate Nathan Englander, *Ministry of Special Cases* (New York: Knopf, 2007); Rivka Galchen, *Atmospheric Disturbances* (2008); and Nicole Krauss, *Great House* (2010).

83. In addition to the best-selling genre novel *The Nanny Diaries* and its sequels, a number of more aesthetically ambitious works have updated the Victorian governess narrative for twenty-first-century scenes; most are set in wealthy American households. See Lori Tharps, *Substitute Me* (New York: Atria Trade, 2010); Suzanne Berne, *A Perfect Arrangement* (Chapel Hill, N.C.: Algonquin Books, 2001); Mary Dermansky, *Bad Marie* (New York: Harper Perennial, 2010); Victoria Brown, *Minding Ben* (New York: Hyperion-Voice, 2011); Mona Simpson, *My Hollywood* (New York: Knopf, 2010); Tracy Davis, *My Husband Ran Off with the Nanny and God Do I Miss Her* (Booksurge, 2010); and the opening sections of Francine Prose, *My New American Life* (2011).

84. For a fuller treatment of the cultural history of the bourgeois family home, see Marjorie Garber, *Sex and Real Estate: Why We Love Houses* (New York: Pantheon, 2000).

85. The phrase is Davis's in *Planet of Slums*.

86. For subtle readings of urbanism in contemporary African American literature, see Madhu Dubey, *Signs and Cities: Black Literary Postmodernism* (Chicago: University of Chicago Press, 2003).

87. Marcus, *Apartment Stories*.

4. IDEOLOGY, TERROR, AND APOCALYPSE

1. Francis Fukuyama, *The End of History and the Last Man* (New York: Penguin 1992), 1.

2. Francis Fukuyama, *America at the Crossroads: Democracy, Power, and the Neoconservative Legacy* (New Haven, Conn.: Yale University Press, 2006), and *The Origins of Political Power: From Prehuman Times to the French Revolution* (New York: Farrar, Straus and Giroux, 2011).

3. Alain Gresh, "Neither with the West Nor Against It," *Le Monde diplomatique*, March 2011.

4. Michel Foucault, "Useless to Revolt?" in *Power*, vol. 3 of *The Essential Works of Foucault, 1954–1984*, ed. James D. Faubion (New York: New Press, 2001), 449–453.

5. John Locke, *Of Civil Government: The Second Treatise* (1689; New York: Dover, 2002), 102.

6. On Lenin, see Slavoj Žižek, *On Belief* (New York: Routledge, 2001), 113–124; on Mao, see Rebecca E. Karl, *Mao Zedong and China in the Twentieth-Century World* (Durham, N.C.: Duke University Press, 2010).

7. Alain Badiou, "The Communist Hypothesis," *New Left Review* 49 (2008): 1789–1848.

8. David A. Zimmerman, *Panic! Markets, Crises, and Crowds in American Fiction* (Chapel Hill: University of North Carolina Press, 2006); Michael Denning, *The Cultural Front: The Laboring of American Culture in the Twentieth Century* (New York: Verso, 1996); Barbara Foley, *Radical Representations: Politics and Form in U.S. Proletarian Fiction, 1929–1941* (Durham, N.C.: Duke University Press, 1994).

9. György Lukács, *The Historical Novel*, trans. Hannah Mitchell and Stanley Mitchell (Boston: Beacon Press, 1962).

10. Linda Hutcheon, *A Poetics of Postmodernism: History, Theory, Fiction* (New York: Routledge, 1988).

11. Walter Benjamin, "Theses on the Philosophy of History," in *Illuminations: Essays and Reflections*, ed. Hannah Arendt, trans. Harry Zohn (1968; New York: Continuum, 1999), 261.

12. Perry Anderson, "From Progress to Catastrophe," *London Review of Books*, July 28, 2011, 28.

13. Lois Zamora, *Writing the Apocalypse: Historical Vision in Contemporary U.S. and Latin American Fiction* (New York: Cambridge University Press, 1989), 1–15.

14. M. O. Grenby, *The Anti-Jacobin Novel: British Conservatism and the French Revolution* (New York: Cambridge University Press, 2001), 43.

15. Anthony Jarrells makes this opposition in "Bloodless Revolution and the Form of the Novel," *Novel* 37, nos. 1–2 (2003–2004): 24–44.

16. Nigel Smith, *Literature and Revolution in England, 1640–1660* (New Haven, Conn.: Yale University Press, 1994); Carol Clark D'Lugo, *The Fragmented Novel in Mexico: The Politics of Form* (Austin: University of Texas Press, 1997); Cathy N. Davidson, *Revolution and the Word: The Rise of the Novel in America* (New York: Oxford University Press, 1986); Edward Larkin, *Thomas Paine and the Literature of Revolution* (Cambridge: Cambridge University Press, 2005); Nicola J. Watson, *Revolution and the Form of the British Novel, 1790–1835: Intercepted Letters, Interrupted Seductions* (New York: Oxford University Press, 1994).

17. Andrew Stauffer, *Anger, Revolution, and Romanticism* (New York: Cambridge University Press, 2005); Kevin M. F. Platt, *History in a Grotesque Key: Rus-*

sian Literature and the Idea of Revolution (Stanford, Calif.: Stanford University Press, 1997).

18. Revisionists include Grenby, *Anti-Jacobin Novel*; Paul Downes, *Democracy, Revolution, and Monarchism in Early American Literature* (New York: Cambridge University Press, 2002); and Victor Ehrlich, *Modernism and Revolution: Russian Literature in Transition* (Cambridge, Mass.: Harvard University Press, 1994).

19. James T. Siegel, *Fetish, Recognition, Revolution* (Princeton, N.J.: Princeton University Press, 1997).

20. Susan Suleiman develops this position in *Authoritarian Fictions: The Ideological Novel as Literary Genre* (New York: Columbia University Press, 1983).

21. Giorgio Agamben, *Homo Sacer: Sovereign Power and Bare Life*, trans. Daniel Heller-Roazen (Stanford, Calif.: Stanford University Press, 1998).

22. Caren Irr, *The Suburb of Dissent: Cultural Politics in the United States and Canada During the 1930s* (Durham, N.C.: Duke University Press, 1998), chap. 4.

23. Jürgen Habermas's account of the rise of modern formalist liberalism is in *The Structural Transformation of the Public Sphere: An Inquiry into a Category of Bourgeois Society* (1962; Cambridge, Mass.: MIT Press, 1991).

24. Theda Skocpol, *States and Social Revolution: A Comparative Analysis of France, Russia, and China* (New York: Cambridge University Press, 1979), 170.

25. Here, I summarize Walter Benn Michaels's argument in *The Shape of the Signifier* (Princeton, N.J.: Princeton University Press, 2006).

26. See also Christopher Sorrentino, *Trance* (New York: Farrar, Straus and Giroux, 2005), another recounting of the Hearst kidnapping.

27. Michael Hardt and Antonio Negri, *Multitude* (Cambridge, Mass.: Harvard University Press, 2005), 32.

28. The opposite motif dominates contemporary journalism, however, as David James Clark documents in "Representing the Majority World: Famine, Photojournalism and the Changing Visual Economy" (Ph.D. diss., Durham University, 2009).

29. Elaine Scarry, "Injury and the Structure of War," *Representations* 10 (1985): 1–51.

30. See, for example, Ngugi wa Thiongo's account of drought and longing in *Petals of Blood* (London: Heinemann, 1977) or Paul Bowles's exploration of the conditions that foster anticolonial uprisings in Morocco in *The Spider's House* (New York: Random House, 1955).

31. Skocpol, *States and Social Revolution*, 5.

32. For example, Forest D. Colburn asserts that socialist ideologies cause failed revolutions in *The Vogue of Revolution in Poor Countries* (Princeton, N.J.: Princeton University Press, 1997).

33. Slavoj Žižek, "Seize the Day: Lenin's Legacy," *London Review of Books*, July 25, 2002.

34. Neil Lazarus argues that post-independence writers conflated political and social revolution in *Resistance in Postcolonial African Fiction* (New Haven, Conn.: Yale University Press, 1990).

35. Manning Marable, "Against Power," *Transition* 64 (1994): 143.

36. Jeremy D. Popkin, "Facing Racial Revolution: Captivity Narratives and Identity in the Saint-Domingue Insurrection," *Eighteenth-Century Studies* 36, no. 3 (2003): 511–533.

37. Bell describes his spiritual practices in Jack Stephens, "Madison Smartt Bell," *BOMB* 73 (2000).

38. Amy Elias discusses Bell's trilogy in *Sublime Desire: History and Post-1960s Fiction* (Baltimore: Johns Hopkins University Press, 2001).

39. On apocalyptic fiction, see Zamora, *Writing the Apocalypse*; Malcolm Bull, ed., *Apocalypse Theory and the Ends of the World* (New York: Blackwell, 1995), and *Seeing Things Hidden: Apocalypse, Vision, and Totality* (New York: Verso, 2000); and Slavoj Žižek, *Living in the End Times* (New York: Verso, 2010).

40. Michael André Bernstein rejects deterministic "backshadowing" in *Foregone Conclusions: Against Apocalyptic History* (Berkeley: University of California Press, 1994), preferring "sideshadowing" and narratives of quotidian survival.

41. Postwar apocalyptic writing often advocates changes in environmental or nuclear policy. See Jacqueline Foertsch, "'Extraordinarily Convenient Neighbors': African-American Characters in White-Authored Post-Atomic Novels," *Journal of Modern Literature* 30, no. 4 (2007): 122–138.

42. Klaus Scherpe, "Dramatization and De-dramatization of 'the Era': The Apocalyptic Consciousness of Modernity and Post-Modernity," *Cultural Critique* 5 (1986–1987): 96.

43. Foertsch, "Extraordinarily Convenient Neighbors," 124.

5. TOWARD THE WORLD NOVEL

1. Lawrence Buell, however, tries to bridge the distance between the great American national novel and the world novel in "The Unkillable Dream of the Great American Novel: *Moby-Dick* as Test Case," *American Literary History* 20, nos. 1–2 (2008): 132–155.

2. These features of the world novel have been identified by Rita Barnard, "Fictions of the Global," *Novel* 42, no. 2 (2009): 207–215; Vilashini Coopan, *Worlds Within: National Narratives and Global Connections in Postcolonial Writing*

(Stanford, Calif.: Stanford University Press, 2009); and Michael Valdez Moses, *The Novel and the Globalization of Culture* (New York: Oxford University Press, 1995).

3. Benedict Anderson, *Under Three Flags: Anarchism and the Anti-Colonial Imagination* (New York: Verso, 2005); Malcolm Bradbury, *No, Not Bloomsbury* (New York: Columbia University Press, 1987); Guy Reynolds, *Apostles of Modernity: American Writers in the Age of Development* (Lincoln: University of Nebraska Press, 2008); Timothy Brennan, *At Home in the World: Cosmopolitanism Now* (Cambridge, Mass.: Harvard University Press, 1997); Maxine Hong Kingston, "The Novel's Next Step: If Someone Could Create the Global Novel, We'd All Have a Sequel," *Mother Jones*, December 1989, 37–41.

4. Joseph Slaughter, *Human Rights, Inc.* (New York: Fordham University Press, 2007).

5. Michael Denning, *Culture in the Age of Three Worlds* (New York: Verso, 2004), 51–53.

6. The film theorist Rick Altman has developed a rigorous structuralist language for genre in "A Semantic/Syntactic Approach to Film Genre," *Cinema Journal* 23, no. 3 (1984): 6–18.

7. Bruce Robbins, "The Worlding of the American Novel," in *The Cambridge History of the American Novel*, ed. Leonard Cassuto (New York: Cambridge University Press, 2011), 1099, 1100.

8. Caroline Hamilton, *One Man Zeitgeist: Dave Eggers, Publishing. and Publicity* (New York: Continuum, 2010).

9. Malcolm Bradbury, "Second Countries: The Expatriate Tradition in American Writing," *Yearbook of English Studies* 8 (1978): 15–39.

10. Carolyn Forché, "Expatriate," *Iowa Review* 12, nos. 2–3 (1981): 82.

11. Deborah L. Parsons, *Streetwalking the Metropolis: Women, the City, and Modernity* (New York: Oxford University Press, 2000), 135.

12. On feminist and colonial reconsiderations of the urban expatriate, see ibid. See also Gary Edward Holcomb, "The Sun Also Rises in Queer Black Harlem: Hemingway and McKay's Modernist Intertext," *Journal of Modern Literature* 30, no. 4 (2007): 61–81; and Alexandra Peat, *Travel and Modernist Literature: Sacred and Ethical Journeys* (New York: Routledge, 2011).

13. For more on modernist ethics, see Marilyn Adler Papayanis, *Writing in the Margins: The Ethics of Expatriation* (Nashville: Vanderbilt University Press, 2005); Martin Halliwell, *Modernism and Morality: Ethical Devices in European and American Fiction* (New York: Palgrave, 2001); and Peat, *Travel and Modernist Literature*.

14. Contemporary expatriate writing more closely resembles the post-independence African novel of international migration. L. Losambe lists that form's themes: "nasty weather, European [or American] decaying morality, racism, loneliness resulting from Europeans' keen sense of individuality and Europeans' [or Americans'] excessive concern with the material at the neglect of the spiritual" ("Expatriate Characters in the Early African Novel," *Phylon* 27, no. 2 [1986]: 148).

15. Saskia Sassen, *The Global City: New York, London, Tokyo* (Princeton, N.J.: Princeton University Press, 1991).

16. Paul Theroux, "Tarzan Is an Expatriate," *Transition* 32 (1967): 13–19.

17. Nina Baym, "Melodramas of Beset Manhood: How Theories of American Fiction Exclude Women Authors," *American Quarterly* 33, no. 2 (1981): 123–139.

18. Sergei Eisenstein, "Constanta or Whither the *Battleship Potemkin*," in *Writings, 1922–34*, vol. 1 of *Selected Works*, ed. and trans. Richard Taylor (London: BFI, 1988), 69.

19. Barnard, "Fictions of the Global," 214.

20. Anderson, *Under Three Flags*.

21. Herbert Marcuse, *One-Dimensional Man: Studies in the Ideology of Advanced Industrial Society* (Boston: Beacon Press, 1964).

PRIMARY WORKS

Abani, Chris. *GraceLand*. New York: Farrar, Straus and Giroux, 2004.

———. *The Virgin of Flames*. New York: Penguin, 2007.

Adichie, Chimamanda Ngozi. *Half of a Yellow Sun*. New York: Anchor, 2007.

Adrian, Chris. *The Children's Hospital*. San Francisco: McSweeney's, 2006.

Alarcón, Daniel. *Lost City Radio*. New York: Harper, 2007.

Alison, Jane. *Natives and Exotics*. New York: Mariner, 2006.

Alvarez, Julia. *In the Name of Salomé*. New York: Plume, 2001.

Anam, Tahmima. *A Golden Age*. New York: Harper, 2007.

Aridjis, Chloe. *Book of Clouds*. New York: Grove Press, 2009.

Atta, Sefi. *Everything Good Will Come*. New York: Interlink, 2004.

Atwood, Margaret. *The Year of the Flood*. New York: Doubleday/Nan. A. Talese, 2009.

Banks, Russell. *The Darling*. New York: HarperCollins, 2004.

Bell, Madison Smartt. *All Souls' Rising*. New York: Penguin, 1996.

———. *Master of the Crossroads*. New York: Vintage, 2004.

———. *The Stone That the Builder Refused*. New York: Vintage, 2006.

Berberian, Viken. *Das Kapital*. New York: Simon & Schuster, 2007.

Berlinski, Mischa. *Fieldwork*. New York: Picador, 2008.

Brockmeier, Kevin. *The Brief History of the Dead*. New York: Pantheon, 2006.

Bromell, Henry. *Little America*. New York: Knopf, 2002.

Buruma, Ian. *The China Lover*. New York: Penguin, 2008.

Cameron, Peter. *Andorra*. New York: Picador, 1997.

———. *The City of Your Final Destination*. New York: Picador, 2002.

Caputo, Philip. *Acts of Faith*. New York: Vintage, 2005.

Carey, Peter. *Parrot and Olivier in America*. New York: Random House, 2009.

Chabon, Michael. *The Adventures of Kavalier & Clay*. New York: Random House, 2000.

Chandra, Vikram. *Sacred Games*. New York: HarperCollins, 2007.

Chikwava, Brian. *Harare North*. New York: Random House, 2009.

Choi, Susan. *American Woman*. New York: Harper, 2003.

——. *A Person of Interest*. New York: Viking, 2008.

Cole, Teju. *Open City*. New York: Random House, 2011.

Coleman, Carter. *The Volunteer*. New York: Grand Central, 1998.

Coupland, Douglas. *Microserfs*. New York: HarperCollins, 1995.

Crace, Jim. *The Pesthouse*. New York: Doubleday, 2007.

Danticat, Edwidge. *The Dew Breaker*. New York: Knopf, 2004.

Dasgupta, Rana. *Solo*. New York: Houghton Mifflin, 2010.

Davis, Kathryn. *Versailles*. Boston: Back Bay, 2003.

Dean, Debra. *The Madonnas of Leningrad*. New York: Morrow, 2006.

Deb, Siddhartha. *The Point of Return*. New York: HarperCollins, 2002.

De Robertis, Carolina. *The Invisible Mountain*. New York: Random House, 2009.

Díaz, Junot. *The Brief Wondrous Life of Oscar Wao*. New York: Penguin, 2007.

Doerr, Anthony. *About Grace*. New York: Scribner, 2004.

Dooling, Richard. *White Man's Grave*. New York: Picador, 1994.

D'Souza, Tony. *Whiteman*. New York: Harcourt, 2008.

Eggers, Dave. *What Is the What: The Autobiography of Valentino Achak Deng: A Novel*. San Francisco: McSweeney's, 2006.

Eggers, Paul. *Saviors*. New York: Harcourt, 1999.

Eugenides, Jeffrey. *Middlesex*. New York: Farrar, Straus and Giroux, 2002.

Farah, Nuruddin. *Links*. New York: Riverhead, 2003.

Ferris, Joshua. *Then We Came to the End*. New York: Little, Brown, 2007.

Firouz, Anahita. *In the Walled Gardens*. New York: Little, Brown, 2002.

Foer, Jonathan Safran. *Everything Is Illuminated*. New York: Houghton Mifflin, 2002.

Forna, Aminatta. *The Memory of Love*. New York: Grove Press, 2011.

Franzen, Jonathan. *Freedom*. New York: Farrar, Straus and Giroux, 2010.

Freudenberger, Nell. *The Dissident*. New York: Ecco, 2006.

Galchen, Rivka. *Atmospheric Disturbances*. New York: Picador, 2008.

García, Christina. *Monkey Hunting*. New York: Knopf, 2003.

Ghosh, Amitav. *The Glass Palace*. New York: Penguin, 2000.

Grushin, Olga. *The Dream Life of Sukhanov*. New York: Penguin, 2006.

Gunesekera, Romesh. *Heaven's Edge*. New York: Grove Press, 2002.

Habila, Helon. *Measuring Time*. New York: Norton, 2007.

Hagedorn, Jessica. *Dream Jungle*. New York: Viking, 2003.

Hamid, Mohsin. *The Reluctant Fundamentalist*. New York: Harcourt, 2007.

Haslett, Adam. *Union Atlantic*. New York: Nan A. Talese/Doubleday, 2010.

Hazzard, Shirley. *The Great Fire*. New York: Farrar, Straus and Giroux, 2003.

Hemingway, Ernest. *The Sun Also Rises*. 1926. New York: Scribner, 2006.

Hemon, Aleksandar. *The Lazarus Project*. New York: Riverhead, 2008.

——. *Nowhere Man*. New York: Vintage, 2004.

Hobbet, Anastasia. *Small Kingdoms*. New York: Permanent, 2010.

Isegawa, Moses. *Abyssinian Chronicles*. New York: Vintage, 2001.

Iweala, Uzodinma. *Beasts of No Nation*. New York: Harper Perennial, 2005.

Jacobs, Mark. *Stone Cowboy: A Novel*. New York: Soho, 1997.

Jen, Gish. *World and Town*. New York: Knopf, 2010.

Jin, Ha. *War Trash*. New York: Random House, 2004.

Kalfus, Ken. *The Commissariat of Enlightenment*. New York: Ecco, 2003.

——. *PU-239 and Other Russian Fantasies*. New York: Washington Square Press, 2000.

Khadivi, Laleh. *The Age of Orphans*. New York: Bloomsbury, 2009.

Krauss, Nicole. *Great House*. New York: Norton, 2010.

Kunzru, Hari. *My Revolutions*. New York: Dutton, 2008.

——. *Transmission*. New York: Penguin, 2004.

Kushner, Rachel. *Telex from Cuba*. New York: Scribner, 2008.

Lederer, William J., and Eugene Burdick. *The Ugly American*. 1958. New York: Norton, 1999.

Lee, Chang-Rae. *The Surrendered*. New York: Riverhead, 2010.

Lewycka, Marina. *A Short History of Tractors in Ukrainian*. New York: Viking, 2005.

Lim, Shirley Geok-lin. *Joss and Gold*. New York: Feminist Press at the City University of New York, 2001.

Louie, David Wong. *The Barbarians Are Coming*. New York: Putnam, 2000.

Mantel, Hilary. *Wolf Hall*. New York: Macmillan, 2009.

Marcom, Micheline Aharonian. *The Daydreaming Boy*. New York: Riverhead, 2004.

——. *Draining the Sea*. New York: Riverhead, 2008.

——. *Three Apples Fell from Heaven*. New York: Riverhead, 2001.

Matar, Hisham. *In the Country of Men*. New York: Viking, 2006.

McCann, Colum. *Let the Great World Spin*. New York: Random House, 2009.

McCarthy, Cormac. *The Road*. New York: Knopf, 2006.

Mda, Zakes. *The Madonna of Excelsior*. New York: Picador, 2005.

Meek, James. *The People's Act of Love*. London: Cannongate, 2006.

Meidav, Edie. *The Far Field: A Novel of Ceylon*. Boston: Houghton Mifflin, 2001.

Menéndez, Ana. *Loving Che*. New York: Atlantic Monthly, 2004.

Mengestu, Dinaw. *The Beautiful Things That Heaven Bears*. New York: Riverhead, 2008.

———. *How to Read the Air*. New York: Riverhead, 2011.

Mengiste, Maaza. *Beneath the Lion's Gaze*. New York: Norton, 2009.

Messud, Claire. *The Emperor's Children*. New York: Vintage, 2007.

Meyer, Philipp. *American Rust*. New York: Spiegel & Grau, 2009.

Min, Anchee. *Becoming Madame Mao*. New York: Houghton Mifflin, 2000.

Mishra, Pankaj. *The Romantics*. New York: Anchor, 2001.

Mountford, Peter. *A Young Man's Guide to Late Capitalism*. New York: Mariner, 2011.

Mueenuddin, Daniyal. *In Other Rooms, Other Wonders*. New York. Norton, 2009.

Mukherjee, Bharati. *Desirable Daughters*. New York: Hyperion, 2003.

Nwaubani, Adaobi Tricia. *I Do Not Come to You by Chance*. New York: Hyperion, 2009.

Ochsner, Gina. *The Russian Dreambook of Color and Flight*. New York: Houghton Mifflin, 2010.

O'Neill, Joseph. *Netherland*. New York: Vintage, 2009.

Orner, Peter. *The Second Coming of Mavala Shikongo*. New York: Little, Brown, 2006.

Oyeyemi, Helen. *The Icarus Girl*. New York: Nan A. Talese/Doubleday, 2005.

Ozick, Cynthia. *Foreign Bodies*. New York: Houghton Mifflin, 2010.

———. *Heir to the Glimmering World*. New York: Houghton Mifflin, 2004.

Pasulka, Brigid. *A Long Long Time Ago and Essentially True*. New York: Houghton Mifflin, 2009.

Patchett, Ann. *Bel Canto*. New York: HarperCollins, 2001.

Phillips, Arthur. *Prague*. New York: Random House, 2003.

Powers, Richard. *Plowing the Dark*. New York: Picador, 2000.

Prose, Francine. *My New American Life*. New York: Harper, 2011.

Raban, Jonathan. *Waxwings*. New York: Pantheon, 2003.

Rachman, Tom. *The Imperfectionists*. New York: Pantheon, 2011.

Rosenberg, Robert. *This Is Not Civilization*. New York: Mariner, 2005.

Rush, Norman. *Mortals*. New York: Vintage, 2004.

Russo, Richard. *The Bridge of Sighs*. New York: Knopf, 2007.

Scibona, Salvatore. *The End*. New York: Riverhead, 2009.

Shacochis, Bob. *Swimming in the Volcano*. New York: Scribner, 1993.

Shand, Rosa. *The Gravity of Sunlight*. New York: Soho, 2003.

Shteyngart, Gary. *Absurdistan*. New York: Random House, 2006.

——. *The Russian Debutante's Handbook*. New York: Riverhead, 2002.

Simpson, Mona. *My Hollywood*. New York: Random House, 2010.

Sofer, Dalia. *The Septembers of Shiraz*. New York: Ecco, 2007.

Sontag, Susan. *In America*. New York: Picador, 2000.

Stefaniak, Mary Helen. *The Turk and My Mother*. New York: Norton, 2004.

Suri, Manil. *The Death of Vishnu*. New York: Harper, 2008.

Syjuco, Miguel. *Ilustrado*. New York: Farrar, Straus and Giroux, 2010.

Theroux, Marcel. *Far North*. New York: Farrar Straus and Giroux, 2009.

Thomas, Maria. *Antonia Saw the Oryx First*. New York: Soho, 1987.

Toutonghi, Pauls. *Red Weather*. New York: Random House, 2007.

Tuck, Lily. *The News from Paraguay*. New York: HarperCollins, 2004.

——. *Siam*. New York: Plume, 2000.

Upadhyay, Samrat. *The Guru of Love*. New York: Houghton Mifflin, 2003.

Vapnyar, Lara. *Memoirs of a Muse*. New York: Pantheon, 2006.

Verghese, Abraham. *Cutting for Stone*. New York: Knopf, 2009.

Vida, Vendela. *The Lovers*. New York: Ecco, 2010.

Vollmann, William T. *Europe Central*. New York: Viking, 2005.

Wayne, Teddy. *Kapitoil*. New York: Harper, 2010

Weiss, Philip. *American Taboo: A Murder in the Peace Corps*. New York: Harper, 2004.

Wicomb, Zoe. *David's Story*. New York: Feminist Press, 2002.

Wiley, Richard. *Ahmed's Revenge*. New York: Random House, 1998.

Wray, John. *The Right Hand of Sleep*. New York: Vintage, 2001.

Yamashita, Karen Tei. *I Hotel*. Minneapolis: Coffee House Press, 2010.

BIBLIOGRAPHY

Arseth, Espen J. *Cybertext: Perspectives on Ergodic Literature.* Baltimore: Johns Hopkins University Press, 1997.

Adélékè Adéèkó. "Power Shift: America in the Nigerian Imagination." *Global South* 2, no. 2 (2008): 10–30.

Adorno Theodor W., Else Frenkel-Brunswik, Daniel J. Levinson, and R. Nevitt Sanford. *The Authoritarian Personality.* 1950. New York: Norton, 1993.

Agamben, Giorgio. *Homo Sacer: Sovereign Power and Bare Life.* Translated by Daniel Heller-Roazen. Stanford, Calif.: Stanford University Press, 1998.

Ahmad, Aijaz. "Jameson's Rhetoric of Otherness and the 'National Allegory.'" *Social Text* 7 (1987): 3–25.

Altman, Rick. "A Semantic/Syntactic Approach to Film Genre." *Cinema Journal* 23, no. 3 (1984): 6–18.

American Psychiatric Association. *Diagnostic and Statistical Manual of Mental Disorders.* 4th ed., rev. Washington, D.C.: American Psychiatric Association, 2000.

Amin, Julius. "The Peace Corps and the Struggle for African American Equality." *Journal of Black Studies* 29, no. 6 (1999): 809–826.

Anderson, Amanda. "Character and Ideology: The Case of Cold War Liberalism." *New Literary History* 42, no. 2 (2011): 209–229.

Anderson, Benedict. *Under Three Flags: Anarchism and the Anti-Colonial Imagination.* New York: Verso, 2005.

Anderson, Perry. "From Progress to Catastrophe." *London Review of Books,* July 28, 2011, 24–28.

Anjaria, Ulka. *Realism in the Twentieth-Century Indian Novel: Colonial Difference and Literary Form*. Cambridge: Cambridge University Press, 2012.

Appadurai, Arjun. *Modernity at Large: Cultural Dimensions of Globalization*. Minneapolis: University of Minnesota Press, 1996.

Aravamudan, Srinivas. "In the Wake of the Novel: The Oriental Tale as National Allegory." *Novel* 33, no. 1 (1999): 5–31.

———. *Tropicopolitans: Colonialism and Agency, 1688–1804*. Durham, N.C.: Duke University Press, 1999.

Badiou, Alain. "The Communist Hypothesis." *New Left Review* 49 (2008): 1789–1848.

Bakhtin, Mikhail. *The Dialogic Imagination: Four Essays*. Edited by Michael Holquist. Translated by Caryl Emerson and Michael Holquist. Austin: University of Texas Press, 1982.

———. *Rabelais and His World*. Translated by Helene Iswolsky. Bloomington: Indiana University Press, 1984.

Balina, Marina, Nancy Condee, and Evgeny Dobrenko, eds. *Endquote: Sots-Art Literature and Soviet Grand Style*. Evanston, Ill.: Northwestern University Press, 2000.

Barnard, Rita. "Fictions of the Global." *Novel* 42, no. 2 (2009): 207–215.

Baym, Nina. "Melodramas of Beset Manhood: How Theories of American Fiction Exclude Women Authors." *American Quarterly* 33, no. 2 (1981): 123–139.

Behdad, Ali. *A Forgetful Nation: On Immigration and Cultural Identity in the United States*. Durham, N.C.: Duke University Press, 2005.

Benítez-Rojo, Antonio. *The Repeating Island: The Caribbean and the Postmodern Perspective*. Translated by James Maraniss. Durham, N.C.: Duke University Press, 1992.

Benjamin, Walter. *Illuminations: Essays and Reflections*. Edited by Hannah Arendt. Translated by Harry Zohn. 1968. New York: Continuum, 1999.

Bermingham, Ann. *Landscape and Ideology: The English Rustic Tradition, 1740–1860*. Berkeley: University of California Press, 1989.

Bernstein, Irving. *Promises Kept: John F. Kennedy's New Frontier*. New York: Oxford University Press, 1991.

Bernstein, Michael André. *Foregone Conclusions: Against Apocalyptic History*. Berkeley: University of California Press, 1994.

Birkerts, Sven. *The Gutenberg Elegies: The Fate of Reading in an Electronic Age*. 2nd ed. New York: Macmillan, 2006.

Bissell, Tom. "Destination: Central Asia." June 22, 2006. The Literary Guide to the World." *Salon*, http://www.salon.com/2006/06/22/central_asia/.

——. "Unflowered Aloes: Why Literary Success Is a Product of Chance, Not Destiny." *Boston Review*, April–May 2000.

Blight, David. *Race and Reunion: The Civil War in American Memory*. Cambridge, Mass.: Harvard University Press, 2001.

Boelhower, William Q. "The Immigrant Novel as Genre." *MELUS* 8, no. 1 (1981): 3–13.

Bona, Mary Jo. *Claiming a Tradition: Italian American Women Writers*. Carbondale: Southern Illinois University Press, 1999.

Bousquet, Mark. *How the University Works: Higher Education and the Low-Wage Nation*. New York: New York University Press, 2008.

Boyers, Robert. *Atrocity and Amnesia: The Political Novel Since 1945*. New York: Oxford University Press, 1985.

Bradbury, Malcolm. *No, Not Bloomsbury*. New York: Columbia University Press, 1987.

——. "Second Countries: The Expatriate Tradition in American Writing." *Yearbook of English Studies* 8 (1978): 15–39.

Braudel, Fernand. *The Mediterranean and the Mediterranean World in the Age of Philip II*. 2 vols. Berkeley: University of California Press, 1996.

Breckenridge, Donald, ed. *The Brooklyn Rail Fiction Anthology*. New York: Hanging Loose Press, 2006.

Brennan, Timothy. *At Home in the World: Cosmopolitanism Now*. Cambridge, Mass.: Harvard University Press, 1997.

Brintlinger, Angela. "The Hero in the Madhouse: The Post-Soviet Novel Confronts the Soviet Past." *Slavic Review* 63, no. 1 (2004): 43–65.

Brougher, Valentina G. "The Occult in Russian Literature of the 1990s." *Russian Review* 56, no. 1 (1997): 110–124.

Brown, Nicholas. *Utopian Generations: The Political Horizon of Twentieth-Century Literature*. Princeton, N.J.: Princeton University Press, 2005.

Brown, Wendy. *States of Injury: Power and Freedom in Late Modernity*. Princeton, N.J.: Princeton University Press, 1995.

Buell, Lawrence. "The Unkillable Dream of the Great American Novel: *Moby-Dick* as Test Case." *American Literary History* 20, nos. 1–2 (2008): 132–155.

Buhle, Paul, ed. *Popular Culture in America*. Minneapolis: University of Minnesota Press, 1987.

Bull, Malcolm, ed. *Apocalypse Theory and the Ends of the World*. New York: Blackwell, 1995

——. *Seeing Things Hidden: Apocalypse, Vision, and Totality*. New York: Verso, 2000.

Butler, Judith. *Precarious Life: The Powers of Mourning and Violence*. New York: Verso, 2004.

——. *The Psychic Life of Power: Theories in Subjection*. Stanford, Calif.: Stanford University Press, 1997.

Carollo, Russell, and Mei-Ling Hopgood. "Mission of Sacrifice: Peace Corps Volunteers Face Injury, Death in Foreign Lands." *Dayton Daily News*, October 26, 2003.

Casteel, Sarah Phillips. *Second Arrivals: Landscape and Belonging in Contemporary Writing of the Americas*. Charlottesville: University of Virginia Press, 2007.

Castells, Manuel. *The Rise of the Network Society*. Vol. 1 of *The Information Age: Economy, Society, and Culture*. New York: Blackwell, 1996.

Charles, Laurie L. *Intimate Colonialism: Head, Heart, and Body in West African Development Work*. Walnut Creek, Calif.: Left Coast Press, 2007.

Cheah, Pheng. *Spectral Nationality: Passages of Freedom from Kant to Postcolonial Literatures of Liberation*. New York: Columbia University Press, 2003.

Cheah, Pheng, and Bruce Robbins, eds. *Cosmopolitics: Thinking and Feeling Beyond the Nation*. Minneapolis: University of Minnesota Press, 1998.

Chernetsky, Vitaly. *Mapping Postcommunist Cultures: Russia and Ukraine in the Context of Globalization*. Montreal: McGill–Queens University Press, 2007.

Ch'ien, Evelyn Nien-Ming. *Weird English*. Cambridge, Mass.: Harvard University Press, 2004.

Chow, Rey. "Listening Otherwise, Music Miniaturized." In *The Cultural Studies Reader*, edited by Simon During, 462–478. New York: Routledge, 1996.

Clark, David James. "Representing the Majority World: Famine, Photojournalism and the Changing Visual Economy." Ph.D. diss. Durham University, 2009.

Clifford, James. *Routes: Travel and Translation in the Late 20th Century*. Cambridge, Mass.: Harvard University Press, 1997.

Clowes, Edith W. *Russian Experimental Fiction: Resisting Ideology After Utopia*. Princeton, N.J.: Princeton University Press, 1993.

Clune, Michael. *American Literature and the Free Market, 1945–2000*. Cambridge: Cambridge University Press, 2010.

Coates, John. "Experimenting with Genre: Green [*sic*] and *The Confidential Agent*." *Renascence* 55, no. 1 (2002): 47–64.

Cohen, Bruce J. *Theory and Practice of Psychiatry*. New York: Oxford University Press, 2003.

Colburn, Forest D. *The Vogue of Revolution in Poor Countries*. Princeton, N.J.: Princeton University Press, 1997.

Comaroff, Jean, and John L. Comaroff. "Millennial Capitalism: First Thoughts on a Second Coming." *Public Culture* 12, no. 2 (2000): 305–335.

Coopan, Vilashini. *Worlds Within: National Narratives and Global Connections in Postcolonial Writing*. Stanford, Calif.: Stanford University Press, 2009.

Coronil, Fernando. *The Magical State: Nature, Money, and Modernity in Venezuela*. Chicago: University of Chicago Press, 1997.

Cowart, David. *History and the American Novel*. Carbondale: Southern Illinois University Press, 1989.

——. *Trailing Clouds: Immigrant Fiction in Contemporary America*. Ithaca, N.Y.: Cornell University Press, 2006.

Csikszentmihalyi, Mihaly. *Flow: The Psychology of Optimal Experience*. New York: Harper & Row, 1991.

Curtin, Philip. *Death by Migration: Europe's Encounter with the Tropical World in the Nineteenth Century*. New York: Cambridge University Press, 1989.

Danticat, Edwidge. "Junot Díaz." *BOMB* 101 (2007).

Davidson, Cathy N. *Now You See It: How Technology and Brain Science Will Transform Schools and Business for the 21st Century*. New York: Penguin, 2012.

——. *Revolution and the Word: The Rise of the Novel in America*. New York: Oxford University Press, 1986.

Davis, Mike. *Planet of Slums*. New York: Verso, 2006.

Davis, Rocio. "Oral Narrative as Short Story Cycle: Forging Community in Edwidge Danticat's *Krik? Krak!*" *MELUS* 26, no. 2 (2001): 65–81.

DeKoven, Marianne. "The Politics of Modernist Form." *New Literary History* 23, no. 3 (1992): 675–690.

Denning, Michael. *Cover Stories: Narrative and Ideology in the British Spy Thriller*. London: Routledge, 1987.

——. *The Cultural Front: The Laboring of American Culture in the Twentieth Century*. New York: Verso, 1996

——. *Culture in the Age of Three Worlds*. New York: Verso, 2004.

Derrida, Jacques. "The Law of Genre." Translated by Avital Ronnell. *Critical Inquiry* 7, no. 1 (1980): 55–81.

Desai, Gaurav. "Old World Orders: Amitav Ghosh and the Writing of Nostalgia." *Representations* 85 (2004): 125–148.

Desai, Radhika. "From National Bourgeoisie to Rogues, Failures and Bullies: 21st Century Imperialism and the Unraveling of the Third World." *Third World Quarterly* 25, no. 1 (2004): 169–185.

Diemert, Brian. *Graham Greene's Thrillers and the 1930s*. Montreal: McGill–Queens University Press, 1996.

D'Lugo, Carol Clark. *The Fragmented Novel in Mexico: The Politics of Form*. Austin: University of Texas Press, 1997.

Downes, Paul. *Democracy, Revolution, and Monarchism in Early American Literature*. New York: Cambridge University Press, 2002.

Dubey, Madhu. *Signs and Cities: Black Literary Postmodernism*. Chicago: University of Chicago Press, 2003.

Edelman, Lee. *No Future: Queer Theory and the Death Drive*. Durham, N.C.: Duke University Press, 2004.

Edmondson, Belinda. *Making Men: Gender, Literary Authority, and Women's Writing in Caribbean Narrative*. Durham, N.C.: Duke University Press, 1999.

Edwards, Brian T. *Morocco Bound: Disorienting America's Maghreb, from Casablanca to the Marrakech Express*. Durham, N.C.: Duke University Press, 2005.

Ehrlich, Victor. *Modernism and Revolution: Russian Literature in Transition*. Cambridge, Mass.: Harvard University Press, 1994.

Eisenstein, Sergei. *Writings, 1922–34*. Vol. 1 of *Selected Works*. Edited and translated by Richard Taylor. London: BFI, 1988.

Elias, Amy. *Sublime Desire: History and Post-1960s Fiction*. Baltimore: Johns Hopkins University Press, 2001.

Elliott, Carl. *Better Than Well: American Medicine Meets the American Dream*. New York: Norton, 2003.

Emenyonu, Ernest. *The Rise of the Igbo Novel*. New York: Oxford University Press, 1978.

Eng, David L. "Melancholia in the Late Twentieth Century." *Signs* 25, no. 4 (2000): 1275–1281.

Engerman, David. *Know Your Enemy: The Rise and Fall of America's Soviet Experts*. New York: Oxford University Press, 2009.

Erikson, Erik. "Autobiographic Notes on the Identity Crisis." *Dedalus* 99, no. 4 (1970): 730–759.

Etkind, Alexander. "Stories of the Undead in the Land of the Unburied: Magical Historicism in Contemporary Russian Fiction." *Slavic Review* 68, no. 3 (2009): 631–658.

Ferraro, Thomas J. *Ethnic Passages: Literary Immigrants in Twentieth-Century America*. Chicago: University of Chicago Press, 1993.

——. *Feeling Italian: The Art of Ethnicity in America*. New York: New York University Press, 2005.

Finn, Helena K. "The Case for Cultural Diplomacy: Engaging Foreign Audiences." *Foreign Affairs* 82, no. 6 (2003): 15–20.

Fischer, Fritz. *Making Them Like Us: Peace Corps Volunteers in the 1960s*. Washington D.C.: Smithsonian Institution Press, 1998.

Foertsch, Jacqueline. "'Extraordinarily Convenient Neighbors': African-American Characters in White-Authored Post-Atomic Novels." *Journal of Modern Literature* 30, no. 4 (2007): 122–138.

Foley, Barbara. *Radical Representations: Politics and Form in U.S. Proletarian Fiction, 1929–1941*. Durham, N.C.: Duke University Press, 1994.

Forché, Carolyn. "Expatriate." *Iowa Review* 12, nos. 2–3 (1981): 82.

Foucault, Michel. *Power*. Vol. 3 of *The Essential Works of Foucault, 1954–1984*. Edited by James D. Faubion. New York: New Press, 2001.

Freeden, Michael. *Liberal Languages: Ideological Imaginations in Twentieth-Century Progressive Thought*. Princeton, N.J.: Princeton University Press, 2005.

Frye, Northrop. *Anatomy of Criticism: Four Essays*. Edited by Robert D. Denham. 1957. Toronto: University of Toronto Press, 2006.

Fukuyama, Francis. *America at the Crossroads: Democracy, Power, and the Neoconservative Legacy*. New Haven, Conn.: Yale University Press, 2006.

——. *The End of History and the Last Man*. New York: Penguin, 1992.

——. *The Origins of Political Power: From Prehuman Times to the French Revolution*. New York: Farrar, Straus and Giroux, 2011.

Garber, Frederick. "Self, Society, Value, and the Romantic Hero." *Comparative Literature* 19, no. 4 (1967): 321–333.

Garber, Marjorie. *Sex and Real Estate: Why We Love Houses*. New York: Pantheon, 2000.

Gardaphé, Fred L. *Italian Signs, American Streets: The Evolution of Italian American Narrative*. Durham, N.C.: Duke University Press, 1996.

George, Rosemary Marangoly. *The Politics of Home: Postcolonial Relocations and Twentieth-Century Fiction*. New York: Cambridge University Press, 1996.

Gerring, John. "Ideology: A Definitional Analysis." *Political Research Quarterly* 50, no. 4 (1997): 957–994.

Gikandi, Simon. *Reading the African Novel*. London: Heinemann, 1987.

Gill, Carolyn Bailey, ed. *Maurice Blanchot: The Demand of Writing*. New York: Routledge, 1996.

Gilroy, Paul. *Postcolonial Melancholia*. New York: Columbia University Press, 2005.

Goldstein, Jan. "The Wandering Jew and the Problem of Psychiatric Anti-Semitism in Fin-de-Siècle France." *Journal of Contemporary History* 20 (1985): 521–552.

Grenby, M. O. *The Anti-Jacobin Novel: British Conservatism and the French Revolution*. New York: Cambridge University Press, 2001.

Gresh, Alain. "Neither with the West nor Against It." *Le Monde diplomatique*, March 2011.

Grewal, Inderpal. *Transnational America: Feminisms, Diasporas, Neoliberalisms*. Durham, N.C.: Duke University Press, 2005.

Griswold, Wendy. *Bearing Witness: Readers, Writers, and the Novel in Nigeria*. Princeton, N.J.: Princeton University Press, 2000.

Gruesser, John Cullen. *White on Black: Contemporary Literature About Africa*. Urbana: University of Illinois Press, 1992.

Habermas, Jürgen. *The Structural Transformation of the Public Sphere: An Inquiry into a Category of Bourgeois Society*. 1962. Cambridge, Mass.: MIT Press, 1991.

Habib, Shahnaz. "The Book Bench: Exchange with Daniyal Mueenuddin." *New Yorker*, March 3, 2009.

Hacking, Ian. *Mad Travelers: Reflections on the Reality of Transient Mental Illness*. Charlottesville: University of Virginia Press, 1998.

Halliwell, Martin. *Modernism and Morality: Ethical Devices in European and American Fiction*. New York: Palgrave, 2001.

Hamid, Mohsin. "Now That I've Finally Been Admitted to Britain, It Seems That Everyone Else Suddenly Wants to Leave." *Guardian*, August 6, 2008.

Hamilton, Caroline. *One Man Zeitgeist: Dave Eggers, Publishing, and Publicity*. New York: Continuum, 2010.

Hannam, Kevin, and Irena Ateljevic, eds. *Backpacker Tourism: Concepts and Profiles*. Tonawanda, N.Y.: Channel View Press, 2008.

Harbach, Chad. "MFA vs. NYC." November 6, 2010. *Slate*, http://www.slate.com/articles/arts/culturebox/2010/11/mfa_vs_nyc.html.

Hardt, Michael, and Antonio Negri. *Empire*. Cambridge, Mass.: Harvard University Press, 2001.

Harris, Sharon, ed. *Redefining the Political Novel: American Women Writers, 1797–1901*. Chattanooga: University of Tennessee Press, 1995.

Harvey, David. "Neoliberalism as Creative Destruction." *Annals of the American Academy of Political and Social Science* 610, no. 1 (2007): 21–44.

——. *Spaces of Global Capitalism: Towards a Theory of Uneven Geographical Development*. New York: Verso, 2006.

Hewett, Heather. "At the Crossroads: Disability and Trauma in *The Farming of Bones*." *MELUS* 31, no. 3 (2006): 123–145.

Hickey, Dennis, and Kenneth C. Wylie. *An Enchanting Darkness: The American Vision of Africa in the Twentieth Century*. East Lansing: Michigan State University Press, 1993.

Hill, Christopher L. *National History and the World of Nations: Capital, State, and the Rhetoric of History in Japan, France, and the United States.* Durham, N.C.: Duke University Press, 2008.

Hirsch, Leon V. "The Authenticity of Makonde Art: A Collector Replies." *African Arts* 26, no. 1 (1993): 10, 12, 14, 100.

Hoffman, Elizabeth Cobbs. *All You Need Is Love: The Peace Corps and the Spirit of the 60s.* Cambridge, Mass.: Harvard University Press, 1998.

Holcomb, Gary Edward. "The Sun Also Rises in Queer Black Harlem: Hemingway and McKay's Modernist Intertext." *Journal of Modern Literature* 30, no. 4 (2007): 61–81.

Holloway, David. "The War on Terror Espionage Thriller, and the Imperialism of Human Rights." *Comparative Literature Studies* 46, no. 1 (2009): 20–44.

Holton, Robert. "Kerouac Among the Fellahin: *On the Road* to the Postmodern." *Modern Fiction Studies* 41, no. 2 (1995): 265–283.

Horkheimer, Max, and Theodor W. Adorno. *The Dialectic of Enlightenment.* Translated by Edmund Jephcott. 1944. Stanford, Calif.: Stanford University Press, 2002.

Howe, Irving. *Politics and the Novel.* New York: Horizon, 1957.

Hron, Madeleine. "*Ora na-azu nwa*: The Figure of the Child in Third-Generation Nigerian Novels." *Research in African Literatures* 39, no. 2, (2008): 27–48.

Hutcheon, Linda. *A Poetics of Postmodernism: History, Theory, Fiction.* New York: Routledge, 1988.

Hutchinson, Anthony. *Writing the Republic: Liberalism and Morality in Political Fiction.* New York: Columbia University Press, 2007.

Hutner, Gordon. *What America Read: Taste, Class, and the Novel, 1920–1960.* Chapel Hill: University of North Carolina Press, 2009.

Ikheloa, Ikhide R. "Whiteman: The Heart of Our Darkness." April 27, 2006. Nigerians in America, http://www.nigeriansinamerica.com/articles/997/1/ Whiteman-The-Heart-of-Our-Darkness/Page1.html.

Inglehart, Ronald, Miguel Basáñez, Jaime Díez-Medrano, Loek Halman, and Ruud Luijkx, eds. *Human Beliefs and Values: A Cross-Cultural Sourcebook Based on the 1999–2002 Values Surveys.* Mexico City: Siglo XXI, 2004.

Irr, Caren. *The Suburb of Dissent: Cultural Politics in the United States and Canada During the 1930s.* Durham, N.C.: Duke University Press, 1998.

Jack, Ian. Introduction to "Best of Young American Novelists 2." *Granta* 97, spring 2007, 7–11.

Jacobs, Mark. "A Serious Conversation." *Counterpunch*, June 19, 2003.

Jacobson, Matthew Frye. *Whiteness of a Different Color: European Immigrants and the Alchemy of Race*. Cambridge, Mass.: Harvard University Press, 1998.

Jameson, Fredric. *Archaeologies of the Future: The Desire Called Utopia and Other Science Fictions*. Durham, N.C.: Duke University Press, 2005.

——. "The Cultural Logic of Late Capitalism." In *Postmodernism, or the Cultural Logic of Late Capitalism*, 1–50. Durham, N.C.: Duke University Press, 1991.

——. "Persistencies of the Dialectic: Three Sites." *Science and Society* 62, no. 3 (1998): 358–372.

——. *The Political Unconscious: Narrative as a Socially Symbolic Act*. Ithaca, N.Y.: Cornell University Press, 1981.

——. "Third-World Literature in the Era of Multinational Capitalism." *Social Text* 15 (1986): 65–88.

Jarrells, Anthony. "Bloodless Revolution and the Form of the Novel." *Novel* 37, nos. 1–2 (2003–2004): 24–44.

Jenkins, Henry. *Convergence Culture: Where Old and New Media Collide*. New York: New York University Press, 2006.

Kaplan, Caren. *Questions of Travel: Postmodern Discourses of Displacement*. Durham, N.C.: Duke University Press, 1996.

Karl, Rebecca E. *Mao Zedong and China in the Twentieth-Century World*. Durham, N.C.: Duke University Press, 2010.

Kaussen, Valerie. *Migrant Revolutions: Haitian Literature, Globalization, and U.S. Imperialism*. New York: Rowman & Littlefield, 2007.

Keim, Curtis A. *Mistaking Africa: Curiosities and Inventions of the American Mind*. Boulder, Colo.: Westview Press, 1999.

Kellerman, Aharon. *Personal Mobilities*. New York: Routledge, 2006.

Khamis, Said A. M. "Signs of New Features in the Swahili Novel." *Research in African Literatures* 36, no. 1 (2005): 91–108.

Kingston, Maxine Hong. "The Novel's Next Step: If Someone Could Create the Global Novel, We'd All Have a Sequel." *Mother Jones*, December 1989, 37–41.

Kloppenberg, James. *The Virtues of Liberalism*. New York: Oxford University Press, 1998.

Kluge, P. F. Review of *American Taboo: A Murder in the Peace Corps*, by Philip Weiss. April 7, 2004, Peace Corps Writers, http://www.peacecorpswriters.org/pages/2004/0407/407rvamtaboo.html.

Knight, Charles A. *The Literature of Satire*. Cambridge: Cambridge University Press, 2004.

Kroll, Catherine. "Rwanda's Speaking Subjects: The Inescapable Affiliations of Boubacar Boris Diop's *Murambi*." *Third World Quarterly* 28, no. 3 (2007): 655–663.

Kuhne, Dave. *African Settings in Contemporary American Novels*. Westport, Conn.: Greenwood Press, 1999.

Kumar, Amitava, ed. *Away: The Indian Writer as Expatriate*. New York: Routledge, 2004.

———. "Louder Than Bombs: What's So Hot About Indian Writing?" *Transition* 79 (1999): 80–101.

———. *Passport Photos*. Berkeley: University of California Press, 2000.

Kumar, Krishan, and Ekatarina Makarova. "The Portable Home: The Domestication of Public Space." *Sociological Theory* 26, no. 4 (2008): 324–343.

Laliotou, Ioanna. *Transatlantic Subjects: Acts of Migration and Cultures of Transnationalism Between Greece and America*. Chicago: University of Chicago Press, 2004.

Langford, Barry. *Film Genre: Hollywood and Beyond*. Edinburgh: Edinburgh University Press, 2004.

Larkin, Edward. *Thomas Paine and the Literature of Revolution*. Cambridge: Cambridge University Press, 2005.

Latham, Michael E. *Modernization as Ideology: American Social Science and "Nation Building" in the Kennedy Era*. Chapel Hill: University of North Carolina Press, 2000.

Lazarus, Neil. *The Postcolonial Unconscious*. New York: Cambridge University Press, 2011.

———. *Resistance in Postcolonial African Fiction*. New Haven, Conn.: Yale University Press, 1990.

Leiderman, N. L., and M. N. Lipovetskii. *Sovremannaia russkaia literatura*. Moscow: Editorial URSS, 2001.

Lipovetsky, Mark. "New Russians as a Cultural Myth." *Russian Review* 62, no. 1 (2003): 54–79.

———. *Russian Postmodernist Fiction: Dialogue with Chaos*. Armonk, N.Y.: Sharpe, 2000.

Litman, Jessica. *Digital Copyright: Protecting Intellectual Property on the Internet*. New York: Prometheus, 2001.

Losambe, L. "Expatriate Characters in the Early African Novel." *Phylon* 27, no. 2 (1986): 148–158.

Lovesey, Oliver. "Chained Letters: African Prison Diaries and 'National Allegory.'" *Research in African Literatures* 26, no. 4 (1995): 31–45.

Lukács, György. *The Historical Novel.* Translated by Hannah Mitchell and Stanley Mitchell. Boston: Beacon Press, 1962.

——. *The Theory of the Novel: A Historico-Philosophical Essay on the Forms of Great Epic Literature.* Translated by Anna Bostock. Cambridge, Mass.: MIT Press, 1974.

Luke, Timothy W. "An Apparatus of Answers: Ecologism as Ideology in the 21st Century." *New Political Science* 31, no. 4 (2009): 487–498.

Makdisi, Saree. *Romantic Imperialism: Universal Empire and the Culture of Modernity.* Cambridge: Cambridge University Press, 1998.

Marable, Manning. "Against Power." *Transition* 64 (1994): 113–169.

Marciniak, Katerzyna. *Alienhood: Citizenship, Exile, and the Logic of Difference.* Minneapolis: University of Minnesota Press, 2006.

Marcus, Sharon. *Apartment Stories: City and Home in Nineteenth-Century Paris and London.* Berkeley: University of California Press, 1999.

Mardorossian, Carine M. "From Literature of Exile to Migrant Literature." *Modern Language Studies* 32, no. 2 (2002): 15–33.

——. *Reclaiming Difference: Caribbean Women Rewrite Postcolonialism.* Charlottesville: University of Virginia Press, 2005.

Maren, Michael. *The Road to Hell: The Ravaging Effects of Foreign Aid and International Charity.* New York: Free Press, 1997.

Marsh, Rosalind. *Images of Dictatorship: Portraits of Stalin in Literature.* London: Routledge, 1989.

Marx, Bill. "Dr. Strangereader: Or How I Learned to Stop Worrying About Suburban Novels and Love International Fiction." *Ploughshares* 26, nos. 2–3 (2000): 204–216.

Marx, John. *Geopolitics and the Anglophone Novel, 1890–2011.* New York: Cambridge University Press, 2012.

Marx, Karl, and Friedrich Engels. *The Family, Private Property and the State.* New York: International Publishers, 1942.

Marx, Leo. *The Machine in the Garden: Technology and the Pastoral Ideal in America.* New York: Oxford University Press, 1964.

Mason, Wyatt. "Volunteers of America" [review of *Whiteman*, by Tony D'Souza]. *New York Times Book Review*, April 14, 2006.

Mbembe, Achille. *On the Postcolony.* Berkeley: University of California Press, 2001.

McCann, Sean. *Gumshoe America: Hard-Boiled Crime Fiction and the Rise and Fall of New Deal Liberalism.* Durham, N.C.: Duke University Press, 2000.

——. *A Pinnacle of Feeling: American Literature and Presidential Government.* Princeton, N.J.: Princeton University Press, 2008.

McCarthy, Kathleen D. *The American Creed: Philanthropy and the Rise of Civil Society, 1700–1865*. Chicago: University of Chicago Press, 2003.

McCarthy, Mary. "The Lasting Power of the Political Novel." *New York Times Book Review*, January 1, 1984.

McGurl, Mark. "The Program Era: Pluralisms of Postwar American Fiction." *Critical Inquiry* 32, no. 1 (2005): 102–129.

Medovoi, Leerom. *Rebels: Youth and the Cold War Origins of Identity*. Durham, N.C.: Duke University Press, 2005.

Meisler, Stanley. *When the World Calls: The Inside History of the Peace Corps and Its First Fifty Years*. Boston: Beacon Press, 2011.

Michaels, Walter Benn. *The Shape of the Signifier: 1967 to the End of History*. Princeton, N.J.: Princeton University Press, 2004.

Miller, Laura. "Are MFA Programs Ruining American Fiction?" May 17, 2011. *Salon*, http://www.salon.com/2011/05/18/mfa_programs/.

——. Review of *Whiteman*, by Tony D'Souza. May 16, 2006. *Salon*, http://www.salon.com/2006/05/16/desouza/.

Mitchell, W. J. T. *Picture Theory: Essays on Verbal and Visual Representation*. Chicago: University of Chicago Press, 1994.

Mitter, Siddhartha. "Ebony and Ivoirité: War and Peace in Ivory Coast." *Transition* 12, no. 4 (2003): 30–55.

Moretti, Franco. "Conjectures on World Literature." *New Left Review* 1 (2000): 54–68.

——. *Graphs, Maps, Trees: Abstract Models for a Literary History*. New York: Verso, 2005.

Morley, David. *Home Territories: Media, Mobility, and Identity*. New York: Routledge, 2000.

Morris, Jeremy. "From *Chudak* to *Mudak*? Village Prose and the Absurdist Ethics of Evgenii Popov." *Modern Language Review* 99, no. 3 (2004): 696–710.

Moses, Michael Valdez. *The Novel and the Globalization of Culture*. New York: Oxford University Press, 1995.

Moyo, Dambisa. *Dead Aid: Why Aid Is Not Working and How There Is a Better Way for Africa*. New York: Farrar, Straus and Giroux, 2009.

Mukherjee, Menakshi. "The Anxiety of Indianness: Our Novels in English." *Economic and Political Weekly*, November 27, 1993, 2607–2611.

Muller, Gilbert. *New Strangers in Paradise: The Immigrant Experience and Contemporary American Fiction*. Lexington: University Press of Kentucky, 1999.

Munro, Martin. *Exile and Post-1946 Haitian Literature: Alexis, Depestre, Ollivier, Laferrière, Danticat*. Liverpool: Liverpool University Press, 2007.

Mwangi, Evan. *Africa Writes Back to Self: Metafiction, Gender, Sexuality.* Albany: State University of New York Press, 2009.

Naficy, Hamid. *An Accented Cinema: Exilic and Diasporic Filmmaking.* Princeton, N.J.: Princeton University Press, 2001.

Nesbitt, Nick. *Voicing Memory: History and Subjectivity in French Caribbean Literature.* Charlottesville: University of Virginia Press, 2003.

Newfield, Christopher. *Unmaking the Public University: The Forty-Year Assault on the Middle Class.* Cambridge, Mass.: Harvard University Press, 2008.

Newman, Judie. *Fictions of America: Narratives of Global Empire.* New York: Routledge, 2007.

Ngugi wa Thiong'o. *Writers in Politics: Essays.* London: Heinemann, 1981.

Oates, Nathan. "Political Stories: The Individual in Contemporary Fiction." *Missouri Review* 30, no. 3 (2007): 156–171.

Ogata, Sadako. *The Turbulent Decade: Confronting the Refugee Crises of the 1990s.* New York: Norton, 2005.

Ogundele, Wole. "Devices of Evasion: The Mythic Versus the Historical Imagination in the Postcolonial African Novel." *Research in African Literatures* 33, no. 3 (2002): 132.

Ohmann, Richard. *Politics of Knowledge: The Commercialization of the University, the Professions, and Print Culture.* Middletown, Conn.: Wesleyan University Press, 2004.

Okafor, Dubem, ed. *Meditations on African Literature.* Westport, Conn.: Greenwood Press, 2001.

Oliver, Kelly, and Benigno Trigo. *Noir Anxiety.* Minneapolis: University of Minnesota Press, 2002.

Ong, Aihwa. *Flexible Citizenship: The Cultural Logics of Transnationality.* Durham, N.C.: Duke University Press, 1999.

Packer, George. "Third World, Second Hand." *Mother Jones,* June 1989, 42–43.

Palakeel, Thomas. "Third World Short Story as National Allegory?" *Journal of Modern Literature* 20, no. 1 (1996): 97–102.

Paley, Morton D. *Apocalypse and Millennium in English Romantic Poetry.* New York: Oxford University Press, 1999.

Papayanis, Marilyn Adler. *Writing in the Margins: The Ethics of Expatriation.* Nashville: Vanderbilt University Press, 2005.

Parks, Tim. "The Dull New Global Novel." *New York Review of Books,* February 9, 2010.

Parsons, Deborah L. *Streetwalking the Metropolis: Women, the City, and Modernity.* New York: Oxford University Press, 2000.

Parthé, Kathleen. "The Righteous Brothers (and Sisters) of Contemporary Russian Literature." *World Literature Today* 67, no. 1 (1993): 91–99.

——. *Russian Village Prose: The Radiant Past*. Princeton, N.J.: Princeton University Press, 1992.

Peat, Alexandra. *Travel and Modernist Literature: Sacred and Ethical Journeys*. New York: Routledge, 2011.

Pfau, Thomas. *Romantic Moods: Paranoia, Trauma, and Melancholy, 1790–1840*. Baltimore: Johns Hopkins University Press, 2005.

Platt, Kevin M. F. *History in a Grotesque Key: Russian Literature and the Idea of Revolution*. Stanford, Calif.: Stanford University Press, 1997.

Polsby, Nelson W. *Political Innovation in America: The Politics of Policy Initiation*. New Haven, Conn.: Yale University Press, 1984.

Popkin, Jeremy D. "Facing Racial Revolution: Captivity Narratives and Identity in the Saint-Domingue Insurrection." *Eighteenth-Century Studies* 36, no. 3 (2003): 511–533.

Pound, Ezra. *The ABC of Reading*. 1934. New York: New Directions, 1960.

Reynolds, Guy. *Apostles of Modernity: American Writers in the Age of Development*. Lincoln: University of Nebraska Press, 2008.

Robbins, Bruce. "The Worlding of the American Novel." In *The Cambridge History of the American Novel*, edited by Leonard Cassuto, 1096–1106. New York: Cambridge University Press, 2011.

Rodríguez, Ileana. *House/Garden/Nation: Space, Gender, and Ethnicity in Postcolonial Latin American Literatures by Women*. Translated by Robert Carr and Ileana Rodríguez. Durham, N.C.: Duke University Press, 1994.

Rothberg, Michael. *Traumatic Realism: The Demands of Holocaust Representation*. Minneapolis: University of Minnesota Press, 2000.

Rudnicki, Robert W. *Percyscapes: The Fugue State in Twentieth-Century Southern Fiction*. Baton Rouge: Louisiana State University Press, 1999.

Sabin, Margaret. *Dissenters and Mavericks: Writings About India in English, 1765–2000*. New York: Oxford University Press, 2002.

Sassen, Saskia. *The Global City: New York, London, Tokyo*. Princeton, N.J.: Princeton University Press, 1991.

Scarry, Elaine. "Injury and the Structure of War." *Representations* 10 (1985): 1–51.

——. *On Beauty and Being Just*. Princeton, N.J.: Princeton University Press, 2001.

Scheingold, Stuart A. *The Political Novel: Reimagining the Twentieth Century*. New York: Continuum, 2008.

Scherpe, Klaus. "Dramatization and De-dramatization of 'the Era': The Apocalyptic Consciousness of Modernity and Post-modernity." *Cultural Critique*, no. 5 (1986–1987): 95–129.

Schreier, Benjamin. *The Power of Negative Thinking*. Charlottesville: University of Virginia Press, 2009.

Sexton, Jamie. "US 'Indie-Horror': Critical Reception, Genre Construction, and Suspect Hybridity." *Cinema Journal* 51, no. 2 (2012): 67–86.

Shacochis, Bob. Review of *American Taboo: A Murder in the Peace Corp*, by Philip Weiss, July 20, 2004. *Salon*. Http://www.salon.com/2004/07/20/weiss/.

Sharpe, William. Review of *Politics and the Novel*, by Irving Howe. *Political Science Quarterly* 108, no. 1 (1993): 206–207.

Shea, Renee. "The Dangerous Job of Edwidge Danticat." *Callaloo* 19, no. 2 (1996): 382–389.

Shields, David. *Reality Hunger: A Manifesto*. New York: Knopf, 2010.

Shneidman, N. N. *Russian Literature, 1995–2002: On the Threshold of the New Millennium*. Toronto: University of Toronto Press, 2004.

Shriver, Sargent. "Two Years of the Peace Corps." *Foreign Affairs*, July 1963, 694–707.

Siddiqi, Yumna. "Police and Postcolonial Rationality in Amitav Ghosh's *The Circle of Reason*." *Cultural Critique* 50 (2002): 175–211.

Siegel, James T. *Fetish, Recognition, Revolution*. Princeton, N.J.: Princeton University Press, 1997.

Skocpol, Theda. *States and Social Revolution: A Comparative Analysis of France, Russia, and China*. New York: Cambridge University Press, 1979.

Slaughter, Joseph. *Human Rights, Inc.: The World Novel, Narrative Form, and International Law*. New York: Fordham University Press, 2007

——. "Master Plans: Designing (National) Allegories of Urban Space and Metropolitan Subjects for Postcolonial Kenya." *Research in African Literatures* 35, no. 1 (2004): 30–51.

Smith, Nigel. *Literature and Revolution in England, 1640–1660*. New Haven, Conn.: Yale University Press, 1994.

Snel, Guido. "The Footsteps of Gavrilo Princip: The 1914 Sarajevo Assault in Fiction, History, and Three Monuments." In *History of the Literary Cultures of East-Central Europe*, vol. 1, *Junctures and Disjunctures in the 19th and 20th Centuries*, edited by Marcel Cornis-Pope and John Neubauer, 202–215. Amsterdam: Benjamins, 2004.

Snyder, Robert Lance. "Eric Ambler's Revisionist Thrillers: *Epitaph for a Spy, A*

Coffin for Dimitrios, and *The Intercom Conspiracy*." *Papers on Language and Literature* 45, no. 3 (2009): 227–260.

Sommer, Doris. *Foundational Fictions: The National Romances of Latin America.* Berkeley: University of California Press, 1993.

Speare, Morris Edmund. *The Political Novel: Its Development in England and America.* New York: Oxford University Press, 1924.

Stauffer, Andrew. *Anger, Revolution, and Romanticism.* New York: Cambridge University Press, 2005.

Steger, Manfred B., and Jennifer M. Gidley, "Guest Editors' Introduction." *New Political Science* 31, no. 4 (2009): 423–430.

Suleiman, Susan. *Authoritarian Fictions: The Ideological Novel as a Literary Genre.* New York: Columbia University Press, 1983.

Szalay, Michael. *Hip Figures: A Literary History of the Democratic Party.* Stanford, Calif.: Stanford University Press, 2012.

Szeman, Imre. "Who's Afraid of National Allegory? Jameson, Literary Criticism, Globalization." *South Atlantic Quarterly* 100, no. 3 (2001): 803–827.

Tamburri, Anthony Julian. *A Semiotic of Ethnicity: In (Re)cognition of the Italian/American Writer.* Albany: State University of New York Press, 1998.

Thapa, Manjushree. "Reaching One's Own People, Reaching the World." *Manoa* 13, no. 3 (2001): 37–53.

Theroux, Paul. "Tarzan Is an Expatriate." *Transition* 32 (1967): 13–19.

Thurschwell, Adam. "Writing and Terror: Don DeLillo on the Task of Literature After 9/11." *Law and Literature* 19, no. 2 (2007): 277–302.

Todorov, Tzvetan. "The Origin of Genres." *New Literary History* 8 (1976–1977): 159–170.

——. *The Poetics of Prose.* New York: Blackwell, 1978.

Twark, Jill E. *Humor, Satire and Identity: East German Literature in the 1990s* Berlin: de Gruyter, 2007.

"20 More Under 40." June 16, 2011. The Millions, http://www.themillions.com/2010/06/20-more-under-40.html.

Updike, John. "Botswana Blues" [review of *Mortals*, by Norman Rush]. *New Yorker*, June 2, 2003.

Virilio, Paul. "After Architecture: A Conversation." *Grey Room* 3 (2001): 32–53.

Viscusi, Robert. *Buried Caesars, and Other Secrets of Italian American Writing.* Albany: State University of New York Press, 2006.

Viswanathan, Gauri. "The Ordinary Business of Occultism." *Critical Inquiry* 27, no. 1 (2000): 1–20.

——. *Outside the Fold: Conversion, Modernity, and Belief*. Princeton, N.J.: Princeton University Press, 1998.

Wainaina, Binyavanga. "How to Write About Africa." *Granta* 92: "The View from Africa," winter 2005.

Waine, Anthony. "Anna Seghers's *Transit*: A Late Modern Thriller—Without Thrills." *Neophilologus* 89 (2005): 403–418.

Walkowitz, Rebecca, *Cosmopolitan Style: Modernism Beyond the Nation*. New York: Columbia University Press, 2006.

Wallace, David Foster. "E Unibus Pluram: Television and U.S. Fiction." *Review of Contemporary Fiction* 13, no. 2 (1993): 151–193.

Watson, Nicola J. *Revolution and the Form of the British Novel, 1790–1835: Intercepted Letters, Interrupted Seductions*. New York: Oxford University Press, 1994.

Wegner, Phillip. *A Life Between Two Deaths, 1989–2001: U.S. Culture in the Long 1990s*. Durham, N.C.: Duke University Press, 2009.

Weisenberger, Steven. *Fables of Subversion: Satire and the American Novel, 1930–1980*. Athens: University of Georgia Press, 1995.

Whalen-Bridge, John. *Political Fiction and the American Self*. Urbana: University of Illinois Press, 1998.

Wiemann, Dirk. *Genres of Modernity: Contemporary Indian Novels in English*. Amsterdam: Rodopi, 2008.

Williams, Nicholas M. *Ideology and Utopia in the Poetry of William Blake*. Cambridge: Cambridge University Press, 1998.

Willmott, Glenn. *Unreal Country: Modernity in the Canadian Novel in English*. Montreal: McGill–Queens University Press, 2002.

Wilson, Julie. "Backpacker Icons: Influential Literary 'Nomads' in the Formation of Backpacker Identities." In *The Global Nomad: Backpacker Travel in Theory and Practice*, edited by Greg Richards and Julie Wilson, 123–148. Tonawanda, N.Y.: Channel View Press, 2004.

Witt, Doris. *Black Hunger: Food and the Politics of U.S. Identity*. New York: Oxford University Press, 1999.

Wofford, Harris. "The Future of the Peace Corps." *Annals of the American Academy of Political and Social Science* 365 (1966): 129–146.

Womack, Kenneth, and Amy Mallory-Kani, "'Why Don't You Just Leave It Up to Nature?': An Adaptationist Reading of the Novels of Jeffrey Eugenides." *Mosaic* 40, no. 3 (2007): 157–173.

Wood, James. "Thinking" [review of *Mortals*, by Norman Rush]. *New Republic*, June 23, 2003.

Wright, Derek, ed. *Contemporary African Fiction*. Bayreuth: Bayreuth African Studies, 1997.

Yúdice, George. *The Expediency of Culture: Uses of Culture in the Global Era*. Durham, N.C.: Duke University Press, 2003.

Zabrowska, Magdalena. *How We Found America: Reading Gender Through East European Immigrant Narratives*. Chapel Hill: University of North Carolina Press, 1995.

Zalman, Amy. "Gender and the Palestinian Narrative of Return in Two Novels by Ghassan Kanafani." In *Literature and Nation in the Middle East*, edited by Yasir Suleiman and Ibrahim Muhawki, 48–78. Edinburgh: Edinburgh University Press, 2006.

Zamora, Lois. *Writing the Apocalypse: Historical Vision in Contemporary U.S. and Latin American Fiction*. New York: Cambridge University Press, 1989.

Zaretsky, Eli. *Secrets of the Soul: A Social and Cultural History of Psychoanalysis*. New York: Vintage, 2004.

Zimmerman, David A. *Panic! Markets, Crises, and Crowds in American Fiction*. Chapel Hill: University of North Carolina Press, 2006.

Zimmerman, Jonathan. "Beyond Double Consciousness: Black Peace Corps Volunteers in Africa, 1961–1971." *Journal of American History* 82, no. 3 (1995): 999–1028.

Žižek, Slavoj. *Living in the End Times*. New York: Verso, 2010.

——. *On Belief*. New York: Routledge, 2001.

——. "Seize the Day: Lenin's Legacy." *London Review of Books*, July 25, 2002.

——. "The Violence of Liberal Democracy." *Assemblage*, April 1993, 92–93.

INDEX

Numbers in italics refer to pages on which tables appear.